Travels through American History
in the Mid-Atlantic

TRAVELS THROUGH AMERICAN HISTORY

in the MID-ATLANTIC

A GUIDE FOR ALL AGES

CHARLES W. MITCHELL

With Maps by Elizabeth Church Mitchell

Johns Hopkins University Press
Baltimore

© 2014 Johns Hopkins University Press
All rights reserved. Published 2014
Printed in the United States of America on acid-free paper
9 8 7 6 5 4 3 2 1

Johns Hopkins University Press
2715 North Charles Street
Baltimore, Maryland 21218-4363
www.press.jhu.edu

Library of Congress Cataloging-in-Publication Data
Mitchell, Charles W., 1954–
    Travels through American history in the Mid-Atlantic : a guide for all ages /
Charles W. Mitchell ; with maps by Elizabeth Church Mitchell.
        pages cm
    Includes bibliographical references and index.
    ISBN 978-1-4214-1514-7 (pbk. : acid-free paper) — ISBN 978-1-4214-1515-4
(electronic) — ISBN 1-4214-1514-3 (pbk. : acid-free paper) — ISBN 1-4214-1515-1
(electronic) 1. Middle Atlantic States—History. 2. Virginia—History. 3. Middle
Atlantic States—Guidebooks. 4. Virginia—Guidebooks. 5. Historic sites—
Middle Atlantic States—Guidebooks. 6. Historic sites—Virginia—Guidebooks.
I. Title.
    F106.M658 2014
    974—dc23   2014002573

A catalog record for this book is available from the British Library.

*Special discounts are available for bulk purchases of this book. For more information,
please contact Special Sales at 410-516-6936 or specialsales@press.jhu.edu.*

Johns Hopkins University Press uses environmentally friendly book materials,
including recycled text paper that is composed of at least 30 percent post-
consumer waste, whenever possible.

For Betsy, who always rides shotgun;
and for Abbie and Alec, who are always good sports
on their picaresque travels with Charley

CONTENTS

Preface   ix
Acknowledgments   xv

1 Jamestown, Williamsburg, and Yorktown   1
Side Trip: Jamestown Settlement

2 St. Mary's City   16
*Side Trips: John Wilkes Booth Escape Trail;
Point Lookout State Park; Sotterley Plantation;
Solomons Island*

3 Fort Frederick   30
Side Trips: Hagerstown; Western Maryland Rail Trail

4 Independence National Historical Park   38
*Side Trips: African American Museum in Philadelphia;
Philadelphia History Museum; Rittenhouse Square*

5 Valley Forge   48
Side Trip: Brandywine Battlefield State Park

6 Fort McHenry and the Star-Spangled Banner
National Historic Trail   59
*Side Trips: The Star-Spangled Banner Flag House;
Shot Tower; Fells Point; Hampton National Historic Site*

7 The Baltimore & Ohio Railroad Museum   71
*Side Trips: Irish Railroad Workers Museum; Mt. Clare
Museum House; Thomas Viaduct, Patapsco State Park; Babe
Ruth Birthplace and Museum / Sports Legend Museum*

8 The Chesapeake & Ohio Canal   82
*Side Trips: Monocacy National Battlefield; Cumberland;
Clara Barton National Historical Site; Williamsport*

9 Harpers Ferry 97
Side Trip: Ball's Bluff Battlefield Regional Park

10 Civil War Richmond 107
Side Trips: Museum of the Confederacy, Richmond and Appomattox; James Madison's Montpelier

11 Antietam 120
Side Trips: Frederick; Crampton's Gap / Gathland State Park; Shepherdstown

12 Civil War Washington 133
Side Trips: Ford's Theater National Historic Site; Arlington National Cemetery; George Washington's Mount Vernon

13 Gettysburg 146
Side Trips: The David Wills House; Eisenhower National Historic Site; Union Mills Homestead; Taneytown

14 Fredericksburg, Chancellorsville, the Wilderness, and Spotsylvania 158
Side Trips: George Washington's Ferry Farm; George Washington Birthplace; Stratford Hall; Brandy Station

15 Cedar Creek and Belle Grove National Historical Park 170
Side Trip: Winchester

16 Petersburg and the Road to Appomattox 179
Side Trips: Thomas Jefferson's Monticello; Ash Lawn–Highland

Index 195

PREFACE

With the possible exception of New England, no part of the United States features as many historically significant points in as compact a space as the mid-Atlantic region. Southern and midwestern sites, for all their grandeur, are often dispersed across far greater distances. The richness of this midregion's historical geography is a catalog of the momentous decisions and conflicts that have shaped our nation, and they range from southern Virginia to Pennsylvania. Each has become defined by events that over time have bestowed a lasting historical identity: Valley Forge as symbol of the American Revolution; Fort McHenry as bulwark against the assault on Baltimore during the War of 1812; Gettysburg as the genesis of a national reconciliation that began even before the end of the Civil War. Others, such as the multidimensional Chesapeake & Ohio Canal and Harpers Ferry, span the centuries of American history. Because the region is rich in Civil War history, the book features many destinations from that conflict, but the area offers a wide variety that begins with the colonial era.

Long-standing interest in our nation's history has drawn me to the historical landscape of my native region. Some places I visited on school field trips. I developed a passing acquaintance with others, often on weekend pilgrimages with our children. In the 1990s I wrote travel stories on a number of sites for the Sunday feature section of the Baltimore *Sun*, an endeavor that led to deeper exploration of historical attractions that families could enjoy over the course of a two- or three-day weekend. In 2007 I published *Maryland Voices of the Civil War* (also with Johns Hopkins University Press), a thematic collection of letters, diaries, and other contemporary accounts of Marylanders grappling with the profound issues of the Civil War in a loyal slave state on the border. The twelve years devoted to that work further stoked my interest in the significance of historical places and their rich stories—of the sites themselves and the people, famous and unknown, who shaped those stories.

Bookstore shelves teem with travel books and guides to such destinations. Few, however, offer much historical depth, tending more toward sightseeing while lacking context; and even fewer address the mid-Atlantic region from this perspective. Indeed, one finds regional road atlases and guides to B&B's and books dedicated to specific topics such as hiking, biking, camping, beach vacations, annual events, waterways, architecture, fossil-collecting, lighthouses, rail trails, scenic backroads, traveling with children, traveling with dogs, festivals, used bookstores, and even ghosts. Still other works are devoted to specific states in the mid-Atlantic region. Many are useful and well done. But *Travels through American History in the Mid-Atlantic* offers historical context leavened with quotes from the letters and diaries of those who witnessed and sometimes made history at these places, helping to illuminate the complex issues individuals faced at key moments in our national story. Quotations are given verbatim, with spelling and punctuation as the writer or speaker intended, to better capture the flavor of the era.

We live in a time when historical literacy, particularly among the young, is sadly lacking. The many significant historical sites in this part of our nation can be a pleasurable way to address that deficiency, for they offer an engaging spectrum of age-inclusive, interactive activity, ranging from the nearly sedentary to the strenuous. The leisurely stroll through the museum and visitor center at the Gettysburg Battlefield and the two-hour hike up Loudoun Heights for the panoramic view of Harpers Ferry nicely illustrate this variety. The reenactment each December of street fighting between Union and Confederate troops in Fredericksburg, Virginia, is sure to become a vivid family memory of a weekend trip. And the serious student of early American history, who may know that George Washington was a principal founder of what became the Chesapeake & Ohio Canal Company, comes away with an appreciation of life on that canal after seeing the small houses of the lock tenders who awaited the approach of the mule-pulled cargo boats, alerted by horns blaring in daylight and lanterns swinging in darkness. And new historical sites of compelling interest appear from time to time, such as the Harriet Tubman Underground Railroad Byway, on Maryland's Eastern Shore.

Americans should appreciate that while cataclysmic events, military campaigns, and the exploits of the famous and infamous can provide historical framework, individuals and groups often supply the context and color that enrich the canvas. The diary of a Pennsylvania farmer serving in the Continental Army during the winter of 1777–1778 at Valley Forge reveals a dimension of those extraordinary three months found neither in Washington's writings nor in books about the Revolutionary War. The young New Jersey soldier's letter to his family recounting the terror of the dawn surprise attack by Confederate troops at the 1864 battle of Cedar Creek, in the Shenandoah Valley, conveys a deeply personal perspective on that crucial engagement. The recollection of the colonial militia officer at Fort Frederick, in western Maryland, of a visit in the 1750s from neighboring Cherokees—whose chief "invited us to Smoak a Pipe with him"— helps illuminate relations between colonists and Native Americans in the mid-eighteenth century. And the amusing aside of the soldier at Fort Ethan Allen in Arlington, Virginia, finding tedious his duty to guard the nation's capital during the Civil War—"the only thing we have to record is a remarkable dream of one of the men, in which he saw the Confederates scaling the parapet," he wrote—sheds light both on the extensive network of fortifications around Washington, D.C., and, on a personal level, the weary monotony faced by young men itching to fight.

The destinations in these pages illuminate both the majestic and everyday events that have helped shape our American experience, from its origins to the mid-nineteenth century. Chapters, arranged chronologically, encompass the colonial and revolutionary eras, the War of 1812, and the Civil War—from the mid-seventeenth century to 1865. All but four of the destinations are part of the National Park Service system. Side trips suggest lesser-known sites travelers might visit en route or while in the area—for example, a short detour from Harpers Ferry or Antietam Battlefield leads to Shepherdstown, West Virginia, just across the Potomac River. The chapters include site features that can escape the notice of visitors, such as the hiking trails at Valley Forge; the only intersection of the Appalachian Trail and the Chesapeake & Ohio Canal, near Harpers Ferry; and the short, albeit steep, climb onto Big Round Top at Gettysburg, overlooked by many who tend to cluster on the adjacent, iconic Little Round Top. National Park Service websites are particularly detailed; travelers should check them for directions, hours, and events. Superintendents' reports on these sites contain impressive detail on the Park Service's multifaceted work, and most offer guides for educators. Many parks have social media options and free mobile apps with up-to-date information that further enhance a visit.

A word about my criteria for choosing these sites: the Baltimore and

Washington, D.C., area serves as the center of a circle extending approximately 150 miles that encompasses most of them. My objective is to illuminate single sites that are synonymous with a specific seminal event or era in American history, and that warrant a day, or perhaps two or three (including travel time), to enjoy fully. By contrast, Annapolis—a city of tremendous historical significance that lies in the geographic range of this book—offers such a broad panorama of America's past that one is hard pressed to choose just one defining event associated with it. Conversely, the first three days in July of 1863 on bucolic farmland surrounding Gettysburg, Pennsylvania, are embedded in our national memory. Hand-drawn maps evoke the historical era and illustrate the period topographic features—the hills, rivers, streams, roads, and mountains—that so heavily shaped what happened at these places. While some of the roads shown on these maps no longer exist, aficionados can compare their locations with present-day thoroughfares and traverse those roads themselves.

Activities appealing to children are an important part of this book. Kids who observe archeologists working at St. Mary's City, watch a Civil War re-enactment, engage the interactive exhibits at a National Park visitor center, hide in the rocky crevasses of Little Round Top at Gettysburg, or explore the Sunken Road on Marye's Heights at Fredericksburg will help mold a rich family experience. Our daughter, Abbie, and her brother, Alec, loved artillery and cavalry demonstrations at Civil War battlefields, camping on the banks of the Potomac River, seeing a reenactment of a French and Indian War battle at Fort Frederick, skipping rocks on the Shenandoah River at Harpers Ferry, and choosing historically accurate souvenirs in gift shops. These experiences, reinforced by opportunities for play-acting—Alec, at age 6, helping spring Confederate prisoners from the jail at Fort McHenry in Baltimore during a living history weekend, then joining the chase for them, wooden musket in hand; and two years later falling victim to a Union Minie ball while serving as flag-bearer during a reenactment of Pickett's Charge at Gettysburg, when I was an embedded journalist with an artillery unit—remain fond memories for us as parents. And perhaps they were formative moments in the later decisions of our kids to study American history.

Researching this book underscored a vital point for me that historians and readers alike should bear in mind—inaccurate claims can appear in print, often in multiple places over the years and at times by reputable scholars. Myth and legend grow around significant events, and like vines on trees, over time obscure what lies beneath. Other writers then unwittingly recycle these inaccuracies, to the point where repetitively cited claims become embedded in the historical record, accepted by posterity as factual. Claims that cannot be substantiated by credible, original source material should be viewed with honest skepticism. Diligent scholarship by public historians and archivists constantly interprets and reinterprets events, unearthing new evidence that reshapes or even contradicts what we previously believed to be true. (Evidence of this process abounds: For example, we continue to learn more about the Underground Railroad, as records of itineraries and places continue to be excavated.) As I encountered such instances in my research, especially in the course of editorial review by the outside experts acknowledged herein, I either excised information or indicated in the text that a particular claim is controversial, or a story likely mythical. I encourage readers wishing sharper clarity about declarative statements to delve into the historical record and find the primary sources and original documents that undergird proper study of the past. Suggestions for further reading at the end of each chapter will, I trust, be useful for some readers.

With copious information about historical places readily available in books and easily found online, why invest time and money to see them in person? The desire to know what came before is in our DNA—it is natural that we are drawn to the powerful forces that shape political conflict and alliances; to grasp the realities of terrain, weather, and illness on the outcome of war; and to build context and meaning around the present. But equally compelling should be the lives of our ancestors and the rhythms that characterized their daily lives, at work and play. Adding our own visual impressions of places and people to what we have previously learned shapes our imagination and creates indelible memories that lead to rich, lasting historical narrative for us all.

So let us put aside the old bromides about our dismal ignorance of history—the visitors who ask rangers why so many Civil War battles were fought in national parks, and the poll some years ago indicating a large percentage of American high school students believed that Malcolm X was a pope—and hit the road to enjoy firsthand the many splendors of America's mid-Atlantic past.

ACKNOWLEDGMENTS

No writer of narrative nonfiction works alone, though in the dark of night one may be forgiven for thinking otherwise. The seed for this book was planted years ago, during my time as a travel writer for the Baltimore *Sun*, and many people along the way have helped me both reshape original articles into finished chapters and write new ones. I thank Bruce Friedland, former features and travel editor at the *Sun*, for his guidance on selecting themes for some of those early travel stories. I am particularly grateful to the historians, archivists, and educators, noted below, who reviewed the chapters for accuracy and helped ensure that they stressed the features of each site that would most engage readers contemplating a visit. Their editorial comments have no doubt made this a far more useful work:

Renee Albertoli, Interpretive Specialist, Interpretation and Education
Independence National Historical Park

James H. Blankenship, Jr., Historian
Petersburg National Battlefield

Eric A. Campbell, Park Ranger-Interpretation
Cedar Creek and Belle Grove National Historical Park

Tracy Chernault, Park Ranger (Interpretation)
Petersburg National Battlefield

Dr. Thomas G. Clemens, Professor Emeritus
Hagerstown Community College

Diane K. Depew, Supervisory Park Ranger
Colonial National Historical Park

David Fox, Interpretive Ranger
Harpers Ferry National Historical Park

Karen M. Gray, Ph.D., C&O Canal NHP headquarters library volunteer
and avocational historian of the C&O Canal

Susan Haberkorn, Secretary
Harpers Ferry National Historical Park

Dr. William Hakkarinen, Member
B&O Railroad Museum and National Railway Historical Society

D. Scott Hartwig, Supervisory Historian
Gettysburg National Military Park

Christian Higgins, Archivist, Cultural Resources Management
Independence National Historical Park

Mike High, Author of *The C&O Canal Companion*

Zachary Klitzman, Executive Assistant
President Lincoln's Cottage, a site of the National Trust
for Historic Preservation

Robert E. L. Krick, Historian
Richmond National Battlefield Park

William Lange, Park Ranger
Valley Forge National Historical Park

Terry Levering, Department of History
Loyola Blakefield High School, Baltimore, MD

Mark Maloy, Park Guide
Frederick Douglass National Historic Site

Erin Carlson Mast, Executive Director
President Lincoln's Cottage, a site of the National Trust
for Historic Preservation

Henry M. Miller Ph.D., RPA
Maryland Heritage Scholar, Historic St. Mary's City

Donald Pfanz, Staff Historian
Fredericksburg & Spotsylvania National Military Park

Frederick N. Rasmussen, reporter and columnist
The Baltimore *Sun*

Patrick A. Schroeder, Historian
Appomattox Court House National Historical Park

Scott S. Sheads, lecturer and author of books and journal articles
on the War of 1812 in the Chesapeake and Park Ranger/Historian
Fort McHenry National Monument & Historic Shrine, National
Park Service

Bob Study, Park Ranger
Fort Frederick State Park

Anna Coxey Toogood, Historian, Cultural Resources Management
Independence National Historical Park

Courtney B. Wilson, Executive Director
Baltimore & Ohio Railroad Museum

The editorial vision of my friend and editor at Johns Hopkins University Press, Robert J. Brugger, has much to do with the structure of this book, as it did with my first one. Crafting a sensible way of organizing this work was no small task, as we met in pubs around Baltimore to explore the reasons why people would want to visit these sites, how to illustrate a travel book in an era when no one needs road maps or photographs of monuments, and the most reader-friendly manner in which to present the chapters—one day a geographic order made sense; the next, the chronological sequence that we eventually chose.

Mary Lou Kenney's excellent editing skills call to mind the old adage that every writer needs an editor. Despite my meticulous review of manuscript and maps prior to arrival on her desk, she caught more than a few errors, word choices, and statements that would likely have confused readers. Her instincts for reconfiguring paragraphs have made the narratives flow more smoothly.

Braxton Mitchell, my father, again supplied valuable research assistance and fact-checking, particularly for the side trips at the end of each chapter. The encouragement of my mother, Polly Mitchell, who did not live to see publication, to never give up helped me get across the finish line. I am grateful to them both for those gifts and their many other contributions to my well-being over the years.

I am indebted more than I can write to my wife, Betsy, whose expertise is an integral part of this book. She accompanied me on virtually every site visit, studying exhibits and films in visitor centers, recording the locations of siege lines and rifle pits, hiking little-used trails, navigating auto tours, planning itineraries, and remembering things I forgot. Her knowledge of Civil War battles and military strategy, which far exceeds my own, was a readily available resource around the clock. She read every chapter and made it better. And the period maps that flowed from her experience as a graphic designer and illustrator speak for themselves on the page. And a shout-out to our kids, Abbie and Alec, now grown, who by joining in many of these adventures helped me to see the many ways children can be actively engaged at these sites.

I would be remiss not to acknowledge my alma mater, St. Paul's School in Brooklandville, Maryland, in this work. On that bucolic campus I was introduced to the marvels of history by Martin D. "Mitch" Tullai and Louis Dorsey Clark and started becoming a writer at the knee of Thomas N. Longstreth.

Travels through American History
in the Mid-Atlantic

JAMESTOWN, WILLIAMSBURG, AND YORKTOWN

Jamestown and Yorktown are the bookends of the British presence in America. The former was the first permanent British settlement in America, while Yorktown—a mere twenty-three miles to the east—saw the ignoble end of that presence, when the surrender of Gen. Charles Lord Cornwallis to Gen. George Washington effectively ended the Revolutionary War. These two sites, connected not only by history but by the Colonial Parkway in Tidewater Virginia, comprise Colonial National Historical Park. The Jamestown site, known as Historic Jamestowne, is administered by a partnership between the National Park Service and the Colonial Williamsburg Foundation (on behalf of Preservation Virginia). Both are scenically situated on the James and York Rivers, respectively. Between them lies Colonial Williamsburg, the third leg of Virginia's "Historical Triangle" and one of the Tidewater's most important colonial towns.

In May 1607, a hundred English men and four English boys rowed ashore and climbed the banks of the James River. They named the defensible settlement they created Jamestown, in honor of their king. The excitement of this new venture soon faded, however, in the face of hunger and disease, until the colonists created a sustainable food supply and an aura of permanence that would attract more settlers. Ill prepared for the steamy, disease-laden Chesapeake tidewater area, the Englishmen had expected a climate similar to the Mediterranean region, and they dressed accordingly in wool and linen clothing. They failed to build cordial relations with the Powhatan Indians, whose thirty tribes were ready to share their "Corne, weomen and Country" with the English, who quickly alienated their new neighbors by making off with their maize and trying to convert them to Christianity. Dr. John Pott tried to solve the "Indian problem" in 1623 by allegedly poisoning them. Relations were at a low from 1609 to 1614, when the English and the Powhatan warred, leading to hundreds of casualties on both sides.

Making matters more difficult for the English was the occurrence of the worst drought in almost 800 years; lacking fresh water, they drank from the James River. River water was pure enough in the spring, but during the summer the salinity content climbed as fresh runoff ceased and the water surrounding the island grew stagnant and contaminated. Salt poisoning took hold as summer wore on. When the suffering colonists drank rum and beer, they became dehydrated and lethargic. "Our drinke (was) cold water taken out of the River ... at low tide full of slime and filth, which was the destruction of many of our men," recorded George Percy, a leader of Jamestown. "We digged a faire Well of fresh water in the Fort of excellent, sweet water which till then was wanting," wrote Capt. John Smith about fresh water eventually found in 1609. But by September, close to fifty men were dead. When the first supply ship arrived at Jamestown in January 1608, only thirty-eight of the original colonists were alive, and most of those only barely. Smith described a frozen colony of three dozen people, hardly "a verie fit place for the erecting of a great cittie" he had envisioned. (Smith returned to England in 1609 after being badly burned in a gunpowder accident.) Indeed, the first scientifically validated instances of survival cannibalism have been documented at Jamestown.

Historic Jamestowne, which sits on a 1,500-acre island acquired in 1934 by the National Park Service, tells how three cultures converged at this site: English, American Indian, and African American. A film at the visitor center provides an orientation to the history and archaeology of the settlement. Exhibits in both the visitor center and the Voorhees Archaearium, just west of the old town center, tell the Jamestown story and the meticulous research and archaeological work that have shed light on its evolution and citizenry. A highlight in the visitor center is the complete clay baking oven excavated in the 1930s—restored after being shattered into over 200 pieces, it was likely used outdoors, where heated stones dropped inside made it sufficiently hot for baking. Daily park ranger tours occur throughout the year and offer rich details about the growth of a society at Jamestown. Just inside the park entrance is the Glasshouse, where demonstrations of seventeenth-century glassblowing techniques illuminate the intricacies of one of Virginia's early industries. The second group of Jamestown arrivals, in 1608, included Germans and Poles recruited to build sawmills and make glass, tar, pitch, and potash. When the London-based Virginia Company, which was financing the establishment of area settlements, sent four Italian glassmakers to the colony in 1621, they got on poorly with the English, one of whom wrote that "a more damned crew hell never vomited." In 1625 the company dispatched French winemakers to Jamestown to expand the colony's product lines, but the venture failed.

The historic town site includes Old Towne and New Towne. Old Towne highlights are the location of the 1607 James Fort, the brick church tower dating to the second half of the seventeenth century, and the 1907 Memorial Church. The tower, with walls three feet thick, is the last remaining structure from the seventeenth century. The church remains active today, hosting weddings and other events. When entering the Memorial Church, look down to see the original foundations dating to 1607 and the 1640s. Sitting in that small unheated structure, listening to a ranger describe the harsh punishments handed down for violating the social codes of that nascent society, one can almost see the men and women of Jamestown asking God to bless their fragile social experiment on the James. The church is also the site of the first whispers of representative government in America—elected burgesses met there in 1619 with the governor and his council to form Virginia's first general assembly.

Walking tours through Old Towne and New Towne allow visitors to conjure the appearance of life in the seventeenth century. The James River laps at the shore. Bricks lining the original foundations mark the

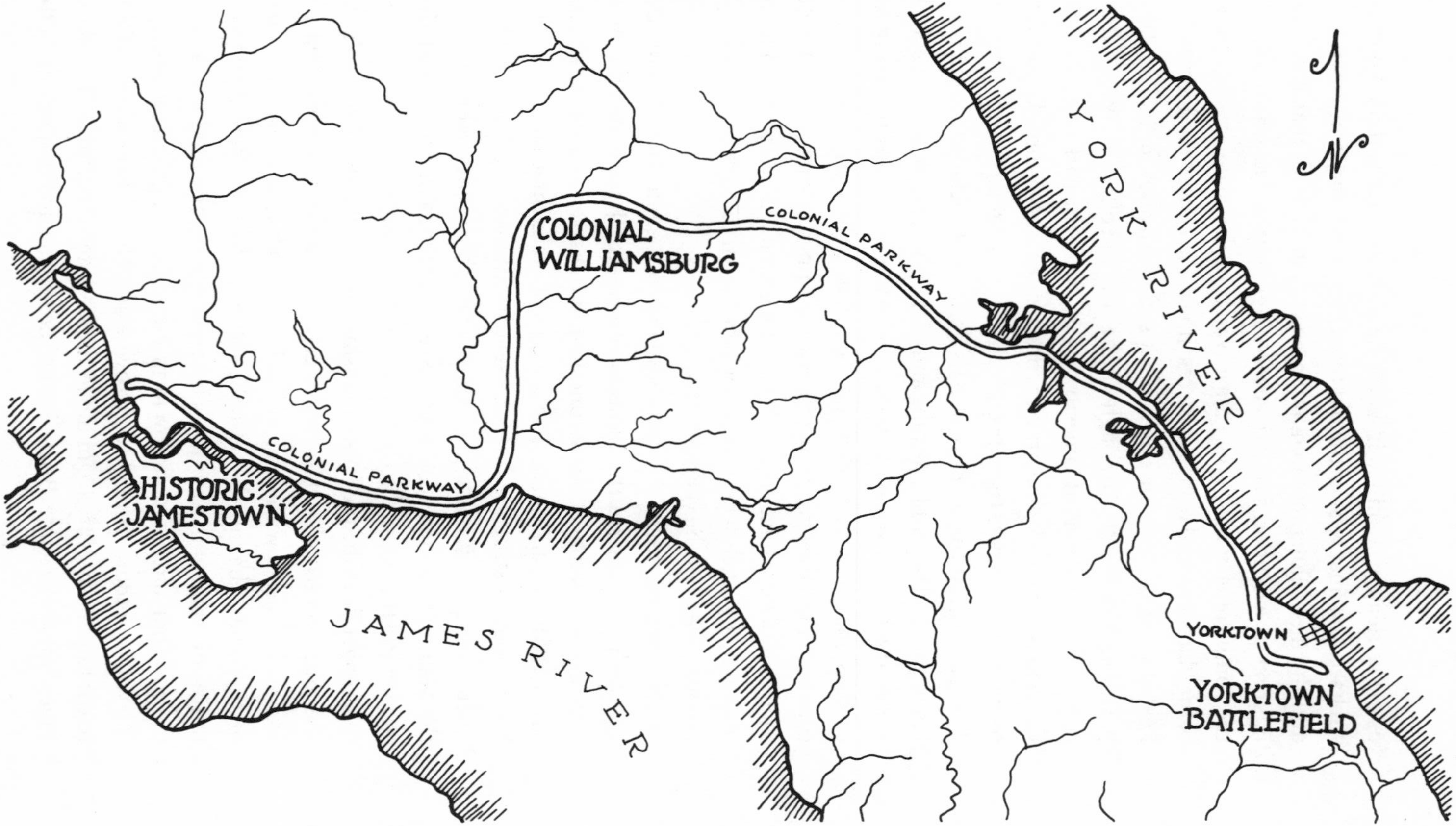

VIRGINIA'S HISTORIC TRIANGLE

YORK RIVER

COLONIAL PARKWAY

COLONIAL WILLIAMSBURG

COLONIAL PARKWAY

HISTORIC JAMESTOWN

JAMES RIVER

YORKTOWN

YORKTOWN BATTLEFIELD

N

locations, sizes, and contours of Jamestown's early houses and taverns, known as ordinaries. Running near the seawall along the James River is the Captain John Smith Chesapeake National Historic Trail, a 3,000-mile, three-state-plus Washington, D.C., water route in and around the Chesapeake Bay that marks Smith's 1608 explorations. Gravestones mark the resting places of some of the earliest Americans. Remains of buildings loom. The New Towne Viewer at the Tercentenary Monument presents computer-generated images that depict the historic appearance of the Jamestown landscape, using archeological objects to reinforce the experience of stepping back in time. The Viewer also incorporates videos showing the remains of buildings and artifacts as they were being excavated.

The first order of business for the English settlers in the spring of 1607 was building a triangular fort for protection, a task they accomplished in a mere nineteen days. More than 90 percent of the fort's land area has been located by experts from the Jamestown Rediscovery Project. More than a million and a half artifacts have been collected from the site since 1994, when the project started. Visitors to Old Towne can see the reproduced fort walls consisting of sharpened stakes—archaeologists have pinpointed the locations of the original stakes below the ground by analyzing changes in soil color caused by their decomposition.

The Voorhees Archaearium, home to more than a thousand artifacts discovered in the soil of the Jamestown fort, is a monument to the settlement. Operated by Preservation Virginia, it stands on the site of the third and fourth state houses, whose foundations are visible under glass in the building's entrance. A striking specimen is the skeleton of an English colonist with a bullet embedded in his leg. A 3-D digital facial reconstruction of the skull of Bartholomew Gosnold, captain of one of the three ships that landed in 1607, generates an image of his face. Other artifacts include cooking utensils, coins, and weapons.

The winter years of 1609–1610 are known as the "Starving Tyme." The colony's population of 500 had dwindled to a mere 60 people, according to one eyewitness account; those colonists survived by eating dogs, cats, roots, and snakes, and were driven to boil the starch from shirt collars to make porridge. Settlers ate "what vermin or carrion soever [they] could light on," wrote one. Though George Percy recorded that "Our men were destroyed with cruell diseases, as Swelling, Flixes, Burning Fevers . . . and some departed suddenly, but for the most part they died of meere famine," historians have concluded that diseases such as typhoid and dysentery, which spread via contaminated water and conferred no immunity, were more lethal than outright starvation. By 1621, colonists had moved inland to establish dozens of plantation sites. The following year, a series of attacks by the Powhatan on English settlements along the James killed 347 settlers. But the young colony rebounded; by 1634 the population had grown to about 5,000 colonists, and tobacco exports that year exceeded 1.5 million pounds. Historians and archaeologists have found clues to daily life at Jamestown and the surrounding region. Clues about the settlers' diet, for example, come from excavation of animal remains and fish bones from twenty-four households at seventeen different sites in Tidewater Virginia and Maryland, such as Jamestown and St. Mary's City (see chapter 2). The sites of storehouses, privies, and wells—the latter often used for rubbish disposal—also yield vital clues about daily life.

The sponsoring Virginia Company sought profits from the gold, silver, and gems believed to be plentiful in the area (in contrast, the Pilgrims, who landed thirteen years after the Jamestown settlers, sought religious freedom, not riches, in the Americas). Though the first ships sailing up the James landed no women, the Virginia Company soon recruited some—many were women of the lower classes whose meager dowries meant poor marriage prospects in England, but all strata of English society were represented—to join the men, with the expectation that they would marry and start families.

In the 1620s surveying began east of the fort for what would become New Towne. Planters and merchants bought lots and began erecting taverns, warehouses, and wharves to accommodate visitors to the capital with business at the courts or who were serving in the general assembly. Facilities were needed to grade, weigh, tax, and ship tobacco from this deep-water port so it could land in the pipes of Englishmen who so coveted sweet Virginia tobacco. As construction techniques evolved from mud-and-stud to multistory timber structures that sat on footings of stone or brick, buildings became more structurally stable, thereby increasing the volume of tobacco that could be harvested and shipped. To-

bacco became the engine of economic growth in the region—John Rolfe, who wed paramount chief Powhatan's daughter Pocahontas, began exporting it to London in 1613; by 1617, it was said, colonists were planting tobacco in the streets of Jamestown. The quiet atmosphere of the site today contrasts starkly with the bustling port of the early seventeenth century, depicted by interpretive signs. Much of the land in and around the town was abandoned starting in 1699, when the capital of Virginia moved inland to Williamsburg after the state house was destroyed by fire; roughly a dozen families remained to farm on the island. Archaeological excavations began in 1934, and today reconstructed foundations sit atop original ones, both to show their locations and protect them.

East on Colonial Parkway, en route to Yorktown, is Colonial Williamsburg, Britain's largest and wealthiest capital in the New World, which tells the story of how diverse peoples grew into a society with western values of liberty and equality. Here the Virginia Convention in June 1776 took a series of bold steps, voting to declare the dissolution of the royal government; empower the Virginia delegation to the Continental Congress (then assembled in Philadelphia) to support independence; pass resolutions of rights; and create a plan for a new state government that would serve as a blueprint for the United States Constitution. As Virginia's capital, Williamsburg was a vital political center, watched closely by the British, who "may destroy the little hamlet of Williamsburg, steal a few slaves, and lose half his army among the fens and marshes of our lower country, or by the heats of our climate," wrote Thomas Jefferson to John Adams in the summer of 1777. The town's 301 acres are a splendid destination for historical tourism, as they feature hundreds of restored, reconstructed, and historically furnished buildings replete with costumed interpreters telling the stories of the men and women of this eighteenth-century city—black, white, Native American, slave, indentured and free— as their colonial speaking style underscores the authenticity.

The original reincarnation of Williamsburg, in the 1920s, was underwritten by John D. Rockefeller, Jr., and its historical narrative tended to exclude any hint of slavery until the 1970s, when African Americans began to portray the slaves who were part of the vital infrastructure of the original town. Not until the mid-1990s did African Americans begin to appear in interpretive depictions of slave marriages and auctions. By 2000 the story of slavery had been incorporated into the educational narrative at Williamsburg, which has since expanded further to include the contributions of free blacks during the Revolutionary period.

Visiting Colonial Williamsburg during the winter months means sparser crowds and the opportunity for immersion into colonial and revolutionary American life. Watch a milliner fashion stylish hats, a cooper craft sturdy barrels, and an instrument maker tune a viola. Wander the cobblestones with horse-drawn carriages and take in some of the finest examples of colonial American brick architecture—a colonial city as it was from 1699 to 1780, inhabited by men such as Thomas Jefferson, George Mason, and Patrick Henry, all members of the Virginia House of Burgesses (and Jefferson also as governor). Listen to the glassblower, blacksmith, and wigmaker explain the fine points of their craft. Stop in a tavern for a pint or a square of spicy gingerbread. Williamsburg's ar-

YORKTOWN BATTLEFIELD

chitectural highlights include the Raleigh Tavern, Governor's Palace and its gardens, and the Capitol. Visit the Abby Aldrich Rockefeller Folk Art Museum. Numerous historically accurate activities abound in the town, for adults and children—favorites include the revolutionary experience of joining an irate mob marching on the Governor's Palace to demand British soldiers return the colony's gunpowder they had seized. Kids can don a rented period costume, play colonial-era games, portray an undercover agent, and experience the life of a soldier in the Revolution.

At the far, east end of the Colonial Parkway is Yorktown, scene of Cornwallis's surrender in October 1781 that ensured American independence from Great Britain. This small village on the west bank of the York River would also host, fourscore and a year later, a Civil War clash as Union troops tried unsuccessfully in 1862 to capture Richmond, the Confederate capital, from the South. The commanders who failed here—Gen.

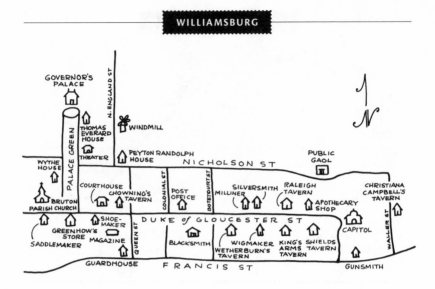

Charles Lord Cornwallis in 1781 and Maj. Gen. George B. McClellan in 1862—were drawn to the deep, navigable waters of the York River to this site just seven miles from the Chesapeake Bay, where the river was close to shoreline and a narrow enclave enabled strategically placed cannon to protect ships in the Yorktown port. The failure of Cornwallis was especially striking. The American Continental Army and the Virginia Militia, together with their French allies, trapped his army, then besieged him from the south while the French Navy blockaded the York River, preventing reinforcements and supplies from reaching Cornwallis. The drive to Yorktown on Colonial Parkway offers scenic river views, swans on ponds, and interpretive signs that describe the sites of historic structures and American Indian villages along the way.

The National Park Service relied on period military maps and excavations to reconstruct the many dimensions of the 1781 siege and subsequent fighting. Get a map of the battlefield at the visitor center, attend a ranger tour, and enlist the kids as Colonial Junior Rangers (Junior Ranger programs are available at most national parks; kids can complete an activity sheet available from the book shop that earns them a free patch and certificate). Kids can also obtain Civil War trading cards available at various sites in the park. See the film, *Siege of Yorktown*, and the exhibits in the museum, which packs a lot into its small quarters to tell the vivid story of the battle on the York River.

A map in the museum that lights up the sequence of events helps tourists visualize the order of battle. Artifacts extracted from the York River and sunken British ships include artillery shells and cannon. Displayed are tools used to dig the siege lines and a uniform button and escutcheon, or wrist plate, from a British Brown Bess musket recovered from the battlefield at Yorktown that was wielded by a man in the 33rd Regiment of Foot. A highlight is walking through the partial replica of the quarterdeck of H.M.S. *Charon*, the largest British warship at Yorktown, viewing its dining tables and sleeping hammocks and hearing the creaking lines and water lapping against the hull—a presentation sufficiently authentic to make one feel the swaying motion that comes from being under sail. The low ceiling and small space for cannon crews show the uncomfortable conditions sailors faced in that era. The cannon were salvaged from the ship's watery grave; other recovered artifacts are displayed before the entrance to the ship.

Upon regaining sea legs, climb the steps to the kids' exhibit to meet 13-year-old John Whitney of Connecticut, a fictional soldier in the American Continental Army. Whitney confesses that he lied about his age to enter the army and talks about his Yorktown experiences, such as making fascines (bundles of large branches) and gabions (stacks of bottomless large baskets built to contain dirt from trenches and earthwork walls) that were components of the fortifications: "You will undertake the collection of Spades, Axes, Hatchets, Shovels, & hilling Hoes & you are hereby empowered to take for the public Use all you can find in the town or adjacent Country," instructed Gov. Thomas Nelson, Jr., on September 15, 1781. "You are also impowered to impress Negroes to bring the tools to such places." Nelson, a signer of the Declaration of Independence, commanded the Virginia militia at the siege of Yorktown; the walls of his home still bear damage from cannonballs fired during the fighting. Nelson's home, which was used as a hospital during the Civil War, is open to the public; hours are posted at the visitor center. The Whitney display includes battle scenes with figures. Before going onto the battlefield, visit the museum shop for a range of books about the Revolutionary War and period toys sure to intrigue the young—the penny whistles, fifes, tabletop ninepins, and spinning tops contrast with twenty-first century items of amusement.

Don't miss George Washington's field tent in the museum. While the outer portion, or marquee, is reproduced, the ceiling, made of wool and linen, is original, as is the sleeping tent. Washington's tents are the only known remaining eighteenth-century American officers' tents—his were inherited by Robert E. Lee's wife from her father, who was Washington's stepson. A slave of Mrs. Lee's protected them from the Union troops who during the Civil War occupied the Lee home, Arlington House, which overlooks the Potomac River in Virginia.

Constructing siege lines is a backbreaking task. The Continental Army worked with their French allies, whose military engineers were highly skilled. "In general our works go on slow, the heavy artillery hard to get up," recorded Col. Richard Butler of the Second Pennsylvania Battalion, 5th Regiment, in his diary. "Indeed, I discover very plainly that we are young soldiers in a siege; however, we are determined to benefit ourselves by experience; one virtue we possess, that is perseverance." Into the second week of October, the Americans and French had constructed thousands of defensive bulwarks, and siege lines began to scar the soft, sandy soil of the rolling landscape. No first-hand accounts support claims that sightseers turned up to watch the construction (nor would General Washington have allowed such), though some citizens did witness the British surrender on October 19.

Two driving routes, the Battlefield Tour (seven miles) and the Allied Encampment Tour (nine miles), permit a thorough inspection of the defenses and siege lines, the small forward forts known as redoubts, the house where British surrender terms were negotiated, and the sites of both Washington's headquarters and the allied camps. Interpretive signs explain the action along the way. Earthworks (some original, some reconstructed) and redoubts convey a sense of how siege lines worked tactically and the extraordinary labors required to construct them. The landscape remains unspoiled, so one can see both how the topography influenced commanders' decisions and the troop movements that led to this American triumph.

The reconstructed redoubts, with pointed stakes, or fraises, protruding at sharp angles from the earthen walls, are striking. Hand-to-hand fighting occurred at Redoubts 9 and 10 (stop D on the driving tour), when American and French troops each successfully assaulted one, moving the allies closer to their enemy now pinned against the steep banks of the York River. General Cornwallis was desperate. "Last evening the enemy carried my two advanced redoubts on the left by storm," he wrote to his commanding officer in New York City, Gen. Sir Henry Clinton, on October 15, 1781. "My situation now becomes very critical." Lt. Col. Alexander Hamilton led the American charge into Redoubt 10, whose reconstructed portion, standing just above the river, can be viewed from outside its earthen walls. The remains of Redoubt 9 are open for inspection as well.

Cornwallis's despair had been growing by the day. One late September night he ordered his men to abandon their outer defensive lines, to consolidate his forces behind his main works while awaiting reinforcements. This maneuver prompted one diarist to note that this offered valuable ground that could otherwise be obtained only by "much labor and many lives." The French blockade of the York River precluded any chance of escape by the English. Conditions for the Redcoats were poor: "We get terrible provisions now," complained a soldier, "putrid meat and wormy biscuits that have spoiled on the ships . . . foul fever is spreading . . . we have had little rest day or night." Between 1,500 and 2,000 blacks—most were slaves promised freedom if they fought as part of a winning British effort, and many infected with smallpox, as were some of Cornwallis's troops—were suddenly released from the British camp, which was running out of food. This decision may have seemed a bioterrorist attack, but the disease did not spread to the American and French lines. Washington ordered the slaves from this group recaptured and placed under guard so their owners might recover them.

The allied bombardment began on October 9. Governor Nelson reportedly urged General Washington himself to fire the first American shot, at Cornwallis's headquarters in the house of Nelson's uncle (also Thomas Nelson). Governor Nelson later ordered his own home bombarded, on the supposition that Cornwallis would move his headquarters there. An early shot crashed into a house where officers of the Scottish 76th Regiment of Foot were dining, killing the British commissary general and wounding others on Cornwallis's staff. French gunners went after the squadron of English ships in the river, scoring direct hits on the *Charon* and two others: "The ships were enwrapped in a torrent of fire," recorded Dr. James Thacher, an American surgeon, in a graphic journal entry. Flames spread "with vivid brightness among the combustible rigging, and running with amazing rapidity to the tops of the several masts … and in the darkness of night, presented one of the most sublime and magnificent spectacles which can be imagined. Some of our shells … were seen to fall into the river and, bursting, throw up columns of water like the spouting of the monsters of the deep."

The British did not last long under this furious fusillade, which by October 17 had "made the Enemies situation so very disagreable—that about the middle of the day his Lordship was induced to send out a flag, with some proposals for a capitulation," remembered one witness. On October 18, surrender terms were drawn up at the eighteenth-century Augustine Moore House, which would later be badly damaged during the Civil War by cannon fire and soldiers who stripped it of wood for campfires. The Moore House, open seasonally, is stop E on the Battlefield Tour; the next, stop F, is Surrender Field, where British troops laid down their arms the following day—some smashing their weapons to the ground in anger. Other notable stops include "The Deposit," the ravine where the allies stored their siege materials until ready for deployment along the lines, and, just beyond, the gristmill dam, which soldiers crossed repeatedly preparing for siege and battle. These sites, not marked on the park map, are on a heavily wooded section of the Battlefield Tour, which includes the location of Washington's Headquarters (stop H), situated between the American and French camps and strategically next to a spring that provided fresh water.

Both George Washington and Charles Lord Cornwallis would thrive in their later careers, while Sir Henry Clinton would labor thereafter to avoid blame for the ignominious surrender to the upstart Americans and their French allies. Perhaps the most vocally distraught British official was Lord North, the prime minister, who took news of the defeat in London as though he were hit by "a ball in the breast," recorded Lord George Germain, the colonial secretary. North, wrote Germain, paced about in a state of great agitation, bellowing "Oh God! Oh God! It is over! It is all over!" And indeed it was.

SIDE TRIP

JAMESTOWN SETTLEMENT, VA: This seventeenth-century town comes alive through film, gallery exhibits, and outdoor living history that describe the cultures of the Powhatan Indians, Europeans, and Africans who converged on this site. Replicas of the three ships that sailed from England to Virginia in 1607 and re-creations of the colonists' fort and a Powhatan village, along with costumed historical interpreters, give a strong flavor of daily life in this Tidewater region. *2110 Jamestown Road, Williamsburg, VA, 23185, 757-253-4838 or 888-593-4682.*

FURTHER READING

Jerome Greene, *The Guns of Independence: The Siege of Yorktown, 1781.* Savas Beatie, 2009.

James Horn, *A Land as God Made It: Jamestown and the Birth of America.* Basic Books, 2006.

Henry P. Johnson, *The Yorktown Campaign and the Surrender of Cornwallis, 1781.* Scholar's Bookshelf, 2006 (first published 1881).

William Kelso, *Jamestown: The Buried Truth.* University of Virginia Press, 2008.

Benjamin Woolley, *Savage Kingdom: The True Story of Jamestown, 1607, and the Settlement of America.* Harper Perennial, 2008.

2

ST. MARY'S CITY

First-time visitors to Historic St. Mary's City can be forgiven for scanning the horizon and, hand to brow, wondering just where the city is. Their bewilderment is understandable. This first settlement and capital of Maryland perished long ago, in a conspiracy of politics, time, and nature. Meticulous research and modern archaeology, however, have led to a gradual restoration of St. Mary's City and its window into seventeenth-century colonial life in the Chesapeake region. This work continues to illuminate how the first European immigrants to Maryland adapted to a landscape dramatically different from the England they had left behind.

St. Mary's City, easily reachable today from Baltimore and Washington, D.C., via Charles County, was situated on the east bank of the St. Mary's River, a spectacular setting for Maryland's first capital and the bustling seat of Maryland government for much of the 1600s. When the legislature and courts were in session, the town teemed with tobacco planters and lawmakers—and those who lived off them: innkeepers, lawyers, clerks, surveyors, court officials, and shopkeepers. At its peak, as many as 300 people lived in the town, enjoying the principles of religious toleration enshrined in its founding. When the capital relocated to Annapolis in 1694, many moved with it.

The departure of the government left a ghost town on the banks of the St. Mary's River. More than 250 years would pass before work began to uncover the mysteries that lay beneath its soil. Fortunately, other than at the adjacent St. Mary's College of Maryland, no development had occurred during that time. Though some site testing was done in the 1930s, serious study and preservation efforts at St. Mary's did not begin until the 1960s, when the Maryland legislature began acquiring land on which the state's first capital stood. The town had become an underground fossil, its remains a mere eight inches below the surface. The National Park Service believes that St. Mary's City, which became a National Historic Landmark in 1968, is likely the most intact seventeenth-century English town surviving in the United States.

Religious strife in England was a major force behind the establishment of Maryland. In the early 1600s, with the Church of England persecuting dissenting Protestants and Catholics, King Charles I granted Cecil Calvert, Lord "Baltemore," title to 12,000 square miles of the northern Chesapeake in 1632. Calvert established a haven of religious liberty there, and he forbade both proselytizing and criticizing the faith of others. Calvert named his new land "Terra Maria," or Maryland, for the King's wife, Henrietta Maria. (The author here discloses that he is descended from the Calverts.)

Cecil's brother Leonard and about 140 Protestant and Catholic passengers set sail from England for this new land in November of 1633 aboard the *Ark* and the *Dove*, which battled storms and dodged pirates as they crossed the Atlantic. The ships arrived at St. Clement's Island, on the Maryland side of the Potomac River, in March of 1634; several weeks later the intrepid adventurers made their way up the St. Mary's River to found the fourth permanent English settlement in North America.

The settlers proceeded to establish a legislature, court system, and the other trappings of a civil society. In 1649, the Maryland Assembly passed "An Act Concerning Religion," which officially codified portions of Calvert's principles of religious toleration and separation of church and state that had been in effect since 1634—the first such practice in America. (Though Cecil Calvert was a Catholic, Maryland was not a Catholic colony; not only were diverse religious views to be tolerated, but the majority of the colony's first settlers were Protestants.) Lord Baltimore's 1661 Oath for Office Holders reinforced these principles: "yo shall Doe Equall Right to the Poore as to the Rich. yow will not . . . directly nor indirectly trouble . . . any person . . . in Respect of his or her religion nor in his or her free exercise thereof within the said Province." Maryland thereby became a harbinger of the democratic ideals that would attend the birth of the United States more than a hundred years later.

St. Mary's City was planned in the baroque style, similar to the great European cities of Rome, Versailles, and Paris. The town was shaped by two symmetrical triangles that met in the center of the town square, itself formed by four buildings. A significant structure sat on the outer points of each triangle. The chapel and state house sat on opposite triangles— a progressive recognition, perhaps, of the notion of church-state separation. St. Mary's has been called an example of the first sophisticated urban planning in America.

Along with the advantages of modern science, establishing the city's contours required extensive detective and forensic work, for no documents or maps of the town exist, and virtually no buildings from colonial America survive anywhere in the Chesapeake region (although a number have survived in New England). Most clues lay in the ground. In 1969 archaeologists began to uncover what the earth had swallowed hundreds of years earlier: nails; oyster shells; foundations of buildings; animal bones; and locations of paths, roads, fences, gardens, and orchards. Today, labor-intensive soil sifting goes hand-in-hand with modern scientific techniques such as analyses of pollen and plant structure. Sites for garbage, now underground and known as middens, are clues to both dietary habits and doorway locations that help historians reconstruct buildings on their original sites. Fragments of clay tobacco pipes reveal the places where people gathered to socialize.

From Baltimore, travel south to St. Mary's on Rts. 301 and 5, passing the towns of Horsehead, Beantown, Loveville, and Burnt Store. Signs note historic spots such as the house (now a museum) of Dr. Samuel Mudd, who was imprisoned for aiding the 1865 escape of John Wilkes Booth in the days immediately following the assassination of President Abraham Lincoln. The Mudd House is part of the John Wilkes Booth Escape Trail that weaves through Charles County and follows the fleeing assassin's route through southern Maryland and across the Potomac River into Virginia.

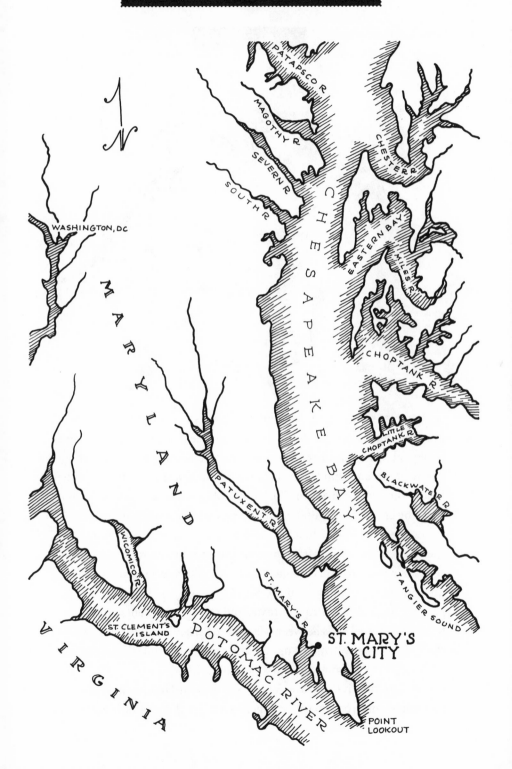

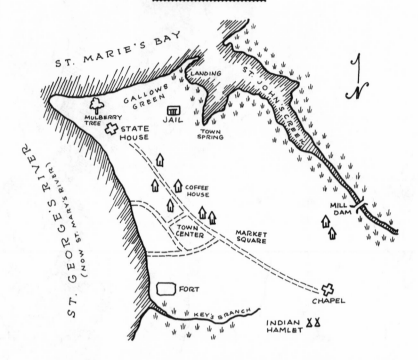

Before visiting, see the Historic St. Mary's City's website for a map, museum hours, the fruits of archeological research, and the interactive "Colonial Kids" feature that, among other offerings, introduces both indentured servant John Halfhead and William Nuthead's print shop, the first in the American South. Once in St. Mary's, visitors can see on foot all of the original town sites and building reconstructions in the historic town. The path mostly follows Aldermanbury Street, the main road of the 1660s town. Stop first at the visitor center museum for a map and see both a panorama of colonial Chesapeake life and a video. Costumed interpreters and exhibits tell the St. Mary's story in engaging human, geographic, and historical contexts, and the special events and activities on many weekends between March and December—churning butter, shooting arrows, watching a militia drill—offer opportunities, especially for children, to imagine the rigors of colonial life.

Settlers first lived at the Woodland Indian Hamlet, a small Native American "Yoacomaco" village, a name at the root of Maryland's

Wicomico County. Luck and timing blessed our English forebears, who were taken in by these nonviolent people who were only too happy to have armed Marylanders on their side as they coexisted peacefully with the belligerent Susquehannocks of the northern Chesapeake. "These Indians are so noble as you can do them noe favor but they will return it," recorded Jesuit colonist Andrew White in his journal. The Yoacomaco taught the settlers how to survive in a landscape drastically different from the fenced grazing lands of England they had known. This new terrain had thick forests and no fields. The English learned to clear small paths of forest by girdling trees to prevent sap from rising, purging them of leaves, and clearing the underbrush with a low fire. As sunlight reached the forest floor, the area could then be planted with corn, beans, and peas (corn became a staple that provided half a settler's calories). The Yoacomaco also showed our ancestors how to set fire rings to drive deer into the river, making them easy prey for the colonists, who coveted venison—the meat of nobility in England but available to even the poorest Maryland servant.

Cold-weather visitors can warm themselves in a "witchott," a thatch-and-wood hut reconstructed using replicated sixteenth-century Chesapeake Indian tools. Smoke from its fire preserved the dry goods, stacked on planks above, and kept mice and mosquitoes away. Others may see a Yoacomaco man make a dugout canoe. As a small fire slowly burns out the center of a log, he scrapes away the charcoal debris and hollows the log, then applies clay to the sides to protect them from the fire. Perched on a nearby log, an English woman weaving a basket may describe her five-month trans-Atlantic journey and her new life at St. Mary's as an indentured house servant. She is a Protestant working for a Catholic master, as was often the case in Maryland, and must work for five years to pay off her passage, not being permitted to marry until her term is up. (Slavery would not take root in the region until the latter part of the century.) She might extol the virtues of the Yoacomaco and—a smile playing at the corners of her mouth—note that she is but one of five women in the colony at that moment.

The Roman Catholic Church has its American origins in St. Mary's City, and one may stand on the spot where, in 1634, it all began. The Society of Jesus obtained land grants in exchange for transporting 10 percent of the new colony's settlers across the Atlantic. The wooden chapel the Jesuits built on their land was burned in 1645 by a Protestant raiding party from England rebelling against the Calverts—making St. Mary's the only known spot where the complex series of military episodes that comprised the English Civil Wars (1642–50) physically touched America. The 1660s-era replacement chapel, the first major brick structure in Maryland, is also long gone, and it is being reconstructed on its original foundation in the shape of a Latin cross, scheduled for completion in 2014.

Colonists worshipped at this site until 1704. Here some 500 early Marylanders lie in unmarked graves, around what was once the most potent symbol of religious toleration in America. Graves within five feet of the brick foundation have been excavated, to permit drainage and stabilization of the bricks. Ground-penetrating radar and other technology have helped researchers locate and mark other graves so the cemetery can eventually be restored to its seventeenth-century appearance.

Careful sleuthing and modern science have helped identify three of those early Marylanders. In 1990, three lead coffins were discovered beneath what had been the chapel floor. This discovery launched Project Lead Coffin, in which experts from NASA, the U.S. Army, the Smithsonian, and other organizations used sophisticated instruments and techniques to excavate the coffins in 1992. In the largest lay a male, identified as Philip Calvert, Chancellor of Maryland and half brother of Cecilius and Leonard Calvert. The second coffin contained a female, believed to be Philip's first wife, Anne Wolseley; the third housed a child, possibly Calvert's by his second wife. Following the chapel's completion, the coffins with the Calvert remains will be returned to their original resting places of 300 years ago, in a burial vault visible to visitors under a glass floor.

A stroll along a mowed path toward the town square, dotted by three-dimensional "ghost frames," shows the rough locations of other structures that engage the imagination. Four buildings define the town square, the physical and social center of St. Mary's. One, a reconstructed store and office called Cordea's Hope, conveys the small scale and simple tastes of early colonial life. An inn called Smith's Ordinary suggests what visitors to the capital would have experienced. The other two—a lawyer's office and Leonard Calvert's home—are depicted by ghost frames.

The Calvert House, once home to Maryland's government, served St. Mary's as part legislative chamber and part tavern (drinking and legislating, as today, being close companions then). Nathaniel Pope, an ancestor of George Washington's and leader of the rebel Protestants, fortified it during the 1645 English attack—thus it is also known as Pope's Fort. Its moat eventually became a disposal site for the detritus of daily colonial life, and a scholarly prism through which to examine St. Mary's society. Its excavation has yielded body armor, an exploded cannon barrel, cannonballs, and evidence of early African-style tobacco pipes. Historic St. Mary's City schedules an annual "Tidewater Archeology" weekend each July, which offers the public a rare opportunity to participate in archeological digs—a particularly engaging activity for children, who will experience uncommon encouragement to dirty their hands.

Adjacent to the square is a gazebo honoring Margaret Brent, a respected landowner chosen by Gov. Leonard Calvert to manage his affairs after his death. Brent made, by colonial standards, a preposterous demand: that she be given not one, but two votes in the Maryland Assembly—one as a property-owning citizen and one as Lord Baltimore's attorney. Her unsuccessful 1648 attempt to vote, doomed by the era in which she lived, endures as the first suffrage attempt in America by a woman.

Farthing's Ordinary, once an inn that provided food, drink, and lodging for travelers with business before the legislature and courts of seventeenth-century Maryland, is today reconstructed and serves as the museum gift shop. Nearby are the original floor and cellar of Garret Van Sweringen's Inn & Coffeehouse, where habitues of St. Mary's gathered to talk and smoke; play dominoes, cards, and chess; and drink beer, coffee, and boiled cider. This establishment was Maryland's first private hotel, catering to the elite. The coffeehouse cellar, next to the kitchen, has yielded a number of colonial artifacts.

Farthing's swarmed with activity when the colonial assembly was in session. Male guests took meals and downed tankards of ale before drifting off to sleep on the floor of the main room, drawing comfort from their own fatigue and what remained of the fire. Female guests reposed with the ladies of the innkeeper's family. The print shop in St. Mary's was owned by William Nuthead, proprietor of the first printing press in England's southern colonies. Visitors to the excavated and reconstructed shop can watch Nuthead's indentured servant print promissory notes, whose value is pegged to tobacco. The Historic St. Mary's City website has an interactive introduction to Nuthead's printing operation—which, being forbidden in many English colonies, was another symbol of the progressive character of St. Mary's City.

Men and women in period dress welcome visitors aboard the *Maryland Dove*, an approximate reconstruction of one of the vessels that landed in 1634. They inform prospective passengers, in old English, that they must wait until spring for passage. The ship's tour is especially great for kids, and a look below decks may well banish any desire to be part of a voyage to America. The cramped, dank space is designed for England-bound hogsheads of tobacco, not human cargo. Two slats that pass for bunks lie forward, adjacent to a small cooking fireplace that looks both appetite-stifling and unlikely to generate warmth. The captain's small quarters are luxurious by comparison. A young crewman points to the wooded spit of land where the *Ark* and the *Dove* first landed at St. Mary's, then marvels at a visitor's camera—"the box with the little man inside who paints wonderful pictures."

Posted on the dock is a notice about the sale of an indentured servant. This poor chap will not likely engender much envy—he has a 40 percent chance of dying from disease before completing his term of servitude, though should he survive it, he will receive "freedom dues"—clothing, an axe and hoe, three barrels of corn, and fifty acres of land. If he fails to marry, however, he risks being sent into military service against the belligerent Susquehannocks to the north. Marriage was no foregone conclusion in the seventeenth-century Chesapeake, where there were at least three men for every woman. On the high bank above the *Dove* is a marker honoring Mathias de Sousa, an indentured man who arrived with the Jesuits in 1634. De Sousa was the first person of African descent to serve in an American legislature, which he did in St. Mary's City in 1642. Little else is known about him.

The next stop is the reconstructed brick State House of 1676, the second such structure in St. Mary's City and one of the first public buildings in Maryland. It hosts public events such as lectures and concerts. (The government purchased the nearby Leonard Calvert House as the first official State House, in the town center—there archeologists discovered a circular ring, which may have been a pit for animal fighting; if so, it would be the oldest such evidence of this sporting activity known to have existed in the colonies.) A key element of the town's baroque design, the State House (reconstructed in 1934) features period legislators' furniture and, on the second floor, an exhibition of documents about the life of Daniel Clocker. Clocker was an indentured servant who completed his term and became a respected landowner in southern Maryland. Documents displayed include legal records and Clocker's household inventory.

In the yard of the adjacent Trinity Church lies the foundation of the original State House, whose bricks were used to build the church around 1830. Highlighting the small cluster of graves in the churchyard is the vault containing the lead coffins housing the remains of Lionel and Anne Copley—Lionel Copley arrived in Maryland in 1692 as the colony's first royal governor. In 1799, when overly inquisitive medical students breached the vault, Lionel was nothing but bone. Anne, however, was fully preserved—though the consequent exposure to oxygen reduced her to bone in five hours. In 1992, a scientific team entered the vault, seeking clues to lead-coffin construction. These Copley coffins, along with those of the Calverts, are the only seventeenth-century lead coffins known to exist in America. Just to the east stood the St. Mary's jail, on another triangle point and now under the road. Archaeologists have deduced its location from the density and distribution of bricks and Dutch roof tile discovered nearby.

Tobacco was the social and economic grease of colonial tidewater society. It was the currency for life's necessities and fine goods from England. One settler described the crop, known also as sotweed, as "our meat, drinke, cloathing and monies." The opportunity to make a good life as a tobacco planter attracted many immigrants to Maryland, thanks to plentiful land and England's insatiable demand for this leaf that, until the soil became exhausted in the early nineteenth-century, flourished in the southern areas of the colony.

The working tobacco plantation of Godiah Spray (not an actual historical figure but a seventeenth-century version of John Doe) puts visitors right into 1661 St. Mary's, courtesy of the dress and period English of Master Spray, a prosperous Catholic owner of 200 acres along St. An-

drew's Creek. His large family includes seven children; he has five indentured servants. Also on his property is a tenant farmer, who pays Spray
one-third of his tobacco crop as rent. Master Spray owns four times as
much land as he did in England. The upstairs sleeping room in his simple, two-story home on the creek is a sign of his prosperity. The Mackall
tobacco barn, near the chapel, dates from 1785 and allows visitors to see
the construction techniques used at that time.

As his wife and daughter weed a vegetable garden and his roosters
scratch about in the dry soil around the house, Master Spray tells of starting life in St. Mary's City. Each adult male settler receives fifty acres of
land, but the surveying costs will saddle him with a debt of 1,200 to 1,400
pounds of tobacco before a seed goes in the ground (one planter could
grow, on average, about 1,500 pounds per year). So waterfront property is
less for the view than for practical reasons: The further inland surveyors
must travel, the more they must be paid. And the further hogsheads of
tobacco must travel to the wharves, to trade for fine goods from England,
the greater the cost and trouble—so proximity to the water has significant
economic value.

More people work much less land in England; in the colonies the
reverse is true, Master Spray explains. Maryland's settlers are astonished
at its vast forests, since in England, where most timber has been cleared,
forested land is a privilege of nobility. Planters keep only livestock that
can roam and fend for itself, for no man wishes to invest in the labor
to build fences. Having to feed animals, such as horses, requires that
more land be used for food, which means less acreage for raising tobacco.
(Spray's genetically accurate seventeenth-century swine run amok on his
wooded land.) The less corn Master Spray grows, the more tobacco he
can plant. This equation allows more luxury items from England, making
his wife happy and more likely to have more children, who can help him
work more land so he can grow more tobacco. So goes the cycle that is
rewarding him and his family with incrementally increasing prosperity.

St. Mary's City should whet the appetite for a visit to St. Clement's
Island, where the Maryland colonists first landed, in March of 1634. This
small state park sits a half-mile offshore in the Potomac River, 45 minutes
northwest of St. Mary's City. After receiving permission to settle from
the Piscataway, the colonists celebrated their safe arrival here on March

25 with a Mass. A forty-foot high cross commemorates both the landing and spot of this first Catholic Mass in Maryland, and March 25 is still marked as Maryland Day in memory of this landing.

St. Clement's remained on stage for major events of the next two centuries. During the Revolutionary War and the War of 1812, the British used the island as a base for plundering the area. In 1864, Confederate raiders damaged the lighthouse, though they spared the keeper's family (the lighthouse was destroyed by fire in 1956 but has been rebuilt). The island can be visited by boat on weekends. The *Tolerance* leaves the museum pier twice daily on Saturday and Sunday for the 15-minute trip and returns an hour and a quarter later (passengers may ride out on the first trip and return on the second). Visitors can enjoy picnic areas with grills, hiking trails, excellent bird-watching opportunities, fishing, and crabbing.

The adjacent Potomac River Museum (with a small admission charge) presents a perspective on the colonists' arrival and early life in Maryland. Exhibits in this St. Mary's County facility include models and portraits of the Calvert legacy, fragments of seventeenth- and eighteenth-century ceramics, period English dolls, and small models of the *Ark* and *Dove* (including a partial passenger list). Artifacts are cleverly displayed in pullout cabinet drawers.

SIDE TRIPS

JOHN WILKES BOOTH ESCAPE TRAIL, WASHINGTON, D.C., MD & VA: After shooting Abraham Lincoln on April 14, 1865, John Wilkes Booth galloped across the Washington Navy Yard Bridge and headed to southern Maryland, planning to cross the Potomac River into Virginia. The trail starts at Ford's Theater and goes south on MD Rt. 5 / 301 through Clinton, home of the Surratt House Museum (site of the tavern where Booth and his band hid weapons); the Dr. Samuel A. Mudd House Museum (where Dr. Mudd tended to Booth's injured leg); Rich Hill (home of Samuel Cox, from which Booth and David Herold were taken to a pine thicket to hide); Port Royal, Virginia (the eighteenth-century ferry town through which the outlaws rode); and other sites—the last of which is the Garrett Farm outside Port Royal, where Union troops apprehended Herold and killed Booth (and where a marker in a highway median is the sole indication of a momentous historical event).

POINT LOOKOUT STATE PARK, MD: The Union opened Hammond Hospital in 1862 for wounded soldiers at this junction of the Potomac River and Chesapeake Bay, just a few miles south of Historic St. Mary's City. Point Lookout was the site of a Union prison camp from 1863 to 1866. Features include boat launch, canoe rental, camp fire programs, camping (tent and cabin), hiking, hunting, picnic area, playground, swimming, and the Civil War Museum / Marshland Nature Center. *11175 Point Lookout Road, Scotland, MD, 20687, 301-872-5688.*

SOTTERLEY PLANTATION, MD: This slave-operated plantation home, 35 minutes north of St. Mary's City, was built in 1703 and is the only tidewater mansion of its era open to the public. Its 95-acre site sits scenically above the Patuxent River in Charles County, with its spectacular Colonial Revival Gardens tended carefully by volunteers. *44300 Sotterley Lane, Hollywood, MD, 20636, 301-373-2280.*

SOLOMONS ISLAND, MD: Located where the Patuxent River meets the Chesapeake Bay, on the southern tip of Calvert County, Maryland, this scenic town with broad river vistas was the site of amphibious invasion training during World War II. It's an ideal detour for strolling the Riverwalk and al fresco dining when visiting the historical attractions of southern Maryland. Exhibits at the Calvert Marine Museum include the Drum Point Light, one of three surviving Chesapeake Bay screw-pile lighthouses, and the bugeye *Wm. B. Tennison.*

FURTHER READING

ADULTS
Lois Green Carr, Philip Morgan, and Jean Russo, *Colonial Chesapeake Society.* University of North Carolina Press, 1988.

Lois Green Carr and Lorena Walsh, *Robert Cole's World: Agriculture and Society in Early Maryland*. University of North Carolina Press, 1991.

John D. Krugler, *English and Catholic: The Lords Baltimore in the Seventeenth Century*. Johns Hopkins University Press, 2004.

CHILDREN

Ann Jenson, *Leonard Calvert and the Maryland Adventure*. Tidewater Publishers, 1998.

Sally Walker, *Written in Bone: Buried Lives of Jamestown and Colonial Maryland*. Carolrhoda Books, 2009.

3

FORT FREDERICK

Four major wars have occurred on American soil. The first protected our ancestral English colonists from the depredations of the French and their native Indian allies, while two were fought to free us forever from the British yoke. The last determined whether America would be one nation or two. One fortification played a role in three of those four wars—Fort Frederick, in western Maryland, which sat out only the War of 1812. Visitors today can inspect this oldest and best-preserved colonial fort in the United States and enjoy a rare opportunity for a taste of life on the eighteenth-century American frontier.

Built in 1756 by the colony of Maryland to protect its English settlers from French soldiers and their Native American allies, Fort Frederick was one of the largest defensive outposts in North America. It was part of a network of forts built in the 1750s along the western frontier of the middle colonies of Pennsylvania, Maryland, and Virginia at the outset of the French and Indian War, which raged from 1756 to 1763. Fort Frederick qualifies as an authentic eighteenth-century fort, being strategically situated, designed, and built according to accepted principles of fortification, and sufficiently large to hold the necessary supplies and materiel to launch offensive operations. (Most fortifications of this time and place were simple blockhouses and stockades surrounding the cabins of the settlers.) Fort Tonoloway, another fort sited fifteen miles west of Hancock, Maryland, is today the site of a state park of the same name, while the larger Fort Cumberland was situated further west, at the junction of the Potomac River and Wills Creek.

Virginia also constructed a chain of forts, eighteen to twenty miles apart, which served primarily as places of refuge for settlers fleeing Indian attacks—although that colony devoted fewer resources to defending its western frontier than to measures designed to ensure internal security and control of slaves. Most of the forts on the Virginia frontier were in what is today West Virginia: Fort Maidstone sat on the south bank of the Potomac River, across from present-day Williamsport, while Fort Ashby was eight miles south of Fort Cumberland. Forts Pleasant and Buttermilk were constructed on the south branch of the Potomac River, near present-day Moorefield. Maintaining discipline among the men in these outposts was essential: George Washington, commanding the Virginia troops, admonished the captain at Fort Ashby about the behavior of the captain's wife: "There are continued complaints to me of the misbehavior of your wife; who I am told sows sedition among the men," he wrote the officer. "If she is not immediately sent from the Camp, or I hear any more complaints of such irregular Behavior upon my arrival there; I shall take care to drive her out myself." Washington also warned him to stop selling rum to his men.

After the French and their Indian allies defeated British general Edward Braddock in 1755 as he marched west to seize Fort Duquesne (now Pittsburgh), British military strategists considered building a new road from Fort Frederick to Fort Cumberland, forty miles to the west. They decided instead on a new route west from Carlisle, Pennsylvania, to the Forks of the Ohio, overseen by Gen. John Forbes. This "Forbes Road" would parallel the line of British forts in southern Pennsylvania that included Fort Morris at Shippensburg, Fort Chambers at Chambersburg, and Fort Loudoun on the west branch of Conococheague Creek, approximately thirty miles north of Fort Frederick.

The absence of a road connecting Forts Cumberland and Frederick in the late 1750s deprived the latter of a role as major base camp for the British western initiative. Fort Frederick thus became a supply repository and is the only surviving colonial fortification that retains original build-

FORTS ON THE COLONIAL FRONTIER

FORT DUQUESNE
FORT PITT

FORT LIGONIER

YOUGHOGHENY RIVER

MONONGAHELA RIVER

PENNSYLVANIA

SUSQUEHANNA RIVER

FORT CARLISLE

FORT MORRIS

FORT CHAMBERS

FORT LOUDOUN

FORT FREDERICK

MONOCACY RIVER

MARYLAND

POTOMAC RIVER

BALTIMORE

ANNAPOLIS

FORT CUMBERLAND

FORT TONOLOWAY

FORT ASHBY

FORT MAIDSTONE

FORT DEFIANCE

FORT PLEASANT

FORT BUTTERMILK

S.BRANCH POTOMAC RIVER

SHENANDOAH RIVER

WEST VIRGINIA

N

MAP SHOWS PRESENT-DAY
STATE BOUNDARIES

ing materials. Today its restored remnants sit atop a bluff overlooking the Potomac River, which forms the border between Maryland and Virginia, in Fort Frederick State Park. This picturesque site along the base of the Appalachian Mountains in the Cumberland Valley is in Maryland's Washington County.

The coastal English settlements of the mid-eighteenth century stretched from present-day Maine to Georgia (Maine was part of Massachusetts until achieving statehood in 1820). The agrarian bounty of the Ohio Valley had been drawing English settlers westward and toward inevitable collision with French settlers moving into the region from Canada. The French and British both enlisted various Native Americans as allies, and the name given the conflict—the French and Indian War—has over time obscured the reasons over which the war was fought. The English settlers on Maryland's frontier were especially vulnerable to attacks by the native Shawnee and other tribes, who, in the words of one historian, ferociously wielded "the tomahawk, the scalping knife, and the torch." Although Fort Frederick was a base of operations for Maryland troops to repel the French and Indian raiding parties, the fact that no military action occurred there led George Washington to describe it as of "no Singular Service to our Country."

Horatio Sharpe, Maryland's proprietary governor from 1753 to 1769, had urged the state legislature to build Fort Frederick, which he named for Frederick Calvert, the sixth Lord Baltimore. This enterprise strained the colony's budget and ushered in a package of new taxes; the fort was to be financed in part by taxing unmarried men, spirits, billiard tables, and Roman Catholics, who—in a contradiction of the ecumenical ethos of the colony's founders—were required to pay double. Governor Sharpe raised 500 provincials and local militiamen to man the fort, noting that "Our Barracks are made for the Reception & Accomodation of 200 men but on Occasion there will be room for twice that number." The fort served as a staging area in 1758 for troops and supplies during the campaign to recapture Fort Duquesne from the French. That year a smallpox epidemic broke out on its grounds. Five years later Fort Frederick became a haven for 700 refugees fleeing the Native Americans, some of whom would later become allies. One officer reported that his men were visited by some Cherokees, whose chief "invited us to Smoak a Pipe with him."

During the Revolutionary War, Fort Frederick served as a prison camp, housing large numbers of British prisoners inside its walls. During the Civil War, Union troops were garrisoned there to protect the Chesapeake & Ohio Canal and Baltimore & Ohio Railroad, and they repeatedly skirmished with Confederates who slipped across the Potomac River into Maryland. For many years following its military service, Fort Frederick either stood abandoned or was farmed privately—for a time its stone walls, built to withstand cannon fire, were used by an enterprising farmer as a livestock pen. For much of the nineteenth and early twentieth centuries, several generations of an African American family owned and farmed the grounds—Nathan Williams, the family patriarch, was the son of Samuel "Big Sam" Williams, a slave who had purchased his own freedom and that of his wife and four children. After the state of Maryland acquired the fort in 1922, the walls—the majority of which are original—were restored and stabilized by the Civilian Conservation Corps in the 1930s, as part of the New Deal. In 1974 Fort Frederick became a National Historic Landmark.

Those stopping by the visitor center in this 585-acre state park are greeted by a display of exhibits on the history of the park and a short orientation film. The fort is a simple walled rectangle of stone, with arrowhead-shaped bastions that once held cannon gun decks protruding from each corner—Governor Sharpe illuminated the importance of stone in a letter to Lord Calvert: only stone, he wrote, "can secure a Garrison against the Savages." Fort Frederick's wooden barracks have been reconstructed and adorned with period clothing and personal effects of enlisted men and their officers who would have served there during the French and Indian War. The original foundation stones of the officers' quarters are visible, although the powder magazine, gun decks, and the catwalks that once accommodated sentries and musket-wielding defenders disappeared long ago. The officers' quarters are small, as were the standard British weekly rations for each man: seven pounds of flour and beef or pork and a pint of rice, with only daily rum rations to mitigate those paltry portions.

Several other buildings sit just outside the fort. Captain Wort's Sutler Shop has tasteful wares, including a variety of historical souvenirs, period children's games, camping supplies, and sundries such as snacks, sodas, and ice cream. Adjacent are a carriage house, barn, and blacksmith shop, also recreated by the Civilian Conservation Corps. The CCC museum tells the story of the fort's restoration and is full of 1700s-era artifacts excavated during reconstruction in the 1930s. Spectators hoping to see reenacted, eighteenth-century-style hand-to-hand combat will be disappointed, however, as the Maryland Park Service bans such activity.

Numerous activities beckon outside the fort's walls, however. The Chesapeake & Ohio Canal—America's longest and skinniest national park—runs through the south side of the park and parallels the Potomac River for 184.5 miles, from Georgetown to Cumberland (see chapter 8). The canal towpath is fertile ground for hiking and cycling (hikers should watch for cyclists all along the canal). Big Pool, a mile-and-a-half natural depression on the canal that was used as a space to turn canal boats and as the winter home for a few, makes for terrific stream-fed fishing. It's also the place to boat (electric motors only, no launch fees), although there is no access to the Potomac River. The wetland just below Beaver Pond, on the river side of the canal, is a bird watcher's haven, inhabited by wood ducks, canvasbacks, osprey, blue herons, and the occasional bald eagle (beavers, having decimated the area, have moved on). The occasional train whistle that echoes through the river valley is a poignant reminder that goods moving west by rail to the Ohio Valley helped bring to an end the canal's once significant role in east-west commerce.

Another feature of the park, just below the canal, is an unimproved campground offering camping pads and grills (latrines are conveniently located). Large group sites are also available at this camp on the banks of the Potomac River, where on summer evenings families grill and kids and their fathers skip stones across the smooth river surface. A short walk to the east of the fort, still on park grounds, leads to a picnic area with a playground in a wooded glen. This spot is ideal for casual al fresco dining and watching for wild turkeys, fox, deer, and the occasional black bear (deer are sufficiently numerous to earn an annual managed hunt). A three-mile hiking trail in the park, the Plantation Trail, is graced by trees native not to the Appalachians but to the Piedmont and Eastern Shore regions, thanks to a Civilian Conservation Corps experiment in the 1930s that introduced sweetgums and several varieties of pines. Another hiking option is the paved Western Maryland Rail Trail, whose south end starts at the Rt. 56 exit on I-70, a half-mile from the park.

Between Memorial Day and Labor Day each year, the park offers a variety of events that illuminates the roles that Fort Frederick has played in American history. Staff members and volunteers in period dress present a variety of programs that orient visitors to eighteenth-century topics such as clothing, cooking implements, and weapons from both the colonial and Native American communities. The French and Indian War Muster, in August each year, features living-history demonstrations and battle re-enactments that allow visitors to experience this little-understood epoch of colonial history up close. The October Ghost Walk is an ideal opportunity to search for the spirits said to haunt the forest, barracks, and the fort itself.

SIDE TRIPS

HAGERSTOWN, MD: Hagerstown, the seat of Washington County, is eighteen miles east of Fort Frederick State Park. Founded in 1762 by Jonathan Hager, the town sat on the Eastern Native American North-South Trading Route, now Rt. 11, and the First National Road, which is Rt. 40. During the Civil War, Hagerstown had the misfortune to lie along the route used by Confederate general Robert E. Lee to and from the battles of both Antietam and Gettysburg. In July of 1864, Confederate troops threatened to torch the town unless they received a ransom of $200,000—although legend says a clerk's error reduced the amount to a more manageable $20,000 that, when paid, allowed Hagerstown to escape destruction (neighboring Chambersburg, Pennsylvania, did not fare as well at the hands of the Rebels, who burned the town when it failed to pay). A walking tour of Hagerstown's Civil War consists of approximately twenty significant sites and is a fitting finish to a weekend in this part of western Maryland. The Jonathan Hager House & Museum, in the Hagerstown City Park, is full of period furnishings. Also in City Park are the Washington County Museum of Fine Arts, the Hagerstown Railroad

Museum and Engine 202, and the Mansion House Art Center. The park also offers lakes, wooded walking trails, and scenic picnic areas.

WESTERN MARYLAND RAIL TRAIL, MD: The Western Maryland Rail Trail in Maryland is a twenty-three-mile-long voyage through American history that parallels a portion of the Chesapeake & Ohio Canal. This paved trail starts a half-mile west of Fort Frederick and runs to the Old Pearre Rail Station and is ideal for walking, jogging, and biking. The main trailhead is in the quaint town of Hancock, at the trail's midpoint. Interpretive signs along the way describe historical sites and remains. Bikers and hikers can enjoy panoramic vistas of the Potomac River. The Rails-to-Trails Conservancy has named this paved trail one of the top dozen rail trails in the United States.

FURTHER READING

Burton K. Kummerow, Christine H. O'Toole, and R. Scott Stephenson, *Pennsylvania's Forbes Trail: Gateways and Getaways along the Legendary Route from Philadelphia to Pittsburgh.* Taylor Trade Publishing, 2008.

INDEPENDENCE NATIONAL
HISTORICAL PARK

The small cluster of buildings on Independence Square that comprises the feature attraction of this national park, on the east side of Philadelphia, is the cradle of American independence. Here the founding Americans laid the groundwork for independence from Britain and the foundation for modern representative government. Our nation's founding documents—the Articles of Confederation, the Declaration of Independence, and the Constitution—were crafted in these buildings, which hosted the Second Continental Congress (1775–1781) and the Constitutional Convention of 1787–1789. During the convention, fifty-five delegates from twelve colonies hammered out the precepts of American government (the thirteenth, Rhode Island, did not participate).

George Washington was appointed commander of the Continental Army here, in 1775. "I can now inform you that the Congress have made Choice of the modest and virtuous, the amiable, generous and brave George Washington Esqr, to be the General of the American Army," John Adams wrote approvingly to his wife, Abigail, in mid-June of 1775. "This appointment will have a great Effect, in cementing and securing the Union of these Colonies." From 1790 to 1800, while the permanent capital at Washington, D.C., was being constructed, this city of 45,000 inhabitants served as the national capital of the new republic. Washington lived in the President's House, a structure at Sixth and Market Streets whose excavation helped reveal the attitudes toward slavery among our founding statesmen. Exhibits there portray Washington's aggressive pursuit of a slave who escaped from the president's household.

The visitor center on Market Street, between Sixth and Fifth Streets, provides an orientation to this multi-faceted park and tickets to tour Independence Hall (free but required), which can also be reserved in advance on the park website. The visitor center, which shares space with the Philadelphia-area tourist authority (helpful for those interested in other area attractions), also has films, exhibits, and literature on the park. The park map includes recommendations for seeing its many attractions most efficiently. Those with several hours might visit Independence Hall, the adjacent Great Essentials exhibit, and the pavilion housing the Liberty Bell and its exhibit on the evolution of freedom in America. Visitors who have a half day should add to that itinerary Carpenters' Hall (where delegates to the First Continental Congress met to air grievances against King George III); Congress Hall (home of the United States Congress from 1790 to 1800 and venue of Washington's second inauguration and John Adams's first); and Franklin Court, site of Benjamin Franklin's house and related buildings. Those devoting a full day to the park should also see the Portrait Gallery in the Second Bank of the United States; the Bishop White and Todd Houses; the Thaddeus Kosciuszko National Monument; and the Edgar Allan Poe National Historical Site. Children can join the Junior Ranger program and complete the booklet by filling in the trading cards of the founders available throughout the park.

Exhibits in the visitor center illuminate major events of the revolutionary era; curators change the exhibits periodically. Two short films illuminate the difficult choices the colonists faced as the Revolutionary War erupted: "Independence" and "Choosing Sides," in which actors portray both patriots and loyalists who tell their stories, employing quotations from period letters and diaries that dramatize the agonizing issues they faced. Viewers are left to contemplate the choices they would have made.

Independence Hall, a World Heritage site, and the Liberty Bell Center are the most popular sites in the park. Independence Hall, where many of our country's great national decisions were made, was then the Pennsylvania State House, a striking example of Georgian architecture completed in the 1730s. The state lent this building for the meetings of the Second Continental Congress; here occurred both Washington's appointment as American commander in 1775 and the adoption of the Declaration of Independence the following year. The heat and humidity of summer in Philadelphia, rarely pleasant in an era with no air conditioning, was worsened because the windows of the State House were kept closed, for reasons of confidentiality and, more importantly, as a barrier to the flies that tormented the delegates day and night. Thomas Jefferson told of swarming flies that bit through the thin silk stockings of the delegates, who swatted and cursed to no avail. Independence Hall's original furniture was destroyed during the British occupation of Philadelphia, but restorations have injected an authentic eighteenth-century flavor into the building. Visitors queue up early on the tree-lined walkways to tour Independence Hall, especially between early May and Labor Day. The $4.4 million renovation of the Independence Hall tower, completed in 2012, has restored its 1828 appearance.

Park rangers conducting tours of Independence Hall sometimes quiz visitors about the identity of Declaration of Independence signers depicted in the portrait hanging in the east wing courtroom. Benches and chairs in the courtroom are original; the iron-caged defendant's box is a grim symbol of eighteenth-century trials. On the other side of the hall is the assembly room, where the Articles of Confederation were signed and both the Declaration of Independence and United States Constitution debated. Several original items remain from the drama of those days, most intriguing, perhaps, the chair George Washington used during the deliberations over the Constitution (he was the president of the Constitutional Convention). This chair features the "rising sun" carving that, according to James Madison, prompted Benjamin Franklin—probably the only other man who could have served in that post—to ponder the position of the sun: "I have often in the course of the session . . . looked at that behind the President without being able to tell whether it was rising or setting. But now at length I have the happiness to know that it is a rising and not a setting sun." On the south side of Independence

Hall is Independence Square, where Philadelphians gathered during the Continental Congress to protest British policies toward the colonies. The park interprets the square's nineteenth-century history, including stories of the return of the Marquis de Lafayette in 1824, slavery, the abolitionist movement, women's rights, and visits by Abraham Lincoln (both prior to and during his presidency). In pleasant weather the square teems with strollers and lunching office workers.

Philadelphia was founded on the Delaware River as a haven for Quakers and was the largest city in America by the time the First Continental Congress met there in 1774. The city was remarkably civilized by the rough standards of that time. Major thoroughfares were lined with brick or stone, and sidewalks of either those materials or tile offered pedestrians some protection from airborne dirt and mud. By the mid-1790s, brick and stone had become the principal materials of construction, wood having been deemed too great a fire danger for a densely populated city. Citizens amused themselves by chatting and singing in front of their homes in warm weather, watching horse races through city streets, and gambling—more gentile social interactions than those of other young American cities such as New York, thanks to Philadelphia's Quaker influence (although Quakers did not approve of gambling). The city's central location and river accessibility made it the ideal gathering place for the delegates arriving from New England and from as far south as Georgia to shape a nation. Many of these men spent more time in Philadelphia boarding houses than in their own homes during this period. John Adams and his wife, Abigail Adams, wrote faithfully to each other for much of his time away; his letters reflected the weighty issues of this moment. "The Business I have had upon my Mind has been as great and important as can be intrusted to Man, and the Difficulty and Intricacy of it is prodigious," wrote John to Abigail on July 24, 1775, two months into the Second Continental Congress. "When 50 or 60 Men have a Constitution to form for a great Empire, at the same time that they have a Country of fifteen hundred Miles extent to fortify . . . an extensive Commerce to regulate, numerous Tribes of Indians to negotiate with, a standing Army of Twenty seven Thousand Men to raise, pay, victual and *officer*, I really shall pity those 50 or 60 Men."

East of Independence Hall is the Portrait Gallery in the Second Bank of the United States, chartered in 1816 as a source of credit for the nation's growing agrarian economy. Portraits of George and Martha Washington and other founders bring the period to life. A curator from the Park Service discusses the gallery in a short YouTube video. The Park Service makes further use of modern technology with "Ring Up History!," brief stories of approximately twenty of the park's sites accessed by dialing a two-digit number on one's cell phone.

Before crossing Chestnut Street to explore the Liberty Bell Center, stop in the Great Essentials exhibit on the west side of Independence Hall. Don't miss the plaque in the ground that marks the spot where Abraham Lincoln stood at a flag-raising ceremony in February 1861 en route to Washington, D.C., for his first inauguration. Great Essentials has original broadsides of the Articles of Confederation, the Declaration of Independence, and the U.S. Constitution as well as the silver Syng inkstand in which the delegates dipped their quill pens to sign the Declaration. A correction made by George Washington on a copy of the Constitution is a powerful reflection of the sometimes acrimonious debates that shaped the final document. The exhibit takes its name from John Adams's contention that these documents represent the "great essentials of society and government." A few steps to the west is Congress Hall, the county courthouse that served as the meeting venue for the United States Congress when the federal government resided in Philadelphia from 1790 to 1800. The House met on the first floor and the Senate on the second. In this building were the deliberations over, and the smooth transfer of, power from George Washington, the first president, to John Adams, the second—an unprecedented occurrence that many Americans today take for granted, but one far from assured in the uncertain days of the nation's infancy.

Many school children are familiar with the Liberty Bell, named by the nineteenth-century abolition movement. The bell was initially cast in a London foundry in 1752 to commemorate the fiftieth anniversary of Pennsylvania's democratic constitution that William Penn granted to the colony in 1701. In 1777 it was spirited off to Allentown to protect it from the British. Photographic exhibits of slavery and abolition, women's suffrage, and the twentieth-century struggle for civil rights—movements that employed the imagery of the Liberty Bell as part of their own struggles for liberty and equality—line the route to the bell itself, which hangs in an open space, at the far end of the pavilion. Despite occasional attempts to damage the bell, only a thin rope line stands between it and its admirers, allowing a sense of intimacy that is underscored by the view of Independence Hall, its original home, in the background.

The Liberty Bell has two cracks—one sustained during testing in 1753 and the other, legend says, as it tolled to mark the death of John Marshall, chief justice of the Supreme Court, in 1835. The last formal ringing occurred on George Washington's birthday in 1846, when, a Philadelphia newspaper recorded, the bell "rang its last clear note on Monday last . . . and now hangs in the great city steeple irreparably cracked and forever dumb."

On the north side of the Liberty Bell Center is the President's House Exhibit. With the judicial branch of the young federal government ensconced in the city courthouse and the legislative in the county courthouse, the executive branch was left to find space elsewhere. A home owned by wealthy Philadelphian Robert Morris became the new presidential residence for both George Washington and John Adams, his successor. During his presidency Washington never lived in the capital city named for him; Adams would be the first chief executive to sleep in the "President's House," later the White House. A portion of the foundation of the kitchen and main house is visible. Narrative exhibit panels describe the various parts of the house and the duties of Washington's staff, which included both indentured servants and slaves. Actors portray the president's slaves in short films shown on flat-screen television monitors mounted on representations of the interior walls of the President's House.

This juxtaposition of the President's House and the Liberty Bell, adjacent to one another, underscores the central paradox of early America's quest for freedom—how could men simultaneously advocate the principles of liberty and equality while sanctioning slavery and even owning slaves? Washington took eight slaves from his Mt. Vernon estate to serve him in Philadelphia; their names are inscribed in stone in the exhibit. The law at the time specified that slaves living in a free state (as Pennsylvania was) for six consecutive months were to be freed, so Washington secretly rotated his back to Virginia to ensure they would not be. The president included his secretary, Tobias Lear, in this deceptive plan: "I wish to have it accomplished under pretext that may deceive both them and the Public," he wrote to Lear, referring to the slaves. When Ona Judge (also known as Oney Judge), a mulatto slave girl who was Martha Washington's personal attendant, learned that she was to be bequeathed to Mrs. Washington's granddaughter, Eliza Custis, she escaped into the night as the Washingtons dined. The president expended considerable resources in an unsuccessful effort to recover her, even sanctioning an advertisement in a local paper noting that Judge had "absconded from the household of the President of the United States." In 2003 the National Park Service began planning an exhibit to show the complex irony of life in the President's House during George Washington's tenure there. A line of small footprints, embedded in the exhibit plaza, moves in a northerly direction through the outline of the house, a powerful symbol of a slave fleeing to freedom.

Declaration House, now reconstructed, is one block west, at Market and 7th Streets. In a rented room on its second floor, Thomas Jefferson drafted the Declaration of Independence in the early summer of 1776. This document would soon be celebrated throughout the states with fireworks, cannonades, church bells, and parades. Though many Americans are taught that the Declaration was signed on the fourth of July, the Continental Congress merely agreed on its final language on that day in 1776. Jefferson's notes explain that, after much deliberation on July 2–4, agreement was reached "in the evening of the last closed. the declaration was reported by the comm[itt]ee, agreed to by the house, and signed by every member present except Mr. Dickinson." Historians believe that it was likely approved late in the morning of July 4–signed only by John Hancock, president of the Continental Congress—and that fifty representatives of the thirteen states signed it at the official signing ceremony on August 2, 1776 (the six others signed in the months following). Celebrations erupted as the messengers galloped into cities and towns shouting the news. John Adams presciently predicted the legacy of the Declaration in a July 3 letter to Abigail that referred to the work of the Congress on July 2: "I am apt to believe that it will be celebrated, by succeeding Generations, as the great anniversary Festival ... It ought to be commemorated ... solemnized with Pomp and Parade with shews, Games, Sports, Guns,

Bells, Bonfires and Illuminations from one End of this Continent to the other from the Time forward forever more." In Worcester, Massachusetts, a group of gentlemen on July 22 offered a pithier toast to the Declaration: "George rejected and Liberty protected."

East on Market Street, between Fourth and Third Streets, is Franklin Court. This group of buildings consists of Benjamin Franklin's courtyard home, a tenant building he owned that faces Market Street, an eighteenth-century-style post office, and his printing office, which includes a period bookbindery. A brick passageway used daily by Franklin leads to a "ghost house" outlined by steel frames that show the contours of this Renaissance man's home. Here the polymath Franklin entertained George Washington with a cask of dark beer when the general arrived in May of 1787 to participate in the Constitutional Convention. A mulberry tree in the yard provided a shady respite for convention delegates to enjoy one another's company in a more casual and collegial setting, with more serious matters likely discussed in the private rooms of the Indian Queen Tavern next door.

Visitors to Franklin Court can peer below the ground to see the outline of the foundation. The underground Benjamin Franklin Museum has a film, interactive exhibits, and computer animations along with numerous artifacts that illuminate Franklin's contributions to political, scientific, and diplomatic life—most intriguing is Franklin's sedan chair, in which he, in poor health, was likely carried to some sessions of the Constitutional Convention to persuade other delegates to compromise on the fundamental principles of the Constitution. A multilayered archaeological adventure awaits visitors to the four-story tenant building, with markers showing detailed building and architectural features of late-eighteenth-century construction. A surviving 1787 insurance survey has helped historians and archaeologists understand the design of the house and many of its artifacts. A ranger in the printing office operates a press just as a period printer did, especially appealing to children who know little of printing beyond today's sophisticated laser printers. Visitors may be surprised to learn that paper in that era was fine indeed, made from cloth rags, usually cotton or linen, and the printing office today employs the same paper (which is also used for United States currency).

The National Constitution Center, two blocks north of the Liberty

Bell Center, is dedicated to our nation's founding document of 1787. This museum was created by an act of Congress in 1988 and is not part of the park. It employs multimedia shows, live performances, public programs, films, photographs, sculpture, and artifacts to tell the story of the Constitution. Permanent exhibitions and presentations include actors portraying people from the era and opportunities to vote for one's favorite U.S. president, recite the presidential oath of office, sit in the seat of a Supreme Court justice, and read about current constitutional issues. In Signer's Hall, visitors can wander amongst life-sized bronze statutes of the delegates and feel a part of that august collection of founders. Each of the forty-two delegates to the Constitutional Convention is represented, ranging from the well-known (James Madison and Alexander Hamilton) to the barely known (Georgia's William Few). Perhaps the most distinctive name belongs to Daniel St. Thomas of Jenifer, a delegate from Maryland and ardent supporter of both independence and a strong central government. All stand in Signer's Hall, ready for congratulatory handshakes from their countrymen for their remarkable achievements in that summer of 1787.

SIDE TRIPS

AFRICAN AMERICAN MUSEUM IN PHILADELPHIA: A block from the park and the National Constitution Center, this museum celebrates the heritage and culture of Philadelphia's African Americans through four exhibition galleries that present black history through the ages. A core exhibit, "Audacious Freedom: African Americans in Philadelphia, 1776–1876," makes innovative use of sound and light technology, while the Children's Corner leads kids on an exploration of the daily lives of Philadelphia children during that hundred-year period. *701 Arch Street, Philadelphia, PA, 19106, 215-574-0380.*

PHILADELPHIA HISTORY MUSEUM: Exhibitions explore more than 300 years of the city's rich past, ranging from William Penn's utopian plans, the city's fabled sports teams, to locally brewed beer. The museum has more than 10,500 objects, including a desk used by George Washington, and 800 works of art. Multimedia presentations and hands-on experiences bring this great American city to life. *15 South 7th Street, Philadelphia, PA, 19106, 215-685-4830.*

RITTENHOUSE SQUARE: Named for David Rittenhouse, an astronomer and leader during the Revolutionary years, the area surrounding this late-eighteenth-century square later became the most desirable residential section of Philadelphia, home to its "Victorian aristocracy." A few mansions from that period still face the square. A circular walk is on its perimeter, while diagonal walkways meet at a central oval. Classical urns and ornamental lampposts highlight the square, which functions today as a public park and venue for art exhibitions and flower markets. *18th and Walnut Streets.*

FURTHER READING

ADULTS

Carol Berkin, *A Brilliant Solution: Inventing the American Constitution.* Mariner Books, 2003.

George Boudreau, *Independence: A Guide to Historic Philadelphia.* Westholme Publishing, 2012.

Christopher Collier and James Lincoln Collier, *Decision in Philadelphia: The Constitutional Convention of 1787.* Ballantine, 2007.

Joseph Ellis, *Founding Brothers: The Revolutionary Generation.* Alfred Knopf, 2000.

Pauline Meier, *American Scripture: Making the Declaration of Independence.* Vintage, 1998.

CHILDREN

Louise Halse Anderson, *Fever 1793.* Simon and Schuster, 2000.

Ann Rinaldi, *Taking Liberty: The Story of Oney Judge, George Washington's Runaway Slave.* Simon Pulse, 2004.

5

VALLEY FORGE

In eastern Pennsylvania, twenty miles west of Philadelphia, where Valley Creek enters the Schuylkill River, lies Valley Forge, one of the most visible symbols of America's successful struggle for independence. Amid these rolling hills is the 2,000-acre site of the Continental Army's camp during 1777–78, the third year of the American Revolutionary War. Valley Forge has long been etched into the American consciousness, a fulcrum of privation and determination during the crucial months when the young Continental Army endured great hardships to acquire the wherewithal to defeat the British Army and establish a new nation.

William Penn granted the land surrounding Valley Forge to his daughter in 1701. By the middle of the century the water-powered Mount Joy iron works stood along Valley Creek, followed shortly by a sawmill and gristmill. As revolutionary fervor grew, these facilities began producing war materiel—a development not unnoticed by the British, who destroyed the forge, sawmill, and military supplies in September 1777.

The fields at Valley Forge saw no fighting during the encampment. The deadly enemies of the Americans there were hunger, weather, and, foremost, disease, and they attacked relentlessly, from December through the following spring. "The whole army is sick and crawling with vermin," complained an officer in March 1778. Over a thousand men died of disease before better sanitation measures and smallpox inoculations helped limit the death toll.

If you visit on a cold winter's day at Valley Forge—especially one with snow on the ground—you will find conditions reminiscent of those faced by the Continental Army. The park is also one of the few places in the United States, along with Washington's home at Mount Vernon, where visitors can see beyond the myths and legends to humanize our first president through his relationships with his officers and men and his wife, Martha, who spent considerable time with him at Valley Forge; and through his few leisure pursuits. A self-guided driving tour; miles of hiking, walking, and horseback trails; and, especially, the faithfully reproduced log-and-clay "hutts" that housed twelve-man squads allow visitors to imagine the difficulties the Americans faced on these hills as they helped lay the foundation for their independence.

The war was going poorly for Washington's army at the close of 1777. British forces under Gen. Sir William Howe had defeated them at Brandywine, Paoli, and Germantown that autumn, and the Continental Congress fled to York, Pennsylvania, when Howe occupied Philadelphia in early December. Doubts were growing over the competence of General Washington and the likelihood that the Continental Army could become the sort of disciplined fighting force that could defeat the British.

General Howe, confident after the recent British victories, surveyed the Continental Army's position at Valley Forge early in December and decided not to attack. He chose to await more conducive fighting weather and enjoy the firesides and ladies of Philadelphia. "Assemblies, concerts, comedies, clubs and the like make us forget that there is any war, save that it is a capital joke," a Hessian officer wrote. (Told that the British commander had taken Philadelphia, Benjamin Franklin replied, "I beg your pardon, but Philadelphia has taken Howe.") So Washington's Continentals won a reprieve until spring to fashion themselves into a competent army.

More than 11,000 officers and men marched into Valley Forge a few days before Christmas in 1777. Many were insufficiently clad against the winter air. "It is amazing to see the spirit of the soldiers when destitute of shoes and stocking marching cold nights and mornings, leaving blood in their footsteps," wrote a soldier of the march. General Washington

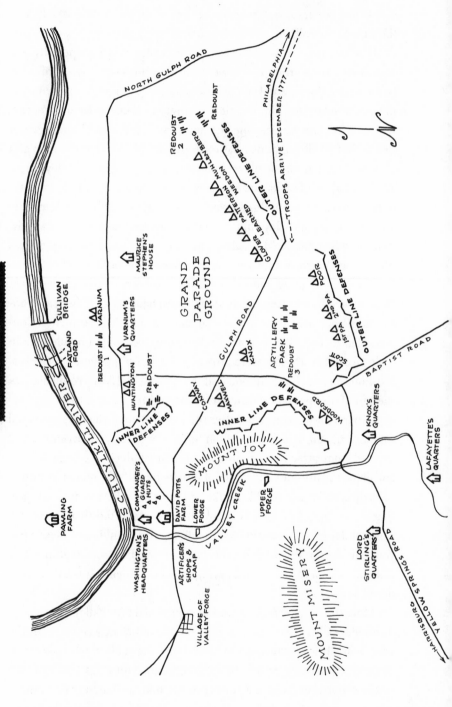

VALLEY FORGE, 1777–78

had chosen the site because it was easy to defend and sufficiently close to Philadelphia to keep watch on the British Army. Supplies had to be purchased, often on credit, from local farmers and sometimes rapacious merchants, or requisitioned by foraging parties who dodged British patrols as they traveled into New Jersey, Maryland, and Delaware. Surreptitious commerce between local farmers and the British had to be stopped. Equipment was scarce and often in disrepair. The men, though industrious and capable, were not thoroughly trained in the routine and drill so crucial to battlefield success in the eighteenth century.

Frustrated by the inadequate clothing and provisions for his men, Washington accused the Congress of believing the "Men were made of Stocks and Stones and equally insensible to frost and Snow." The Continental Congress lacked the power to tax and could do little to implement a stable supply system to provide for the army. Nonetheless, Washington's men were determined to surmount these hurdles. A visitor to the camp under construction reported that he found "nothing like a sigh of discontent at their situation . . . On the contrary, my ears were agreeably struck every evening, in riding through the camp, with a variety of military and patriotic songs and every countenance I saw, wore the appearance of cheerfulness or satisfaction."

Washington's patrician image is stamped indelibly upon our culture: our money; names of our roads, schools, and towns; and advertising campaigns without end. Rarely does a day pass without hearing his name. His ghost is rumored to pray in the snow at Valley Forge. But visiting Valley Forge helps peel away this mythical persona, allowing visitors to see a George Washington who with his men endured a winter they all knew might be their last. More than a hundred years after this iconic story of survival and triumph, Valley Forge became Pennsylvania's first state park, in 1893; it joined the national park system in the bicentennial year of 1976. Adding to the reverence of the site is the absence of suburban sprawl that mars so many of our nation's historical sites—a surprise given the park's proximity to the western suburbs of Philadelphia.

The visitor center has a short film and a map for the ten-mile auto tour of nine stops, known as the Encampment Tour Route. Seasonal open-air trolley tours last 90 minutes and depart from the visitor center. The park offers programs and activities for kids (beginning at age four), who can join the Continental Army and, on the first Saturday morning of the January–April months, participate in a muster complete with dummy muskets and marching maneuvers. The Junior Ranger program has an activity book with assignments about the park's terrain, monuments, artifacts, and the lives of soldiers, with badges awarded on completion. Summer programs have included "story-telling benches," on topics such as "secrets and spies." Audio guides to the auto tour are available, as is cell phone information accessed at each stop. One to two hours by car are sufficient to see the park's terrain and understand why Washington chose it as the Continental Army's winter encampment. Exploring the park on foot or bike allows an even broader perspective.

The visitor center has a collection of Revolutionary-era military artifacts. A creative overview is the chronological "camp panorama" of photographs and key facts, by month—for example, January 1778 notes that 4,000 men were unfit for duty and that Washington considered bringing African American troops from Rhode Island into camp. March saw the start of a smallpox inoculation program. Kiosk touch screens enable visitors to search, by name or regiment, for ancestors who may have been at Valley Forge with Washington.

Camp fortifications were organized into "outer defensive lines" and "inner defensive lines" that aligned with the topography. The "hutts" along this ridge, above the outer defensive line (auto stop two), are symbolic of the conditions the army faced that winter. These huts replicate those constructed by Gen. Peter Muhlenberg's brigade of Virginians and Pennsylvanians; approximately 2,000 were built in parallel lines along streets, along with five earthen forts, known as redoubts, and miles of trenches. Each hut housed twelve soldiers. (One soldier wrote, "have one Dull ax to build a Logg Hutt when it will be done knows not.") Washington awarded prizes to stimulate creative and speedy construction—$12 to the first squad in each regiment to finish its hut, $100 for the best roof without using wood, which was scarce. Thomas Paine likened the scene to "a family of beavers: everyone busy, some carrying logs, others mud, and the rest fastening them together." British general Howe, rocking before a Philadelphia fireside with his mistress, derided the camp as "Logtown."

The huts were "tolerably comfortable," according to soldier accounts.

As older hardwood was depleted, green wood was used for fires; acrid smoke stung the eyes. Many huts were set two feet deep in the ground, creating dank spaces that fostered typhus, typhoid, influenza, and dysentery. The General Orders of March 13, 1778, noted that "Much Filth and nastiness, is spread amongst Ye Hutts, which will soon be reduc'd to a state of putrefaction and cause a sickly camp." Records show that approximately two-thirds of the 2,000 who died at Valley Forge did so during the warmer spring months, when microbes emerged.

The troops knew how to amuse themselves, with drinking a most prevalent recreation. Camp followers—many of whom were wives of men in camp—and local ladies were coveted for dancing. Music was heard often. One diarist declared a violin "excellent in the kind of soft music which is so finely adapted to stir up the tender passions." Washington tried but failed to thwart gambling, which he described as "the foundation of evil"—"this vice shall not, when detected, escape exemplary punishment," he ordered. Exercise was encouraged. Men played "base," a forerunner of baseball. Officers played cricket and bowled with cannon balls, and the general himself occasionally stepped outside to toss a ball with his aides.

A statue of Gen. "Mad Anthony" Wayne, Commander of the Pennsylvania Line, sits at auto stop four on high ground overlooking a broad expanse to the south that would have been a strong defensive position against any British attack on Valley Forge. To the northwest, toward auto stop five, an 1865 covered bridge spans Valley Creek, which flows between Mount Misery and Mount Joy (the encampment extended in parts into modern-day Phoenixville). Easy hikes on any of several trails are found across the bridge onto Yellow Springs Road, just short of Mount Misery, so named by William Penn because he once lost his way on its wooded slopes. More arduous hikes include the Horseshoe Trail that connects to the Appalachian Trail. Non-hikers should continue north on Valley Creek Road (PA Rt. 252).

A parking area on the right is the trailhead for both the paved Valley Creek footpath (it's 1.4 miles to Washington's Headquarters at auto stop five) and the Horseshoe Trail, the latter part of which extends outside the park. Its shorter loop meets the Valley Creek trail at the site of the upper forge and loops back to the lot (40 minutes at an easy pace). An interpretive sign explains the history, archeology, and the basics of eighteenth-century iron-making.

Across the parking lot at the trail head is a colonial manor house once owned by Philander Chase Knox, President Theodore Roosevelt's attorney general and President William Howard Taft's secretary of state. The building is now home to offices and the park library, which is open by appointment and available for special events. Don't confuse this estate with the quarters of Gen. Henry Knox, Washington's artillery commander, on the left just before the bridge. Further west on Yellow Springs Road is Continental Army general William Alexander's (Lord Stirling) quarters, the last historic structure in this direction. None are open to the public, though they are worth a look from the outside.

Re-crossing the bridge and turning left onto Valley Creek Road (PA Rt. 252) leads north to Washington's Headquarters and the Valley Forge Railroad, where the headquarters tour begins. The exhibitions in the station are good background for the visit to the Headquarters, that small house tucked into the elbow of Valley Creek and the Schuylkill River. A series of touch-screen videos in the Valley Forge Train Station shows General Washington talking with his staff aides and impressing upon a visiting member of the Continental Congress the Continental Army's urgent need for provisions.

The replicated period furniture and accessories add to the original walls, woodwork, and floors to give an ambience of authenticity. A case clock on the first floor is a period piece used, at Washington's order, by officers to set their watches, so they would be punctual for meetings. The general and his wife, Martha, who joined him in February 1778, in time to celebrate his 46th birthday, occupied the larger of the two upstairs bedrooms. Staff officers and servants slept elsewhere in the house. From this small house, once owned by Isaac Potts (for whom nearby Pottstown is named), Washington beseeched Congress for supplies, planned (but did not execute) a surprise strike against the British in Philadelphia, co-ordinated intelligence and espionage operations, survived a conspiracy against his command, and inspired a camp that swelled to 20,000 men, larger than the population of Boston. Though menus were often limited, Washington frequently invited officers to dine with him, inviting their counsel and thereby helping cement their loyalty. Virginia colonel Daniel Morgan, who in 1781 won a brilliant victory over the British at Cowpens, proclaimed that "under no other man than Washington will I serve."

Food shortages at Valley Forge were severe at times, especially in those first months. Water was carried in buckets from Valley Creek, several miles from most of the brigades. Because beef, a staple of the Army's diet in good times, was often unavailable, creative culinary use of flour became an art form. The men mixed it with water and baked, fried, or roasted the pasty mass on a stick. Surgeon Albigence Waldo of Connecticut, dining on one of these "fire cakes," lamented his separation from "Ye who Eat Pumkin Pie and Roast Turkies." Cooks soaked vegetables in vinegar to help prevent scurvy. Captain John Lacey recorded a recipe for preparing spoiled pork and hog fodder.

Thirty yards from Washington's Headquarters is a large culvert that takes Valley Creek to meet the Schuylkill River. Behind the house stand the replicated huts of the fifty native-born, property-owning Virginians of Washington's bodyguard corps, known as the "Commander-in-Chief's Guard" or "Lifeguards." The DeWeese house, named for the first manager of the forge, is a short walk south, toward PA Rts. 252 and 23. It served as camp courthouse, where whippings, prison, and death sentences were meted out to deserters and thieves (desertions averaged ten per week).

En route to Redoubt 4 (auto stop six), turn into the parking lot on the right labeled "map" on the park map. Painted on the asphalt is a large map showing that Virginia, North Carolina, and Georgia at that time claimed territory that reached all the way to the Mississippi River.

Bear right off PA Rt. 23 onto West Inner Line Drive and follow it south along the inner line defenses and Redoubt 3 (auto stop seven) and Artillery Park (stop eight, and a good place to let the kids and dogs out to run; the latter, at the least, must be leashed). Beware of dolomite pits, or sink holes, in this area. The redoubts were earthen forts that were manned by fifty to sixty men and anchored the ends of the second defensive line, on the slopes of Mount Joy. Entrenchments flank the entire length of the inner drive. Redoubt 3 (auto stop seven) protected the right flank by plugging the gap between the inner and outer defensive lines, to the south of the encampment. Climb a platform at Redoubt 7 and marvel at the remains of earthworks whose walls were once 10 feet high, and the immense effort the Continentals put forth to construct those fortifications with their eighteenth-century tools.

The East and North Inner Line Drives pass the spots of Maxwell's and Conway's brigades, with a panoramic view of the Grand Parade Ground, in the center of the park, just beyond (and another place to let the kids and dogs run). At the right turn onto PA Rt. 23 (auto stop nine) is a statue of Baron Friedrich von Steuben, the colorful Prussian drillmaster who arrived in February 1778 to oversee the transformation of the army into a disciplined and effective fighting force. Von Steuben codified the drill manual and taught the men to march in cadence, fire in volleys, reload fast and efficiently, and launch bayonet charges and defend against them. When he discovered that bayonets were being used as meat skewers and tent pegs, he erupted in multilingual cursing—screaming in French and German and enlisting help when needed with English words.

On May 6, 1778, the troops assembled at Artillery Park (auto stop eight) to mark France's recognition of the United States. The treaty was read aloud. Arms and dress were inspected. Muskets and thirteen cannon were fired by brigade—the ceremonial *feu de joie*. "The gradual progression of the sound from the discharge of cannon and musketry, swelling and rebounding from the neighboring hills, and gently sweeping along the Schuylkill," recorded a newspaper, "composed a military music more agreeable to a soldier's ear than the most finished piece of your favorite Handel." This French alliance was crucial to the American war effort. French aid—in the form of troops, naval assistance, supplies, and funds—helped escalate the conflict in British minds from a series of skirmishes against rebel upstarts to a major war. To mark the occasion, Washington ordered the soldiers "more than the common quantity of liquor," while acknowledging that it might lead to "some little drunkenness among them."

The early-eighteenth-century farmhouse at auto stop nine is the headquarters of Gen. James Varnum, commander of the Rhode Island brigade. Across the road are a picnic area and earthen remains of Redoubt 1, which guarded a northern escape route across the Schuylkill and major east-west transportation routes. Snow often means dozens of sleds flying down the hillside here, into the Grand Parade. A winter's walk across the Grand Parade brings to mind the hardy men of the Continental Army freezing at morning inspection. On the western edge is the historic trace, an original road through Valley Forge that runs between the Schuylkill River and Artillery Park. Washington's men left the encampment on this road in the spring of 1778. This mile-long, tree-lined trail is popular with snowshoers and cross-country skiers and loops back to the parking lot at Varnum's headquarters.

Some feared that the Valley Forge winter would be the demise of the Continental Army, but the opposite occurred. The rudiments of military training, the creation of a professional officer corps, and the establishment of army branches such as the Corps of Engineers laid the foundation of the United States Army—an American melting pot comprised of Native Americans, blacks, Germans, French, Scots, and Irish, many of whom did not speak English but nonetheless were united behind this common cause. And when General Howe moved north from Philadelphia in July 1778, the Continentals pursued and fought his Redcoats to a draw at Monmouth (and where a woman who soldiered a cannon later became famous as "Molly Pitcher," carrying water to cool the cannon tubes so they would not warp). Over the next three years, the leadership of George Washington and his officers oversaw the transformation of farmers and workmen into a cohesive fighting force that would defeat the world's mightiest army in October 1781, when the British Army surrendered at Yorktown, Virginia.

SIDE TRIP

BRANDYWINE BATTLEFIELD STATE PARK, PA: The British defeat of the Continental Army here in September 1777 allowed British general William Howe to take Philadelphia, home of the Continental Congress, whose members fled first to Lancaster, then to York. Three driving tours of this 50-acre site provide varying perspectives on the fighting; the tenacity of the Americans, though they lost, may have helped dissuade General Howe from attacking them at Valley Forge. *Chadd's Ford, PA, 19317.*

FURTHER READING

ADULTS

Wayne K. Bodle, *The Valley Forge Winter: Civilians and Soldiers in War.* Pennsylvania State University Press, 2004.

Thomas Fleming, *Washington's Secret War: The Hidden History of Valley Forge.* Harper Perennial, 2006.

Lorett Treese, *Valley Forge: Making and Remaking a National Symbol.* Pennsylvania State University Press, 1995.

CHILDREN

Jason Cooper, *Valley Forge.* Rourke Pub Group, 2003.

6

FORT McHENRY AND THE
STAR-SPANGLED BANNER
NATIONAL HISTORIC TRAIL

The War of 1812 began for reasons obscure even to the historically at-
tuned. No less an authority than John Adams wrote during its first year
that "So complicated and so historical had the causes of war become that
no one even in America could explain or understand them." Americans
were furious at the British for supporting Indian raids in the Ohio country and specifically at the Royal Navy for its practice of impressment of
American seamen from U.S. merchant and naval ships. The British, fac-
ing a shortage of seamen in their war with France, claimed they were apprehending deserters—a self-serving definition that in practice included
any American they chose to consider such. The roots of the conflict have
been simplistically rendered as "Free Trade and Sailors' Rights." But the
causes of this war remain opaque in the American declaration of war in
June of 1812, and its bicentennial introduced the opportunity to better
understand this most misunderstood of wars—which is often referred to
as the second war for independence.

Two of its principal sites lie in, or near, Baltimore: Fort McHenry, birthplace of the "Star-Spangled Banner," and North Point State Park, the landing point of the British attack against Baltimore from the east. Sweeping views grace both locations, with none more moving than the one that comes into view at the end of the film, *The Defense of Fort McHenry*, shown in the fort's visitor center. This short movie vividly portrays Baltimore at the time of the British sea assault in September 1814, with panicked citizens clutching valuables as they prepare to flee; and black and white, free and slave digging trenches while British shells explode over the fort. Many flocked to the rooftops to watch, with "the tops of houses covered with men, women and children," recollected one Baltimorean. Nervously watching the British bombardment was George-town lawyer Francis Scott Key, who, during a mission to free an American captive, became aware of the British plan to attack Baltimore. The British commander, Vice Adm. Sir Alexander Cochrane, detained Key aboard an American flag-of-truce vessel anchored in the Patapsco River, from which he observed the engagement. From this vantage point Key intently scanned the horizon through the mist of early morning to see which nation's flag was flying above the fort.

Key's graphic description of the "the rockets' red glare, the bombs bursting in air" portrayed artillery shells with explosive charges, the world's most powerful at the time, that fell behind the walls of the fort amidst its intrepid defenders. These shells and Congreve rockets— the same rockets that had so terrified American militia at the Battle of Bladensburg the previous month—had far more destructive power than the more conventional solid iron cannonballs unleashed by Fort McHenry's guns.

Key polished his lyrics in his Baltimore hotel room a few days after the successful defense of the city, setting them to the tune of an eighteenth-century British drinking song from a gentlemen's social club in London. It rapidly went viral. After its first public airing, in November 1814 at the Holliday Street Theater (near today's War Memorial Plaza), the entire city began singing the song from a printed broadside. Following publication in several Baltimore newspapers, it quickly spread; days later it appeared in a New York paper, and within six weeks was being sung in half of the eighteen states. The song penned by Key became our national anthem in 1931.

The stakes were high in defending Baltimore, the fledging nation's third-largest city, with more than 50,000 inhabitants, a shipbuilding center, and a nest of anti-British fervor. The city was home port for armed privateers that had been preying on British shipping, and had the British seized the city, plunder, pillage, and the torch would surely have been its fate. The successful defense of Baltimore gave a young American nation a historic victory in a war that had until then been full of dismal moments for its militia and military forces.

The fort's museum has iron cannonballs from the battle, dredged from the Patapsco River in 2004. But with relatively few artifacts surviving from the War of 1812, visual narratives of its origins, Francis Scott Key's life, and the fighting itself tell the story of the Battle for Baltimore. Living histories and other events throughout the year help bring to life this war and the U.S. soldiers, militiamen, and citizens who came together to fight it.

The U.S. Congress in 2008 authorized creation of The Star-Spangled Banner National Historic Trail, consisting of water and land routes encompassing approximately 560 miles. The water routes start at Tangier Island, Virginia, a British base during the war; the land routes run north from Solomon's Island, in Maryland's Charles County. War of 1812 sites are numerous in the Chesapeake region and beyond. One guide found more than 800 (including burial grounds), stretching from North Carolina to Pennsylvania—most of which are in Maryland, the scene of more battles, skirmishes, and raids than any other state in the Union.

The trail on land follows the major points of the 1814 British invasion of Maryland, including the Battle of Bladensburg, the British burning of Washington, D.C., and the Battle for Baltimore. Lesser sites include St. Leonard's Creek; Benedict, the Patuxent River site where the British force that marched on Washington landed; and Upper Marlboro and Caulk's Field, site of an August 1814 skirmish in Kent County that is now a well-preserved War of 1812 battlefield. The trail connects to twenty historic landmarks and over a hundred historic sites. Several dozen locations have informational kiosks. The trail offers innovative technological tools that can provide even broader perspectives on the War of 1812: Geocaching, a land-based GPS-aided treasure hunt of more than thirty sites that include parks, forts, and ships and interactive National Oceanic and Atmospheric Administration (NOAA) weather and navigational buoys in the Chesapeake Bay cater to both inquisitive hikers and mariners.

Those wishing to follow the British line of march toward Washington can drive north from the quaint river town of Solomon's Island, at the junction of the Patuxent River and Chesapeake Bay. Cross the river and head north on MD Rt. 235; at Hughesville, take Rt. 231 east to the hamlet of Benedict. Other than a small marker at the turn-off into Benedict, little suggests the town's role in the war. A few houses remain from that time, including one on a hill from which the 4,100-plus enemy force was allegedly spotted disembarking on August 19, 1814. A marker at the Goose Landing Marina shows the location of Camp Stanton, a training center during the Civil War for four regiments in the United States Bureau of Colored Troops, created in 1863.

Continuing north on MD Rt. 381 / 382, follow the Patuxent River, passing west of trail sites Magruders Landing and Nottingham. A detour east at Croom leads to Patuxent River Park, a scenic picnic spot with a river view. Rt. 382 has several "Star-Spangled Banner National Historic Trail" signs that mark the general area, if not the precise path trod by the invaders. Further north is Pig Point, where Commodore Joshua Barney had scuttled all of his thirty-two gunboats and barges on August 22 to forestall their capture by the British. The flat, treeless topography of the Chesapeake gives way to wooded, rolling hills as one journeys northwest toward Washington and away from the Patuxent River and the Chesapeake Bay.

Brig. Gen. William Winder commanded an American force that dug in at Bladensburg, six miles northeast of Washington, to prevent the British from marching on the capital. The inexperience of his men led to miscues, casualties, and the capture by the British of many muskets and cannon on August 24, 1814, a day when the temperature reached 100 degrees. Commodore Joshua Barney, commanding the U.S. Flotilla Service in the Chesapeake, was wounded and captured outside Bladensburg. He was granted parole and carried by litter into the town of Bladensburg, despite his saucy assertion to British admiral George Cockburn that the Americans pronounced his name "Cock-burn" rather than the proper British "Coburn." With the Americans in full retreat and Barney a prisoner, the British veered southwest toward the nation's capital. The affair was a humiliating disaster for the young American forces.

British troops marched unmolested into the largely deserted city on the evening of August 24. They set fire to most government buildings, including the White House and the U.S. Capitol, though resourceful First Lady Dolley Madison saved portraits and vital government documents by orchestrating their removal to safe havens. A Washington resident, Margaret Bayard Smith, recounted how her family was "roused on Tuesday night by a loud knocking—on the opening of the door, Willie Bradley called to us, 'The enemy are advancing, our own troops are giving way on all sides and are retreating to the city. Go for Gods sake go.' He spoke in a voice of agony, and then flew to his horse and was out of sight in a moment."

Another British invading force, under Capt. James Gordon, sailed up the Potomac River. Gordon found no resistance from Fort Washington, situated on a bluff overlooking the river, below the capital—the fort's commanding officer, said to be drunk, ordered the fort abandoned. The city of Alexandria, unable to mount a defense, surrendered to Gordon on August 29; his men made off with twenty-one prize vessels, filled with flour, tobacco, cotton, and other merchandise. The British, perhaps impressed by the good manners of the town's residents, spared Alexandria the torch. The Americans themselves set fire to the Washington Navy Yard, to keep its munitions from British hands. Gordon's move likely diverted the attention of the American defenders from the British squadron that sailed up the Patuxent River to land troops at Benedict for their march on Washington.

The British Army and Navy then combined in a two-pronged sea and land assault directly against Baltimore. Early in September, ships sailed north up the Chesapeake Bay, where the naval force commanded by Vice Adm. Sir Alexander Cochrane moved into the Patapsco River to attack Baltimore and Fort McHenry from the east, with Cochrane vowing that the city "ought to be laid in ashes." The army landing force under Maj. Gen. Robert Ross continued to North Point, a peninsula just east of Baltimore. The action in this area, while no less important to the successful defense of Baltimore and the outcome of the war, has been heavily overshadowed by the heroics of the Fort McHenry defenders and its tale of Francis Scott Key and "The Star-Spangled Banner."

To reach North Point, pass through Edgemere on North Point Road

(MD Rt. 20), then turn right onto Bay Shore Road into North Point State Park. An attractive waterfront with picnic areas, a large fountain, and piers for fishing and wading greet visitors (the visitor center is closed during the winter months). A left turn out of the park, back onto North Point Road, leads to the peninsula's end and both Fort Howard State Park and the Fort Howard V.A. facility. The British had scouted the strategic advantages of this approach to Baltimore—a simple landing from Old Road Bay, on the east side of the peninsula, a road easily passable by men and supplies; naval flanking support for their troops; and a rural, sparsely populated countryside unlikely to provide serious impediment to the attack on Baltimore, a mere fifteen-mile march west.

The Baltimore militiamen had ample reason to fight to the death, for the British planned no leniency for their city of Anglophobes, which they would destroy or spare only by extorting a steep ransom. "I do not like to contemplate scenes of blood and destruction," wrote a British officer to his wife, "but my heart is deeply interested in the coercion of these Baltimore heroes, who are perhaps most inveterate against us of all the Yankees." Such sentiments had many Baltimoreans in a state of panic following the defeat at Bladensburg and the sacking of Washington. "All is now confusion and consternation here," reported the Baltimore correspondent of a New York newspaper at the end of August. "Everybody moving that can get off, under the full expectation that the enemy will be here tomorrow night." Few saw much point in resisting the seasoned British force. "I think the only way to save the town will be to capitulate," wrote Pvt. Henry Fulford, a veteran of the fiasco at Bladensburg, which had become known to some as the Bladensburg Races because of the speed at which the Americans had fled under fire.

Baltimore City authorities thought otherwise, however, and prepared to put up a fight. They placed Maj. Gen. Samuel Smith, a Revolutionary War hero and U.S. senator, in charge of the Baltimore defenses. The thousands of defenders who poured in from Pennsylvania and Virginia reinforced the worst fears of a population terrified at the threat of the British invasion force. Smith quickly began drilling militiamen and organizing a formidable defense. Citizen working parties of black and white, free and slave, wielded pickaxes and shovels to fortify the city's southern and eastern sides, especially Hampstead Hill, "a placid green east of town" now known as Patterson Park (some of the 1812 cannon in the park are authentic). "White and black are all at work together. You'll see a master and his slave digging side by side. There is no distinction whatsoever," noted a young woman. Troop barracks and gun platforms were hastily erected; trenches were dug and earthworks built. The gun battery and observatory on Baltimore's Federal Hill went on high alert. Baltimore banks lent $663,000 to the effort, while individuals did what they could: 3,000 bricks from one and two bundles of lint from another, while a third contributed five barrels of whiskey. Baltimore in short order boasted a land-and-water defensive arc extending from Bel Air Road to the northeast across Hampstead Hill to the harbor—dozens of guns and more than 15,000 defenders. A chain of observation posts along the shore, with horse relays every ten miles, provided intelligence on the movements of the British fleet.

The British commander, Maj. Gen. Robert Ross, landed at North Point before dawn on September 12, planning to attack Baltimore the next day. Ross had nearly 5,000 men, consisting of marines, sailors, and a battalion of "disciplined Negroes," all carrying eighty rounds of ammunition. The blacks were likely escaped slaves known as "Colonial Marines," who were promised land and freedom in Nova Scotia by the British in exchange for their service. The heat rose as the men moved inland. A confident Ross laughed as his sailors vainly chased pigs and chickens, and proclaimed to a farmer who fed breakfast to him and his officers that he would "sup in Baltimore tonight—or in hell." His prophecy proved correct when a sharpshooter blew him from his horse. There is little consensus on the color of the general's horse (white or black) or who felled him— Henry McComas and Daniel Wells, young apprentices in the business of making saddles, being two likely possibilities. Both men, part of an advance skirmish line, died that day. Ross's corpse was sent to Nova Scotia in a hogshead of rum; his arrival in hell is as yet unconfirmed. The British forces, after warily eyeing the American defenses on Hampstead Hill for a night, withdrew, with the two forces so close to one another that one American, Lieut. Jacob Crumbaker, recalled that he "could hear the hogs squeal as [the British] killed them in their camp."

On Sunday, September 11, Baltimoreans anxiously awaited the arrival of British ships seen the day before sailing north up the Chesapeake Bay.

Many attended church services. The Rev. John Gruber of the Light Street Methodist Church beseeched the Lord to "bless King George, convert him, and take him to heaven, as we want no more of him." A thousand militia and citizens now manned the fort's ramparts. "Our alarm guns were fired twenty minutes past twelve, since then the bells rang, drums beating, the houses generally lighted; we have all been up since that second," wrote Baltimorean Deborah Cochrane to a friend. "We know not the hour when we may be attacked." The American defenses, overseen by Maj. George Armistead, included sunken ships in the Patapsco River and gun batteries at adjacent forts.

The British bombardment began at dawn on September 13. Over the next twenty-four hours more than 1,800 shells were fired at Fort McHenry; remarkably, only four defenders died. British bomb ships could launch 200-pound shells at targets two and a half miles distant. An observer noted that "one bomb pierced the centre of the flag"—possibly creating the same hole seen in the flag today at the Smithsonian Museum of American History. One newspaper reported that the power of each shell drove a ship "two feet into the water by the force of it, thus straining every part from stem to stern." Afternoon wind and rain aided the defenders, and the fort's guns, more than fifty of which France had loaned, repulsed the British assault.

Fort McHenry, the first of sixteen fortifications authorized by Congress in 1794 to protect the east coast, is an integral part of the War of 1812 experience. In October 1824, the Marquis de Lafayette visited the fort to pay homage to its gallant defenders ten years prior. The original Star Spangled Banner would be raised as he entered, and encomiums offered to those who drove the English fleet to "retire disgracefully after a bombardment of 48 hours" (the bombardment actually lasted 25 hours). The fort continued to play an instrumental role in Baltimore history, serving during the Civil War as an interrogation and detention center for captured Confederates, political prisoners, spies, and suspected disloyalists (including a grandson of Francis Scott Key)—most of whom were held briefly before either release or transfer north to a Union prison camp. The fort was later the site of a park and a hospital during World War I that was razed in 1927.

Annual events at the fort include both War of 1812 and Civil War living history weekends, with visitors able to see a soldier's life in camp and demonstrations of musket-firing and cavalry maneuvers. The fort's stone jail and its Confederate prisoners intrigue children especially; the inevitable prisoner escapes set off wild pursuit by Union jailors, kids trailing close behind to help capture the fugitives.

From downtown Baltimore take Key Highway south to a right turn onto Lawrence Street, with an immediate left turn onto Fort Avenue and the short drive to the fort. The large guns on the grounds are all originals, including Civil War–era muzzleloaders, last fired on July 4, 1903. Looking from the east rampart one can imagine the twenty-vessel British fleet two miles east, with the Chesapeake Bay ten miles beyond. The opposite shoreline was a grassy one at the time, before industrial activity encroached. Runners and bikers populate the paved trail on the perimeter of the fort's peninsula. The southern portion of the trail overlooks tidal salt marshes that are being restored to resemble those that surrounded the fort in 1814, and is adjacent to a cluster of Japanese maple trees planted to honor the fort's defenders. The magazine, built to withstand artillery fire, is in this area, a haven for migrating birds.

Widely respected for his energy and vision, Samuel Smith did not ride his successful defense of Baltimore—achieved against overwhelming odds—to the White House, as Andrew Jackson did his 1815 victory over the British at New Orleans in the same war. But Smith and his intrepid men did emulate Jackson by sending the British packing, and in so doing helped ensure the success of the fledgling American republic.

SIDE TRIPS

THE STAR-SPANGLED BANNER FLAG HOUSE, BALTIMORE: This 1793 building was the home of Mary Pickersgill, who sewed the flag that inspired Francis Scott Key's lyrics that later became our national anthem. Hear the stories of the defense of Baltimore mounted by citizens and soldiers during one of the few times the United States has been invaded by a foreign power. Exhibits include a variety of period artifacts, including a fragment of the flag that flew over Fort McHenry and a drum used by an

American soldier during the bombardment. *844 East Pratt Street, Balti-more, MD, 21202, 410-837-1793.*

SHOT TOWER, BALTIMORE: This facility, made of approximately 1 million red bricks and rising more than 234 feet, manufactured lead shot from 1828 to 1892. Molten lead dropped from a platform at the top of the tower and passed through a sieve and into cold water. When hardened, dried, and polished, the shot was sorted into 25-pound bags, with a million bags produced per year. The Shot Tower was the tallest structure in the United States until the Washington Monument in the nation's capital was completed after the Civil War; fewer than a dozen such towers remain today. This National Historic Landmark has irregular visiting hours but at the least deserves a close look when passing by its location, on the southeast corner of Fayette and Front Streets.

FELLS POINT, BALTIMORE: One of the oldest sections of Baltimore, this National Historic District is home to an eclectic blend of restaurants, shops, and colorful watering holes fronting cobblestone streets. Founded in 1763, Fells Point can boast that Frederick Douglas was a resident after he fled his Eastern Shore slave master, before he escaped north in 1838. Many of the residences and commercial buildings were erected in the eighteenth and nineteenth centuries, and the area retains the ambience of its seafaring origins. Fells Point is a popular venue for television and cinema, having hosted filming of the movie *Tin Men* and the television series *Homicide: Life on the Streets.* En route, stop at the Civil War Museum at the old President Street Railroad Station (601 President Street) for background on Baltimore's colorful Civil War story, beginning with the Pratt Street Riot on April 19, 1861, which saw the first bloodshed of the Civil War.

HAMPTON NATIONAL HISTORIC SITE, BALTIMORE COUNTY: This Georgian mansion, built just after the Revolutionary War by the Ridgely family, tells the multigenerational story of iron and agricultural production and the indentured servitude and slavery that made it all possible. The effects on the family of the economic and political changes brought about by the Civil War come to life at this magnificent site (1,500 acres at its apogee in the eighteenth century), only nineteen miles north of Fort McHenry. Slave quarters still stand, and the renovated mansion is worth the visit. *535 Hampton Lane, Towson, MD, 21286, 410-823-1309.*

FURTHER READING

ADULTS

Ralph E. Eshelman and Burton K. Kummerow, *In Full Glory Reflected: Discovering the War of 1812 in the Chesapeake.* Maryland Historical Society Press and the Maryland Historical Trust Press, 2012.

Donald R. Hickey, *The War of 1812: A Short History.* University of Illinois Press, 2012.

Donald R. Hickey, Ralph E. Eshelman, and Scott S. Sheads, *The War of 1812 in the Chesapeake: A Reference Guide to Historic Sites in Maryland, Virginia, and the District of Columbia.* Johns Hopkins University Press, 2010.

Walter Lord, *The Dawn's Early Light.* Johns Hopkins University Press Bicentennial Edition, 2012 (first published 1972).

Steve Vogel, *Through the Perilous Fight: Six Weeks That Saved the Nation.* Random House, 2013.

CHILDREN

Susan C. Bartoletti, *The Flag Maker.* Sandpiper, 2007.

7

THE BALTIMORE & OHIO
RAILROAD MUSEUM

Vintage locomotive and rail cars greet visitors at the parking lot of the B&O Railroad Museum, just ten blocks west of Baltimore's famed inner harbor. They are a striking visual introduction to the story of American railroading that awaits in this child-friendly museum and its magnificent Roundhouse. It is difficult to overstate the impact of the Baltimore & Ohio Railroad on both the development of America's railroads and the economy of nineteenth- and twentieth-century Maryland. The great promise of railroading was not lost on Charles Carroll of Carrollton, the noted Marylander who in 1828 was the only living signer of the Declaration of Independence. In July of that year he laid the ceremonial first stone of the Baltimore & Ohio line, a mile west of the station at Mt. Clare, home to today's museum. Carroll considered the occasion "among the most important acts of [his] life, second only to [his] signing the Declaration of Independence, if even it be second to that!"

This 40-acre site is the home of the first passenger station in the world, built in 1829; in 1851 a new brick passenger and freight depot replaced the original wooden structure. Its indoor and outdoor train galleries, films, and interactive exhibits vividly describe this birthplace of

American railroading, and it has earned its designation as a National Historic Landmark and status as a full affiliate of the Smithsonian Institution. Loaded with hands- and feet-on activities for kids, it houses the most comprehensive collection of American railroad artifacts in the world. It's the site of both the first railroad line in the western hemisphere and the nation's oldest continually operating railroad shops, which repair and restore trains even today. Nearby is the first intersection of a rail line and a major road, the place where the B&O crossed the National Road, a few miles west of the museum.

The museum captures the many dimensions of railroading, tracing the invention and evolution of locomotives and both passenger and freight cars. Steam locomotives, originally designed to haul coal, first appeared in the early 1800s, with the earliest models sporting evocative names such as the "Rocket," the "Puffing Billy," the "Tom Thumb," and the "Brother Jonathan." Inventors and engineers constantly redesigned them so they could negotiate the steep grades and curves encountered when, for example, hauling coal through mountainous terrain. Steam locomotives served the railroads well until diesel-electric engines, which required fewer employees to operate and maintain, were introduced in the 1940s. The first passenger cars appeared in the early 1830s and resembled the stagecoaches they would eventually replace. Improvements came quickly as the car evolved from wood to steel, utilized eight wheels for a smoother ride, and added amenities such as heat, air conditioning, and toilets. Early wooden freight cars, aptly called "boxcars," could carry three times their weight, a ratio that increased when steel construction was introduced in the late nineteenth century. Numerous models of locomotives and passenger and freight cars in the Alex. Brown & Sons Gallery illustrate engineering details and the roles each played in the evolution of rail transportation. The push of a button illuminates key components of the engines.

The B&O, the first rail common carrier in the United States, owes its origins to a group of wealthy Baltimoreans who, in the early nineteenth century, recognized the economic threat to Maryland of the new canals opening to transport cargo more efficiently than could the existing wagon-bearing turnpikes on which Baltimore relied. "It is contemplated to make a Rail-way from this City to the Ohio River," wrote Alexander

Brown, a linen merchant turned investment banker, to an English rail-road man in February 1827, the year the railroad received its charter. "If this be accomplished it will resuscitate Baltimore, & . . . will make her in a short time second to no city in the union." Another of those Baltimor-eans, Johns Hopkins, would later allocate $7 million of B&O stock to found a university and hospital. The B&O eventually reached far beyond the Ohio Valley, extending west to Chicago and St. Louis.

In 1828, a 1,000-acre land grant from James Carroll, a distant cousin of Charles Carroll of Carrollton, provided the first right-of-way for the Baltimore & Ohio. On July 4, 1828, close to 60,000 Baltimoreans paraded to the site to see the first stone laid during the inaugural festivities that marked this extraordinary development in industry and transportation. A repair yard opened at Mt. Clare in 1830, and was followed two years later by the world's first passenger station. That same year the company completed thirteen miles of track west to Ellicott's Mills—a Baltimore newspaper advertisement proclaimed this passenger service the first of its kind in America. (The small station in Ellicott City, operated by the B&O Railroad Museum, is now the oldest in the country.) In an early experiment, tests of rail cars under sail were conducted, and horse-drawn cars were used until displaced by locomotives in 1831. The westward line reached Harpers Ferry, Virginia, in 1834 (see chapter 9). The next year, passenger service began between Mt. Clare and Washington, D.C., mak-ing the B&O the first railroad running into the national capital. The station in Ellicott City with its stories, living histories, and exhibits de-scribes life in a small nineteenth-century town. Visitors can take in both this station and Mt. Clare, now operated by the B&O Railroad Museum, with discounted fees.

In the 1840s, as the B&O steadily, if slowly, stretched closer to the lucrative markets of the Ohio Valley and beyond, the Chesapeake & Ohio Canal Company had the same objective (George Washington, showing his entrepreneurial stripes, was a cofounder of its forerunner, the Potow-mack Company). The Canal Company coincidentally turned over its first, ceremonial spadeful of dirt on July 4, 1828, with President John Quincy Adams presiding, at virtually the same moment the B&O laid its first stone. The race between the two enterprises for capital and access to land along the Potomac River lasted for decades, until litigation temporarily halted the work of both companies at Point of Rocks, Maryland. The B&O's engineering prowess and business model, coupled with the canal's propensity to flood and shut down in places for lengthy repairs, ultimately won the day for the B&O, which reached Wheeling, Virginia, and the Ohio River in 1853. The canal reached Cumberland, Maryland, and went no further (see chapter 8).

The B&O Railroad Museum is an especially engaging place for kids of all ages. Younger ones will enjoy the fruits of the museum's award-winning partnership with the Smithsonian in early childhood education, which employs a range of interactive activities to stress reading, word recognition, and understanding colors and shapes (such as circles representing train wheels). The Roundhouse—where more than twenty-two engines and cars surround a 60-foot turntable that is used to move them in and out—has stations for play and learning that pulsate with excited kids coloring, building, and enjoying educational games, with adults either joining the fun or relaxing on rockers. Choo Choo Blue, a graphic young steam locomotive, asks kids for help throughout the museum in understanding different aspects of railroading. Look for the variety of locomotive designs in the Roundhouse—while straight rail lines could use the pioneering English design, steep grades and sharp curves required new, heavier-duty types of engine pistons. A 25-minute, three-mile round trip, seasonally narrated train ride takes passengers from the B&O Museum to Mt. Clare Mansion. Completed in 1757, this building was once the center of a colonial-era agricultural and industrial complex, site of Baltimore's largest Union encampment during the Civil War, and near the spot where Charles Carroll of Carrollton sank spade into soil in 1828. The museum's website includes educational resources for social studies teachers and parents. Ambitious young people between ages eight and twelve might consider applying for the museum's position of Director of Fun, a volunteer who works with the museum staff to create new and engaging experiences for young visitors.

Few realize that our current-day time zones and synchronized time that regiment modern life stemmed from the needs of railroads. Running trains called for a more efficient method for measuring seconds and minutes than using the imprecision of gauging the sun's position in the sky—a method that left their rolling stock and employees prone to deadly accidents. The railroad companies devised synchronized time to coordinate schedules for train arrivals and departures in 1883; towns, police, fire departments, and businesses quickly adopted the scheme. Congress eventually imposed uniformity by enacting the "Standard Time Act" in March 1918. The railroads required train crews to carry accurate timepieces, which were often in the form of pocket watches. The museum's "Clock Room," adjacent to the Brown Gallery, has dozens of ticking clocks and types of pocket watches once used along the rail lines. A brief film explains this evolution from estimating time based on the sun's position to a precise system of measurement that made the trains run more safely and on time.

The B&O played a major role in the Union war effort. At the outbreak of the Civil War, the B&O owned 236 locomotives; maintained 3,579 passenger and freight cars; and employed more than 4,000 people. Following an April 19, 1861, attack on Massachusetts troops passing through the city by a Baltimore mob, the line and its president, John Work Garrett, received numerous threats over the railroad's plans to transport soldiers through Maryland. One warning directed at Garrett came from "one hundred of us, Firm, Respectable, Resolute men—[who] have determined & sworn to each other, to destroy 'every' bridge & tear up your Track on both lines of your Road . . . if you carry another Soldier over either line of your Road after Saturday April 20th . . . spare us Dear Sir this to us unpleasant duty," read the letter signed by "The Secretary." Early in the war, the tracks at Harpers Ferry were unprotected from Rebel raiding parties that torched bridges, tore up miles of track, and derailed trains; the B&O collected and reused much of the iron to rebuild the track. The commander of the New York 7th Infantry Regiment explained why a company was dispatched to Mt. Clare in the summer of 1861 for guard duty: "A serious riot had occurred among the workmen at Mt. Clare, originating in an attempt on the part of the Union to expel from the premises all persons suspected of secession sympathies."

The company's line ran west through Maryland and into Virginia at Harpers Ferry, then crossed back into Maryland at Cumberland before passing back into Virginia (West Virginia did not become a state until its secession from Virginia in May 1863). Late in May 1861, with Harpers Ferry under Confederate control, Gen. Thomas "Stonewall" Jackson employed a clever ruse to destroy track and trap and seize more than 400 B&O locomotives and cars from the B&O shops at Martinsburg, thereby striking a damaging blow both to the railroad and the transport of Union soldiers. The Rebels also destroyed sections of the Chesapeake & Ohio Canal at Harpers Ferry. (In 1872, President John Garrett would offer a job to the Confederate officer responsible for the Martinsburg operation, Thomas Sharp, commending his ability to "steal several million dollars worth of railroad equipment, move it on a dirt road a hundred miles, and place it on another fellow's road.")

In March 1862, Garrett pleaded with Secretary of War Edwin Stanton for protection for the rail line west of Harpers Ferry: "Refugees at Winchester informed our men that [Gen. Stonewall] Jackson expressed astonishment that the B&O Road could be opened soon, and a vicious determination to destroy it again at once," wrote Garrett, who asked for appropriate protection for the railroad, "in view of the great importance attached by the enemy to its destruction as well as the great necessity to the interests of the country to maintain it." During the Civil War, Harpers Ferry changed hands between the sides frequently, and the B&O's railroad bridge spanning the Potomac River was destroyed nine times. More than 140 attacks against B&O track, cars, and bridges were documented during the war. The federal government relied on the railroad to haul coal out of the Ohio Valley to piers in Baltimore and other trans-shipping sites. "It is said we shall all soon be in the dark here, unless *you can* bring coal to make gas," wrote President Lincoln to Garrett in January 1865. "I only write now to say, *it is very important to us*; and not to say that you must *stop* supplying the army to make room to carry coal. Do all you can for us in *both matters*."

Clacking machines lure those finishing in the Clock Room into an interactive exhibit that tells the intriguing story of the creation and evolution of the telegraph. Samuel Morse sent the first telegraph message— "What Hath God Wrought?"—from the United States Supreme Court building in Washington, D.C., to the Baltimore & Ohio's Washington Station, at New Jersey Avenue and C Street. The historic communication was then relayed to the railroad's station at Mt. Clare in Baltimore. Telegraph lines were strung along railroad rights of way, and in 1882 the B&O, looking to capitalize on this exciting new technology, started a telegraph company. But five years later the B&O sold the enterprise to Western Union, which would eventually own the market for telegrams.

Visitors can try to interpret Morse code and see its evolution from flickering signal lamps to the clicks along an electromagnetic telegraph wire to sounds via radio telegraphy. By 1858, a transatlantic cable allowed telegraph messages to cross the sea floor. In the museum's exhibit a telegraph machine clacks out a message, dated May 14, 1861, warning of Confederate attempts to seize locomotives and cars at the B&O's bridge over the Monocacy River in western Maryland. One can tap out a telegraph message, peruse an 1853 map of telegraph-station locations in the United States, and follow instructions to make a telegraph machine. This technology became a vital communications tool in the Civil War, as the Signal Corps of both armies used telegraphy for command and control of their armies in the field. Supplanted by more modern tools of communication, the need for this once-indispensable feature of nineteenth-century American life withered away. The last telegram sent in the United States went out on January 27, 2006.

The Roundhouse is home to a wide variety of engines as well as passenger and freight cars and is the capstone to the visual and interactive histories in the exhibit areas. Huge photographs on the walls depict the many bygone dimensions of the Baltimore & Ohio Railroad. With the sounds of horns and moving trains lending an air of authenticity, adults and children climb into locomotive cabs to turn knobs, pull valve handles, and read gauges. A platform leads to a post-office car with cubby holes for mail sorting and a "catch arm" for snagging mail bags on the fly; a video in the car shows men who once worked sorting mail on the trains explaining and demonstrating their craft. In a Civil War exhibit, next to the engines, lifelike models of workers and soldiers stand rigidly at attention. Fires burn. Heating stoves sit stoically at the end of Civil War–era passenger cars. On rails sit two Civil War–era boxcars, the only two in existence. Wooden boxes at various locations in the Roundhouse contain examples of the fuels used to power locomotives (coal and wood), and the freight the B&O carried during the Civil War (coffee, shoes, mail, military equipment). Young visitors are encouraged to identify the contents of the boxes before opening the lids. Essential railway tools are displayed. A Civil War musket, lifted from a rack, makes one wonder how such a heavy gun was carried for any length of time in the field. Children fill their own haversacks, making choices for the limited number of items a soldier in the Civil War would have carried. A large train carousel spins nearby, full of smiling children.

For moving passengers and freight, the B&O became an engineering and business model for railroads around the nation. Some of its business practices were progressive for the time. In 1855 it was the first railroad to hire women, employing four to work at its Baltimore station, and in 1927 hired Olive Dennis, a Cornell-trained civil engineer, to oversee passenger service and draw up plans for car interiors and seating. Dennis, the first civil engineer hired by a railroad, designed the now-collectible blue transferware china, depicting B&O locomotives and attractive scenes along its routes, which for decades graced the railroad's dining cars. In the last decade of the nineteenth century, the B&O hired train "hostesses," later known as stewardesses, to see to the needs of female passengers and their children. In the early part of the twentieth century, 200 maids were employed to work on long-distance trains, providing manicures, hairdressing services, cleaning, and child care. On-board dining services first appeared during the Civil War, though at that time the food was prepared at stations and kept warm until ready to be put aboard. In the 1920s B&O began preparing food on board and serving patrons in plush dining cars, offering fresh oysters and other bounty plucked from Maryland's waters. President Franklin D. Roosevelt rode the rails frequently and often had a B&O chef in his traveling company to prepare his meals. As did other railroads, the B&O hired "Red Caps" to carry passenger baggage through the stations, to and from trains. A 1916 issue of the Baltimore & Ohio employee magazine noted the professionalism of the line's Red Caps: "The poor woman with babies and baggage, who is making her way with difficulty to the day coach claims his attention to an equal degree with the handsomely gowned woman with the expensive luggage who is on her way to chair car or sleeper." The railroad introduced its first air-conditioned passenger car, the "Martha Washington," in 1930.

Outside the Roundhouse, platforms permit visitors to peer into passenger cars. Model trains run on an outdoor display. The North Carshop houses a number of engines and cars too large for the Roundhouse. Interpretive signs include a description of track workers the B&O employed for vegetation control and track inspection; these men and women became known as "Gandy Dancers," railroad slang of unknown origin, for their chanting and swaying in unison as they worked. A re-purposed former train shed, "Education Station," and two restored passenger cars double as venues for kids' birthday parties. The museum exit, back through the Roundhouse, takes visitors to the first stone, the tools used to embed it into the ground, and an animated bust of an aged Charles Carroll of Carrollton, whose mouth and head move as he speaks of his age and frailty but his eternal faith in the power of the railroad to bring lasting change to the United States.

In 1963 the Baltimore & Ohio Railroad merged with the Chesapeake and Ohio Railroad, creating a rail system of 11,000 miles that stretched from the Atlantic Ocean to the Mississippi River and from the southern borders of Virginia and Kentucky to the Great Lakes. In 1980, the combined company, known as Chessie, merged with Seaboard Coast Lines Industries and took the name CSX. By 1984, employment by CSX had declined by more than half in the prior twenty years, mirroring that of rail workers nationally. Though the original company has disappeared, visitors exiting the B&O Railroad Museum will have touched one of the largest collections of archival railroad materials in the United States and, through the engaging stories of the men and women who made it possible, absorbed the tale of one of the nation's greatest railroads.

SIDE TRIPS

IRISH RAILROAD WORKERS MUSEUM, BALTIMORE: Of the many immigrants arriving in Baltimore between 1840 and1850, many were Irish who settled in southwest Baltimore and went to work for the Baltimore & Ohio Railroad. This non-staffed museum showcases the places where the Irish lived, worked, worshipped, and were buried. It consists of two renovated alley houses, one of which is furnished as a period home that illuminates the lives of the Irish family who lived there in the 1860s. The other house features exhibits on Irish-American history and local neighborhood life. *918 Lemmon Street, Baltimore, MD, 21223, 410-669-8154.*

MT. CLARE MUSEUM HOUSE, BALTIMORE: This 1760 colonial home and National Historic Landmark is one of the best examples of Georgian architecture in Baltimore. Built by Charles Carroll, Barrister (a leading Maryland patriot, not to be confused with Charles Carroll of Carrollton), Mt. Clare was the center of Georgia Plantation, the name of Carroll's original property, and today illuminates the lives of the enslaved Africans and indentured servants who toiled there. The museum features nearly 3,000 objects from the eighteenth and nineteenth centuries, particularly paintings, furniture, and decorative arts. Highlights include English and Chinese export objects and sixteen family portraits by noted artists such as Charles Willson Peale and Robert Edge Pine. A 25-minute, three-mile round trip, seasonally narrated train ride takes passengers from the B&O Railroad Museum to Mt. Clare. *1500 Washington Boulevard, Baltimore, MD, 21230, 410-837-3262.*

THOMAS VIADUCT, PATAPSCO STATE PARK, MD: This stone masonry railroad bridge spans the Patapsco River and the Patapsco Valley gorge in Maryland, between Relay and Elkridge. It is the second oldest railroad bridge still in use in the world—only the nearby Carrollton Viaduct is older—and has been in continuous operation since it opened in 1835. During the Civil War, a Union artillery battery guarded the bridge to thwart Confederate sabotage on the critical rail line that carried troops and supplies. Freight traffic still moves on a daily basis. The bridge, a National Historic Landmark, has survived the great flood of 1868, Hurricane Agnes in 1972, and two major floods that caused widespread destruction in the Patapsco Valley.

BABE RUTH BIRTHPLACE AND MUSEUM / SPORTS LEGENDS MUSEUM, BALTIMORE: These two historic sites, just blocks apart, offer visitors a varied sports experience. George Herman "Babe" Ruth's birthplace, at 216 Emory Street (where the Babe was born in 1895), sheds light on Ruth's early life and remarkable baseball career. His childhood home is a mere several hundred yards from the Sports Legends Museum and the adjacent Oriole Park at Camden Yards, where the Baltimore Orioles now play. The Sports Legends Museum, in the Baltimore & Ohio Railroad's Camden Station that opened in 1856, covers much ground, serving as the official museum site of the Orioles and now-departed but still loved Baltimore Colts. The stories of other Maryland professional teams are here, along with exhibits on the Negro Leagues. The museum also houses Maryland's Athletic Hall of Fame. In a classic example of mission creep, the Sports Legends Museum also offers a small exhibit on Lincoln and the Civil War, on grounds that Lincoln passed through the station several times. *216 Emory Street and 301 West Camden Street, Baltimore, MD, 21201, 410-727-1539.*

FURTHER READING

ADULTS

James Dilts, *The Great Road: The Building of the Baltimore & Ohio 1828–1853.* Stanford University Press, 1993.

Thomas J. Greco and Karl D. Spence, *Dining on the B&O: Recipes and Sidelights from a Bygone Age.* Johns Hopkins University Press, 2009.

Festus P. Summers, *The Baltimore and Ohio in the Civil War.* Stan Clark Military Books, 1993.

Daniel Carroll Toomey, *The War Came by Train: The Baltimore & Ohio in the Civil War.* B&O Railroad Museum, 2012.

CHILDREN

Margaret Talbott Stevens, *ABC Choo Choo Book*, B&O Railroad Museum, 2005.

8

THE CHESAPEAKE
& OHIO CANAL

The crowd cheered on Independence Day, 1828, when President John Quincy Adams, standing before a crowd of dignitaries and commoners, thrust a shovel into some dirt. The festive occasion was the groundbreaking for the Chesapeake & Ohio Canal, designed to follow the Potomac River west for approximately 200 miles, from the rocky gorge of Little Falls, just above Georgetown, likely either to Cumberland, Maryland, or the mouth of the Savage River, allowing water-borne commerce to eventually cross the mountains and reach the Ohio River at Pittsburgh and the Ohio Valley. President Adams called the canal America's "third great step," after the Declaration of Independence and the Constitution, and loftily likened it as a "Wonder," to the Colossus of Rhodes and the Pyramids of Egypt. Though the canal would eventually stretch 184.5 miles, from the wharves at Georgetown to Cumberland, it never got to Pittsburgh. After operations ceased in 1924, the canal soon became an overgrown ditch.

The canal and its towpath—from which mules pulled the cargo-laden boats—have achieved immortality, however, as the C&O Canal National Historical Park, our nation's skinniest and perhaps most multidimensional national park. With striking vistas and eye-popping sites such as Great Falls, the Monocacy Aqueduct, and the Paw Paw Tunnel, its smooth towpath today teems with hikers, joggers, and bikers enjoying this shaded corridor through the Potomac Valley. At Great Falls and Williamsport, visitors can ride a canal boat and, at Great Falls, see how a lock operated to send boats smoothly along the canal's changing elevations. Visitors should check the park's website for a schedule of events.

On that hot July 4, Adams inaugurated a canal that already claimed a distinguished history. The many days George Washington spent surveying the Potomac River Valley made him dream of extensive commerce on the river. He envisioned canals skirting the powerful falls and rapids of the Potomac, allowing vessels to ply the river and make possible trade west of the Appalachians. Washington believed that these trade links with the Ohio Valley would also cement relations with its German, Irish, and Scotch-Irish settlers who felt little allegiance to the United States.

Negotiations between Maryland and Virginia in 1785 conferred upon the Patowmack Company the right to use the river for navigation. Washington, the most revered man in the land, became its first president. (The Articles of Confederation forbade states to make such agreements, and this venture helped lead to the Constitutional Convention two years later.) By 1802 the Patowmack Company had constructed five canals and bypasses and removed major impediments from the river, rendering the river theoretically more navigable. Even as it often operated in the red, the company's investment in the canal nourished river traffic: From 1800 to 1822, close to 14,000 boats, riding the river's southeastern current, carried over $9 million worth of cargo into Georgetown alone. But obstacles remained—water levels had great variance, the river's powerful flow precluded upstream cargo, and large trees propelled by the current torpedoed boats, costing lives and goods. A safer, more reliable way of harnessing the river had become imperative.

When the Canal Convention convened in 1823, delegates—who included Washington's nephew, Bushrod Washington, and Francis Scott Key—devised plans for expanding trade on the Potomac. Within two years the states of Maryland and Virginia and the federal government chartered the Chesapeake & Ohio Canal Company, with ambitious plans for the canal to parallel the Potomac and Youghiogheny Rivers, with a twenty-mile overland route connecting the two until joining the Ohio River in Pittsburgh. Mules and horses on an adjacent towpath would pull canal boats in both directions, and a system of lift locks would permit the boats to negotiate the changes in elevation. Feeder dams from the Potomac would supply water to the canal and regulate its level. Sales of stock would raise the necessary funds.

This "Great National Project" ultimately included 184 miles of canal and the adjoining 12-yard-wide towpath, 75 locks, 7 dams, a 3,100-foot tunnel, and 11 stone aqueducts to carry it over the rivers and streams flowing southward into the Potomac. The effort likely employed tens of thousands of men over the decades. The initial cost was expected to be $4.5 million, for the first phase of work that would take the canal to Cumberland. But labor violence, disease, money shortages, and floods would triple its cost and almost double the construction schedule.

Another enemy lay in wait: As President Adams turned the first spade of canal dirt on that Independence Day in 1828, Marylander Charles Carroll flipped a shovelful of Baltimore soil and launched the Baltimore & Ohio Railroad. The great trade race to the west was underway. For decades, canal and railroad battled one another to win the race to the Ohio Valley. Wily B&O land-purchasing agents stymied the canal's progress at Point of Rocks, the narrow passage between the Potomac and Catoctin Ridge. Although a four-year-long court battle eventually found for the canal, Baltimore businessmen successfully prodded the Maryland legislature to keep the B&O on track, though fears that its high-pitched train whistles would terrorize the animals plodding along the towpath did not materialize.

In 1832 cholera swept through the squalid camps of largely foreign canal workers, the disease likely introduced by newly arrived Irish laborers. Whiskey disrupted work and fueled fisticuffs among the lonely and homesick men. Violence in January 1834 near Williamsport prompted President Andrew Jackson to dispatch U.S. troops, an unprecedented federal intervention in American labor strife. A particularly violent episode in 1839 near Little Orleans saw a large mob of Irishmen attack German workers in their camp—one man was badly beaten and another thrown into a fire.

When the canal finally reached Cumberland in 1850, years behind schedule and $9.5 million over budget, the railroad was already there, having arrived eight years earlier. The "Great National Project" would go no farther toward the Ohio Valley. The canal operated uneasily for the next seven-plus decades. During the Civil War, Confederates attacked its aqueducts and sabotaged locks and berms to drain sections in an effort to disrupt coal and arms shipments. Flood damage was frequent. Nonetheless, in 1875, the canal's busiest year, approximately a million tons of coal traversed the waterway, which at its peak was plied by approximately 500 boats annually, carrying, in addition to coal, lumber, corn, wheat, flour, dry goods, and other cargo.

The canal boats were 92 feet long and 14.5 feet wide, and fit snugly into the seventy-five locks between the Appalachian Mountains at Cumberland and sea level at Georgetown. Living quarters were astern. Mules and horses not being used on the towpath were rested in stables in the bow and dined from "hay houses" amidships. Cargo was carried in the holds. Canaling was often a family affair, with eighteen-hour workdays common. Danger lurked everywhere. One drunken boatman fell into a lock and was crushed between his boat and the lock wall. The long workdays and Spartan conditions led to trouble. "You had to be pretty rough to be on the Canal," recounted one old boatman, decades later. "We'd go fighting all the time . . . made no difference who you hit." Fear crept in as the sun fell: "It was lonely," wrote another, years later. "I was half afraid . . . you'd see that little bow lamp back 100 feet. You were scared at night. It was another world." In 1916 a pipe burst and sprayed steam into the cabin of a canal boat docked along the wall adjacent to the Georgetown Power Co. plant. Captain Sam Spong's three children, asleep in the cabin, were literally cooked to death, and their mother badly scalded trying to save them. In 1992 a researcher discovered that one of Spong's sons had carved his name onto a stone atop the wall of Lock 16, a disquieting reminder of a young life lost on this commercial waterway.

Photographs of the period show the flow of life on the canal in the late-nineteenth century and early-twentieth century: A mother, bent over her washboard, gazes at her children (tethered to the deck so as not to go overboard); grinning, grizzled drivers lead mules along the towpath; happy lock-tender families pose in front of their small, trim homes; and mules strain in the Cumberland Basin to start boats bound for

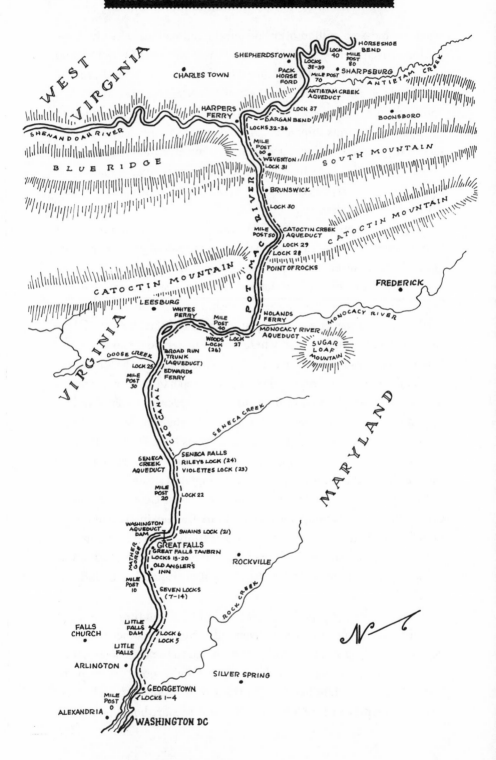

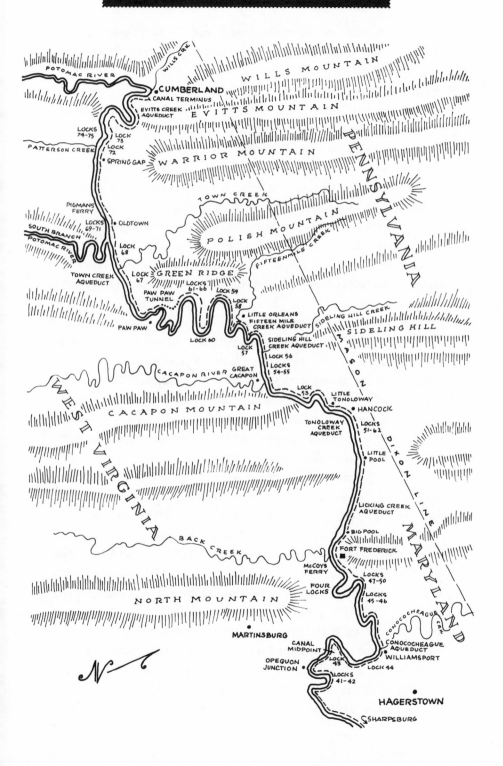

Georgetown, loaded with 100-plus tons of coal. The lock tenders, alerted to approaching boats by a cacophony of bugles, conch shells, lanterns, bells, horns, and shouts, would emerge from their houses at all hours to operate the locks. They trapped muskrats that were blamed for small leaks in the canal berms, earning a 25-cent bounty for each one killed.

Travel this serpentine national park from one end to the other or in sections. The elevation from Georgetown to Cumberland is a gradual 605 feet, with 160 feet of elevation occurring over the lower 14.3 miles. The towpath beckons pedestrians and bikers, watered sections allow boating and fishing, and short side trails lead to intriguing artifacts of the canal's history. Check with one of the six visitor centers, at Georgetown, Great Falls, Brunswick, Williamsport, Hancock, and Cumberland, for a schedule of events along the canal. Approximately thirty hiker-biker campsites (accessible via foot or bike) are along the towpath, with B&Bs and motels in nearby towns.

The chic K-Street shops and upscale cafes overlooking the Potomac River at National Harbor, near the canal's eastern terminus in Georgetown, are a far cry from most of its forested acreage. Mile zero is the Tidewater Lock, where Rock Creek joins the Potomac. Walk past the Thompson Boat Center along Rock Creek Parkway and follow signs to the visitor center on Thomas Jefferson Street, headquarters for a variety of interpretive activities. Rangers and reenactors give lift-lock demonstrations and a colorful history of the canal boat.

Tastefully renovated nineteenth-century buildings that flank the canal along the towpath include old Georgetown mills. Pass under the old bridges and enjoy the view of boat traffic on the wide Potomac. The clock tower of the Capital Traction Company, which ran horse-drawn (and later electric) streetcars in Washington, stands sentinel. Mile one passes under the Key Bridge and the remains of the Alexandria Aqueduct, which once took the canal over the Potomac River to Alexandria via the Alexandria Canal. Bikers, roller-bladers, and pedestrians speed along the Capital Crescent Trail, a hard-surface railtrail alongside the towpath that follows the roadbed of the Georgetown Branch of the B&O Railroad to Bethesda, and a crushed-stone trail on to Lyttonsville, in west Silver Spring (the ultimate destination is downtown Silver Spring).

Four miles farther west, below the Chain Bridge, is Fletcher's Boat

House, which rents boats and sells snacks and fishing gear. Across the towpath from the 1801 Abner Cloud House is a popular fishing spot and shady picnic area with grills and tables; across the river loom the cliffs of Virginia. During the Civil War, Union troops guarded the Chain Bridge, used by soldiers traveling to and from Union Army camps on the Virginia side. One Union private, asleep at his post here, was spared execution by a compassionate President Abraham Lincoln.

Terrific hiking trails are found at Great Falls, as are habitat for eagle, hawk, woodpecker, osprey, great blue heron, and cormorant, among others; 160 bird species that make a first-rate birding site; and a surprisingly unruly river slashing through Mather Gorge, reminiscent of wild rivers in the western United States. A tavern added to the lock tender's house here opened in 1831 as an inn. Strangers often had to share beds, and a marriage certificate and 50 cents allowed couples privacy. The building now serves as a visitor center, where books, artifacts, and DVDs illuminate the canal's history and the devastating floods it has suffered. Costumed interpreters and period music aboard the *Charles F. Mercer* (April–October) allow passengers to enjoy the gentle sway of a mule-pulled boat. The towpath here is flanked by wooded hills, with the ducks and heron dining in the canal and bald eagles soaring above. The seven hiking trails here range from easy to rugged, and catwalks cross roiling Potomac side channels to the bedrock terrace forest of Olmsted Island and a grand view of the primary falls. The remains of a mine just off the Gold Mine Loop Trail are the sole reminder of the gold that once attracted prospectors to Great Falls.

The wooded and rocky terrain of the Billy Goat Trail surprises with its sandy enclaves and panoramas of the river and Mather Gorge. Water, sturdy shoes, and a sharp eye for the blue trail markers are necessary for this two-hour adventure, which can be enjoyed by hardy children over six with an adult closely behind on the verticals. Great Falls is one of the most popular destinations along the canal, and off-season visits offer better views and fewer people.

Eight miles upriver from Great Falls is the Seneca Aqueduct and Riley's Lock (#24), named for its longtime tender—the only spot on the canal where aqueduct and lock were built as one structure. Girl Scouts in period garb conduct seasonal tours of the restored lock house and tell the lock keeper's family story. Red sandstone from the Seneca Creek quarry used in the aqueduct gives the towpath its reddish sheen, and the ruins of a stonecutting mill are in the woods on the berm upstream, a short distance from the aqueduct.

At Whites Ferry, the *Gen. Jubal A. Early* carries passengers, vehicles, and bikes across the Potomac, as nearby in 1864 its namesake Confederate general led his army across the river. The only remaining ferry service of the hundred-plus that once operated along the Potomac, the ferry is a vivid and expedient passage across the river into Virginia if driving (when floating trees snag the wire cable, the crew snaps to with a chain saw). After crossing into Virginia, consider the brief detour to Ball's Bluff Regional Park in Leesburg, where in October 1861 a small Union force that included U.S. senator Edward Baker of Oregon was decimated by Confederate riflemen. Baker, a close friend of President Lincoln's, was killed in the engagement.

A canal highlight lies 6.7 miles upriver from Whites Ferry: the seven-arch, 516-foot Monocacy Aqueduct, accessible by car via Rt. 28, twelve miles south of Frederick. Confederate troops crossed the Monocacy just below the aqueduct on their way to Antietam in 1862, and a Rebel attack on Washington was delayed and possibly thwarted upriver two years later at the Battle of Monocacy. Rebels tried unsuccessfully to destroy the aqueduct in September 1862, when their tools could not drill into the stone. A picnic area and boat launch are at Nolands Ferry, an ancient Potomac crossing for Indians and where the colonial-era Carolina Road crossed the river (south from Frederick via Rt. 85).

Harpers Ferry, where the Potomac and Shenandoah Rivers and the states of Maryland, Virginia, and West Virginia converge, is a third of the way to Cumberland (mile 60.7). Its history, stunning perch above the rivers, and small hotels and B&B's make it a great spot for respite (see chapter 9). The Appalachian Trail joins the towpath at Weverton and, for two and a half miles into Harpers Ferry, hikers are on both. Buried in the lore of John Brown's 1859 assault on the federal arsenal in Harpers Ferry is the fact that a member of his gang once tended a lock across the river while gathering pre-raid intelligence. A half-mile west is the trailhead for Maryland Heights, with panoramic views of the town and river valleys below. Stories of ghosts in the early 1900s include one said to haunt the remains of a frame house above Lock 36. Several miles west of the Antietam Creek Aqueduct, at Lock 38, lies historic Shepherdstown, West Virginia, well worth the one-mile jaunt west over the river via Rt. 34.

Williamsport, at the canal's 100-mile mark, was an eighteenth-century ferry site at the upper end of the canal, with past and present linked to the Potomac River. The park's visitor center is in the Cushwa warehouse, named for the company whose dealing in coal and other commodities had made Williamsport a true canal town by the start of the Civil War. In 1996 the Potomac deposited over five feet of water in the warehouse; the flood line is marked today on the wall inside the building. Adjacent is the three-arch Conococheague Aqueduct, which takes the canal over the river of the same name. In 1920 the aqueduct's upstream parapet collapsed and sent a canal boat crashing into the river below—the captain jumped clear and the driver was able to release the mules, sparing injury to man and beast. The large lock tender's house at Lock 44 and the lock have been restored. Eight miles west of Williamsport is Four Locks (Locks 47–50), in close proximity to take the canal across Prather's Neck to avoid a four-mile bend in the Potomac River.

Lock House 49 was occupied by four generations of the Taylor family, who, as did many lock tenders, supplemented their income by farming near their house (now one of the "Canal Quarters" lock houses available for rent from the C&O Canal Trust). The lock house and restored mule barn overlook the Potomac. A store that once stood next to Lock 48 peddled black powder, hams, candy, groceries, and household supplies to passing boatmen and the community that flourished around Four Locks. Enjoy fish plucked from the river at this sleepy spot in the wooded picnic area.

At mile 112 the canal passes through Fort Frederick State Park. Inside the park are the remains of Fort Frederick, one of the nation's best-preserved colonial forts and sole survivor of the eighteenth-century fortifications built along the river and its tributaries (see chapter 3). Union troops garrisoned here during the Civil War skirmished with Rebels who forded the Potomac River and slipped across the canal. Hiking trails abound, as do fish in Big Pool, where records reveal that one of 223 boat captains in 1851 made his winter home. The campground on the riverbank is operated by the state park. The French & Indian War muster, in August each year, offers a vivid glimpse of life on the colonial American frontier.

The Appalachian Mountains begin to rise along this westernmost stretch. Hancock, on the most northern segment of the Potomac, is a mere two miles from the Pennsylvania border. The canal runs a block below the Main Street establishments; the visitor center is in the historic Bowles House, on the berm side of the canal at Lock 52 at the east end of town. The original house was built in 1785 on a 685-acre farm known as Sarah's Fancy. The center is easily accessible from the Western Maryland Rail Trail, near mile marker #9.

The twenty-one-mile paved Western Maryland Rail Trail follows the old Western Maryland Railroad bed from Fort Frederick to Pearre. It's a top-rated U.S. rail-trail that parallels the canal here. The Little Tonoloway Recreation Area, with boat launch and picnic area, sits between the canal and river. Deer, muskrat, skunk, and beaver inhabit the wooded areas along the river; wild turkeys stroll across the towpath.

The Cacapon River joins the Potomac River nine miles west of Hancock, with splendid views of Cacapon Mountain to the east of the river and Sideling Hill to the west. About eight miles west is Little Orleans, whose sole building has one-stop shopping: restaurant, bait shop, and a bar that doubles as the "Mayor's office"—not bad for a town whose off-season population is two. Irish canal workers are buried in the cemetery surrounding St. Patrick's Church, just across Fifteen Mile Creek. A drive-in campsite and boat launch are reached via the underpass on the canal berm.

Perhaps the most stunning site on the canal is the 3,118-foot, 6-million-brick-lined Paw Paw Tunnel. This pre-dynamite construction task required the dangerous use of black powder and primitive hand tools to blast a tunnel to bypass six miles of river bends along the southern edge of the Green Ridge State Forest. The Paw Paw Tunnel took five years to construct and nearly bankrupted the canal company. The narrow tunnel accommodated only one boat at a time, and the rules of the road awarded right of way to the first to enter. On one occasion two stubborn captains, entering simultaneously at opposite ends, refused to yield; a superintendent, failing to resolve the impasse, built a fire at one end that smoked both boats out. The middle of the twenty-minute passage through the

Paw Paw is pitch black, so flashlights are useful. Bikes should be walked through. The wooden railing is a reassuring anchor along the way, and grooves from tow ropes make the walk more evocative. The eerie echoes of the boatmen's songs, as they drifted through the darkness under the mountain, are easy to conjure. Water cascades down the striated rock at the upstream end of the tunnel. Claustrophobics can hike overland on the two-mile Tunnel Hill Trail, taking in views of the Potomac Valley. Day-trippers can reach the tunnel via Maryland Rt. 51 and by walking a half mile. Lock 64 is the scene of a reported grisly 1890s incident in which the lock tender was murdered for his collection of rare coins—and the culprit caught spending them in a Cumberland saloon.

Two and a half miles beyond Potomac Forks, where the river splits into its north and south branches, is Oldtown, settled in the 1740s by Thomas Cresap, scion of a frontier family who hosted George Washington on his journeys west. The house of Cresap's son Michael, built in 1764, still stands, now as a private museum, the Irvin Allen/Michael Cresap Museum (visits by appointment). Its barred basement windows stem from its past as a jail.

The canal crosses a popular fishing site at Green Spring Road. The road leads to a privately owned wooden low-water toll bridge over the Potomac River that is a busy crossing spot between Maryland and West Virginia (tolls are collected on the honor system, at one time in a tin can welded to an iron handle). This crossing structure hardly calls to mind an interstate bridge, which it is.

Eight miles further along the towpath is the Narrows, where the canal snakes between the Potomac River and Iron Mountain before reaching Cumberland. This city was founded in the mid-eighteenth century as a fort and gateway to the west, with the fort a depot and staging area for British and colonial troops during the French and Indian War (1756–1763). A cabin that may have been used by George Washington is the only remaining fort structure; locals believe Washington used it as an office. The *Cumberland*, a full-size replica of a canal boat, is at Canal Place in Cumberland. The visitor center, in the former Western Maryland Railway Station, is open year round, with a stone memorial to Irish canal workers nearby.

Although the B&O beat the canal to Cumberland, for a time there was room for both. An infrastructure of stables, drydocks, warehouses, hotels, and saloons once ringed the boat basins in Cumberland, where there was plenty of action, some no doubt apocryphal. "Sometimes it was pretty rough," recalled one old boatman who worked the canal as a boy in the early 1900s. "I seen people killed . . . they'd be shot in the evening and they'd just . . . let 'em lay there." A bulldog allegedly swam across the basins, towline in mouth, to speed mule and horse hitchings.

Cumberland itself is a great weekend destination, and Lock 75, Old-town, and the Paw Paw Tunnel are within easy reach by car. The Fort Cumberland Walking Trail covers several downtown blocks; its close proximity to the canal terminus makes it an easy detour. That the visitor center has permanent residence in a restored train station is the ironic capstone to the story of the canal's race west against a railroad.

In 1954 the Washington *Post* endorsed a proposal to place a parkway along much of the long-neglected canal and towpath. Supreme Court justice William O. Douglas, hoping the *Post* editors might instead share his vision of canal preservation, invited them to hike the towpath with him, from Cumberland to Georgetown. They accepted. Fifty-eight hikers left Cumberland in March that year, and by the time Douglas and the eight others who had covered the entire distance reached George-town, the issue had attracted national attention. The *Post* modified its stance, recommending preserving as much of the canal as possible, and the parkway plan soon evaporated. Not until 1971 would the efforts of Maryland legislators, local groups, and individuals succeed in preserving the entire canal, its towpath, and its 1200-plus historic structures as a national park.

An annual spring canal hike, sponsored by the C&O Canal Association, honors Douglas, who, along with George Washington, would surely be pleased by the Great Allegheny Passage Trail that now connects Cumberland and Pittsburgh. A segment of the Potomac Heritage National Scenic Trail, the Passage Trail and the C&O Canal now link the Chesapeake Bay and the Ohio Valley for public enjoyment, a lasting tribute to the vision of Washington and the other founders of the "Potowmack Company" so many years ago.

SIDE TRIPS

MONOCACY NATIONAL BATTLEFIELD, MD: This Civil War battlefield, less than two miles south of Frederick, Maryland, is the site of a July 1864 clash between Confederate general Jubal Early, moving east toward Washington, D.C., and the Union prison camp at Point Lookout, Maryland, and Union general Lew Wallace, who futilely tried to stop him. Though Early continued his move eastward, Wallace's troops delayed him sufficiently that Union reinforcements reached Washington in time to repulse the Rebel incursion. Native Americans were in the area since the earliest human occupation of North America, nearly 10,000 years ago, and European explorers and traders arrived in the region in the early 1700s. An array of interactive exhibits in the visitor center and seven miles of walking trails are highlights of this 1600-acre-plus national park site. *5201 Urbana Pike, Frederick, MD, 21704, 301-662-3515.*

CUMBERLAND, MD: Founded in 1787, this city of 21,000-plus residents grew from a stop for those heading west to a major transportation center. It was the starting point of the first National Road (now known as Route 40, or the National Highway), and later home to railroads and the western terminus of the Chesapeake & Ohio Canal. Visit George Washington's Headquarters (where he really slept) and History House, a large Victorian home with period furnishings. Stroll along Washington Street, the site of the original Fort Cumberland; and inspect both the gnomes and gargoyles that adorn the courthouse and the nineteenth-century homes that line this historic thoroughfare. The Western Maryland Railway Station at Canal Place is an original train station that houses the scenic railroad and shops in addition to the C&O Canal visitor center and the Allegany County tourism office. Cumberland is 130 miles from Baltimore; 130 miles from Washington, D.C.; and 100 miles from Pittsburgh.

CLARA BARTON NATIONAL HISTORICAL SITE, MD: Clara Barton lived the last fifteen years of her life in this home, devoting it to the American Red Cross as headquarters, warehouse, and living space. The house is shown by guided tour only, with tours starting on the hour. *5801 Oxford Road, Glen Echo, MD, 20812, 301-320-1410.*

WILLIAMSPORT, MD: This quaint town of 2,000 people on the Potomac River has been home to Native Americans and fur traders, and many settlers passed through on their way west. Skirmishes between Yankees and Rebels during the Civil War were constant, and the Confederate Army moved through the town several times as it invaded and retreated from Maryland. Union cannon sit atop Doubleday Hill as a reminder of Williamsport's strategic import. The town's past and present are linked to the Potomac River, and it's home to a Chesapeake & Ohio Canal National Historical Park visitor center. Ride a replica canal boat, fish in the river, and picnic along the river banks.

FURTHER READING

ADULTS

Chesapeake and Ohio Canal: A Guide to Chesapeake and Ohio Canal National Historical Park, Maryland, District of Columbia, and West Virginia (National Park Service Handbook). Division of Publications National Park Service (U.S.), 1991.

Mike High, *The C&O Canal Companion* (second edition). Johns Hopkins University Press, in press, 2015.

Elizabeth Kytle, *Home on the Canal.* Johns Hopkins University Press, 1996.

Walter S. Sanderlin, *The Great National Project: A History of the Chesapeake and Ohio Canal.* Eastern National, 2005.

CHILDREN

June Behrens and Pauline Brower, *Canal Boats West.* Children's Press, 1978.

Charles S. Furtney, *Tyrconnel: An Antebellum Adventure Along the C&O Canal.* Local History Company, 2004.

Carolyn Reeder, *Captain Kate.* Children's Literature, 2002.

9

HARPERS FERRY

*The passage of the Patowmac through the Blue Ridge is perhaps one
of the most stupendous scenes in Nature. You stand on a very high
point of land. On your right comes up the Shenandoah, having ranged
along the foot of the mountain a hundred miles to seek a vent. On
your left approaches the Patowmac in quest of a passage also. In the
moment of their junction they rush together against the mountain....
This scene is worth a voyage across the Atlantic.*

So wrote Thomas Jefferson in 1783 about Harpers Ferry, whose wooded and
rocky landscape still looks much as it did in his time. The peaks of the Blue
Ridge Mountains frame this historic West Virginia town, whose buildings
sprout on the steep hillside that juts into the scenic junction of the Potomac and Shenandoah Rivers. The strategic location of Harpers Ferry gave
it a coveted status during the Civil War, when the town was alternately
occupied by Union and Confederate forces for much of the conflict.

The colorful history of Harpers Ferry is, like the town itself, multilayered, and conveys the flavor of a nineteenth-century town. Its name
is forever associated with John Brown's dramatic raid in 1859 to seize
weapons from the federal armory there. Brown believed that this spark
would ignite a massive slave insurrection that would cascade into an in-

ferno, the final act of his messianic crusade to exterminate the scourge of human bondage.

In the darkness of October 16, 1859, Brown and eighteen of his men crept into Harpers Ferry from their headquarters at the nearby Kennedy farm and attacked the United States Armory that housed 100,000 rifles and muskets. Brown planned to arm both slaves and free blacks with these stolen weapons, but following a thirty-six-hour battle that claimed sixteen lives—including that of Heyward Shepherd, a free black man and station baggage porter killed by Brown's men—U.S. Marines led by Col. Robert E. Lee and Lieut. Jeb Stuart captured the raiders. This audacious attack stoked primal fears of slave revolts, and the resulting tensions propelled the country closer to civil war. Brown and six of his men were tried and hanged in nearby Charles Town, earning the defiant Brown, in the eyes of some, everlasting martyrdom.

Harpers Ferry National Historical Park occupies over 3,600 acres in West Virginia, Virginia, and Maryland. The park offers two distinct visitor locations—the visitor center on the east side of West Virginia Rt. 340 and the town itself, less than two miles to the southwest. The visitor center, while small, is ranger-staffed, and the area around it includes interpretive signs and the trailheads for the Lower Town Trail (1.6 miles one way) and the Murphy-Chambers Farm Trail (one to three miles with side trails). Visitors should park at the visitor center and ride the free shuttle into town.

The town of Harpers Ferry, first settled in 1733, was named for Philadelphia millwright Robert Harper, who in 1747 bought land and a ferry service to ply the Potomac River with goods and passengers. By 1801 the federal armory along the south bank of the Potomac was producing muskets and what became known as the Harpers Ferry rifle. The National Park Service has outlined the foundations of the armory's warehouse and forging shop foundations, whose buildings at their peak stretched 600 to 800 yards along the Potomac. Much happened at this site: The Baltimore & Ohio Railroad, which connected the eastern seaboard with the Ohio Valley, lacked access to the Maryland side of the Potomac River, so the B&O built an elevated trestle atop the armory wall (see chapter 7). Above the site engineers built a diversion dam, then dug a narrow canal on the river's Harpers Ferry side to supply water power to the armory.

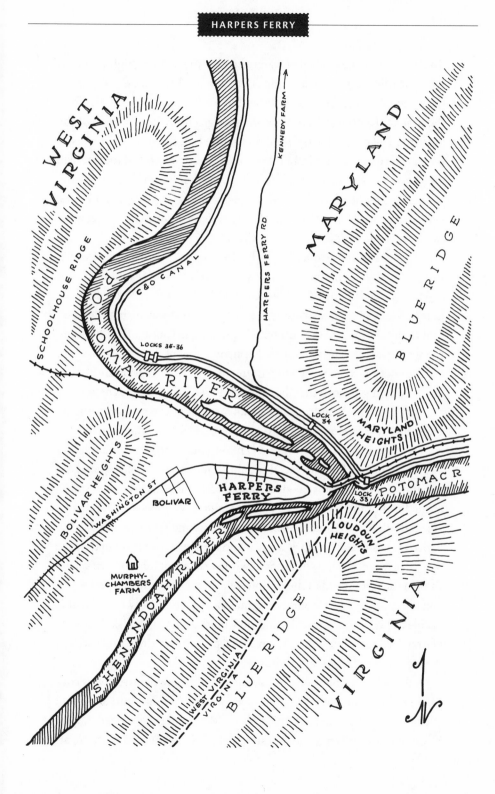

This clever scheme propelled water through the canal at high pressure, where it filled perpendicular pipes, known as "headraces," that drove the water wheels and turbines. Several of the headraces are visible along the base of the armory wall. Interpretive signs describe a handful of the more than 28,000 artifacts found on the site that illuminate the lives of both armory workers and Civil War soldiers—bone-handled toothbrush, pipe bowl, lice comb, belt buckle, bullets, and bugle mouthpiece. On the site also is a replica of the metal-framed boat built for Meriwether Lewis, who arrived in Harpers Ferry in 1803 to purchase guns and supplies for the Lewis and Clark Expedition to the west.

Just south of the armory site is the fire-engine / guard house in which Brown and some of his men barricaded themselves before capture. Known as John Brown's Fort, this only surviving building from the federal armory complex has a peripatetic history. In 1891 it was dismantled and sent to the 1893 World's Columbian Exposition in Chicago, Illinois, then in 1895 to the Murphy-Chambers Farm, now part of the park, and where the foundation remains. The fort remained in that location until 1909 and, sitting high above the Shenandoah River, became a touchstone for the genesis of the American civil rights movement when, in mid-August 1906, the Niagara Movement gathered there to celebrate the goals of John Brown's raid, if not Brown himself. (This organization was co-founded by W.E.B. Du Bois to fight for racial equality and grew into the National Association for the Advancement of Colored People.) An early photograph at the farm of the National League of Colored Women—co-founded by Harriet Tubman to promote women's suffrage and efforts to oppose Jim Crow laws—shows a group of women and men posing in front of the fort; one of the women is the widow of Lewis Leary, one of John Brown's men. In 1909 the fort moved to the campus of Storer College in Harpers Ferry, and today sits 150 feet from its original location in the town, where it is visible in period photographs and now marked by an obelisk. Just west of Arsenal Square and John Brown's Fort, park rangers in period garb tell the story of the raid to rapt visitors.

A few steps to the southeast, at the Point, where the two rivers converge, visitors can cross the footbridge over the Potomac into Maryland and to the Chesapeake & Ohio Canal and Maryland Heights (see chapter 8). From Maryland Heights one can see why Harpers Ferry was easy to attack and difficult to defend during the Civil War, for it had the geographic misfortune to be an asset both sides coveted. The town was a commercial hub by rail and water and featured both the federal armory and a strategic location on the border between Maryland and Virginia. During the war, Harpers Ferry changed hands eight times between the opposing forces. The grind of continuous military operations in the area eroded the town's population from a bustling 3,000 in 1861 to a ghost town with less than 300 people four years later. Some local families earned their wartime livelihoods by baking bread and pies for whichever side happened to control the town. "Our armory is burnt and we have no money and no nothing else," wrote an armory worker on April 18, 1861, after the retreating Union Army torched the complex, to keep its weapons out of the hand of approaching Confederate forces from Virginia (which that very day had voted to secede from the Union).

In the summer of 1861, after Gen. Thomas "Stonewall" Jackson's Confederates vacated the town, a Unionist remarked to a friend, "Well, we have got rid of that lot and have escaped at least with our lives, but what will the next party that comes do with us?" An answer came in a September 1862 letter from a Union soldier that noted how "the hissing and screeching of shot and shell discharged at [them] 'twas a strange medley for a Sabbath day's worship." During a rare calm period, in June 1863, a Union soldier from Maryland encamped at Harpers Ferry told his mother how soldiers went about mending their overcoats: "We generaly patch them up and wear them until they are pretty well gone," wrote Pvt. Robert Kirkwood of the First Maryland Infantry Regiment and one of three brothers fighting for the Union. "I get William to do my patching and mending, he makes a splendid old woman."

Throughout the year, the park vividly brings the Civil War period to life, through ranger-led historical interpretations and reenactments that include the tumultuous election of 1860, living histories, and, of course, John Brown's raid. Summer programs for children include an opportunity for young journalists in period dress to deploy teleprompter and videocam to report on specific Civil War events (kids can sign up to participate when entering the park). The park offers Civil War trading cards, gathered at various places, and a Junior Ranger program for children.

Six themes that illustrate Harpers Ferry's multifaceted past—industry, transportation, natural heritage, John Brown, the Civil War, and African American history—are illuminated by the display in the Master Armorer's House, which doubles as the Park Service information center, on Shenandoah Street. Rangers provide maps and an overview of the area's history, geography, and geology. The exhibits include the six types of muskets and rifles (flintlock, breech-loading, and percussion) manufactured at Harpers Ferry and the spy glass that belonged to John Cook, one of John Brown's men. Cook, who used it to watch the progress of Brown's raid from Maryland Heights, escaped the initial post-raid dragnet but was later caught and executed for his role in it.

Harpers Ferry is a walking town, where visitors could easily be strolling along nineteenth-century streets. Recreated eighteenth- and nineteenth century exhibits—clothing, dry goods, watch-repair, confectionery—line Shenandoah Street and the foot of High Street; visitors can wander into them at their leisure. In a home on one of these streets, a citizen named Walter Eanes told his brother about the impact of the war on the town: "Quite a number of prostitutes have made their appearance here," he wrote in March of 1862, "and when they get fairly started in business we shall find plenty of victims for the Guard House." Other restored buildings in the lower town include the Provost Marshal's Office and the Industry Museum with the machinery used to create the components of a musket—diagrams explain how stocks and barrels were made and assembled. A residential structure on the same block shows the excavation of various features, with queries challenging visitors to see the evolution of the building and how it was modified over the centuries to meet new needs. Steps in the rear lead up into the rocky hillside and to an insightful view of how buildings were fused together; new lots needed for the growing antebellum town were blasted out of the rock, which was often adapted for use as interior walls and hearths. Be sure to see the operating reproductions of nineteenth-century armory machinery. The child-friendly Wetlands Exhibit shows the evolution of the area's river terrain. The Black Voices Exhibit has touch screens and phones that reveal letters that tell stories of freedom and of slavery; artifacts such as tools they used and a cowhide whip—a powerful symbol of slavery's bestial nature—round out the display. The nonprofit Harpers Ferry Historical Association Bookshop is at the end of Shenandoah Street.

Virginius Island lies in the Shenandoah River, to the west, and was once home to factories, mills, and close to 200 residents. During the Civil War it was occupied by Union troops, one of whom was John H. W. Stuckenberg, a Pennsylvania chaplain who complained in October 1862 that throughout the pestilent Harpers Ferry area was contaminated water and food infested by "living creatures ... pork alive with skippers," with his only companions "numerous flies and long legged spiders now and then running over me." Further upstream was Hall's Rifle Works where the manufacture of interchangeable parts was perfected, for the first time anywhere.

The mile-and-a-half walking tour above the lower town lies mostly on the Appalachian Trail. Climb the stone steps near the foot of High Street to the 1782 Harper House, the oldest surviving building in Harpers Ferry and now restored as an 1855 working-class apartment home built by Robert Harper, who died before it was finished. The home's illustrious guest list includes George Washington and Thomas Jefferson. A springhouse and root cellar are embedded into the cool cliff side in the rear. Perched further up the hill are two churches: the 1833 St. Peter's Roman Catholic Church, which advertised its neutrality during the Civil War by flying the British Union Jack (and came through unscathed); and the ruins of St. John's Episcopal Church, site of a Civil War barracks and hospital.

The footpath follows the ridge above the Shenandoah River to Jefferson Rock, an impressive mass of metamorphic rock formed by great heat and pressure in the earth's crust that in 1783 so moved Thomas Jefferson. This spot on the Appalachian Trail offers a panoramic view of the town below, both rivers, and the mountains beyond. Just behind Jefferson Rock a footpath leads up to the Harpers Cemetery, whose old tombstones lean askew and date to 1782. The cemetery's far side spills onto Fillmore Street in upper Harpers Ferry. Storer College, founded as a one-room school after the Civil War to educate newly freed slaves, is a block north, on Camp Hill, named for United States troop encampments from 1798 to 1800. One of the former college buildings now houses a National Park Service training center.

The confluence of rivers, mountains, and trails around Harpers Ferry forms one of the most alluring spots in the mid-Atlantic region. The Appalachian Trail, which traverses fourteen states, passes through the middle of the historic district (the national headquarters of the Appalachian Trail

Conservancy is in the town); across the Potomac River on its Maryland side is the towpath of the Chesapeake & Ohio Canal. The trail crosses the Potomac River on a footbridge built onto the railroad bridge and encircles the south side of the town to join the canal on the Maryland side of the river. Half a mile west along the canal are remains of two structures: Canal Lock 33, which legend says John Cook tended for a time to gather intelligence prior to the arsenal raid; and the Salty Dog Tavern, long known for the potency of its liquor and the frequency of its brawls. Further along is the trailhead for Maryland Heights, looming over Harpers Ferry from the northeast. Hikers can choose from two color-coded trails, both with their own attractions: The longer is 6.5 miles from the Point to the top (about four hours), with intact Civil War fortifications along the way; the shorter is 4.5 miles (about three hours) and leads to the cliffs and a spectacular vista of Harpers Ferry and the valley formed by the rivers.

Historic sights mark the shorter trail: remains of charcoal hearths that fueled the furnaces at the Antietam Iron Works, remnants of Civil War forts and camps, rifle pits and depressions that housed artillery and powder magazines (including the spot where a hapless group of Yankees tossed a live shell into a cooking fire and blew themselves up). Interpretive signs adorn the way. On this trail, graced in spring by blooming dogwood, laurel, and wild roses, one may hear only the wind and the occasional train whistle in the valley below. Wild turkeys scurry at the summit. Hikers should note that neither water nor restrooms are available on the Maryland Heights, and that snakes sometimes sun themselves on its rocks and trails.

Loudoun Heights, across the Shenandoah River from Harpers Ferry in Virginia and West Virginia, is reached via the Appalachian Trail from the foot of Shenandoah Street that crosses the bridge over WV Rt. 340. The trail, roughly a three-hour hike, is an early nineteenth-century military road that allowed armory timber-cutters access to the trees on the Heights; it was used by both sides in the Civil War. Trenches and stone fortifications lie along the crest. The quartz cliffs at the end of the main trail stare across the Potomac River at Maryland Heights.

Bolivar Heights, also part of the park, rises gradually behind Harpers Ferry and includes the adjacent town of Bolivar. This higher ground offers strollers and picnickers a splendid view of Harpers Ferry to the east, framed by Maryland and Loudoun Heights, with Camp Hill / Storer

College in the middle. The Bolivar crest offers quarter-mile and three-quarter-mile trails with rifle pits and signs illuminating Civil War events on the Heights, where Gen. Stonewall Jackson drilled Confederate recruits into an elite brigade in 1861. A year later, on the next ridge to the west (Schoolhouse Ridge), he accepted the surrender of 12,500 Union troops—the largest surrender of United States servicemen prior to the capture of 15,000 federal troops by the Japanese on Bataan in the Philippines during World War II.

Harpers Ferry no longer resembles the town described by John Trowbridge, a writer gathering stories about the ruined cities of the South. "War has changed all," he wrote in his book published in 1865. "Dreary hill-sides present only ragged growths of weeds. The town itself lies half in ruins ... Of the bridge across the Shenandoah only the ruined piers are left; still less remains of the old bridge across the Potomac. All about the town are rubbish, filth and stench." The town today offers much for the historian, the hiker, the biker, the whitewater rafter, the boater, and the fisherman. Shoppers and strollers will enjoy the quaint restaurants (many open only for lunch) and shops with antiques, souvenirs, and Civil War memorabilia along Potomac and High Streets. Visitors may also wish to take the Murphy-Chambers Farm Trail. The trailhead is just across from the main visitor center and leads across an open field to a spectacular view of the Shenandoah River 200 feet below. The Murphy-Chambers House stands a quarter-mile on the left, amid silent fields that in September 1862 saw 5,000 Confederate troops massed against a Union line 1,000 yards away. The federals surrendered to a rebel charge, and Harpers Ferry again changed hands. A side trail slopes down to entrenchments and a redoubt built by Gen. Philip Sheridan's men in August 1864—with Harpers Ferry back in Union control—as protection against Confederate gunboats moving toward the town on the Shenandoah River.

Despite the town's storied history and multiple attractions, however, Harpers Ferry is still defined by John Brown's assault in the darkness of that October night in 1859—thanks to the engaging Park Service programming that explores the planning, execution, and aftermath of the raid. Some say that Brown's spirit still hovers over this small town and its rivers and mountains, even as the debate continues over the extent to which his noble end may have justified his violent means.

SIDE TRIP

BALL'S BLUFF BATTLEFIELD REGIONAL PARK, VA: On October 21, 1861, a small Union detachment was ambushed on the Virginia side of the Potomac River near Leesburg. Trapped on the bluff overlooking the river, many federal soldiers died either sliding down the bluff toward the river or in the river itself, succumbing to the swift current or to Confederate riflemen firing down at them. Col. Edward D. Baker, U.S. senator from Oregon and a close friend of President Abraham Lincoln's, was killed in the engagement. Short hiking trails with interpretive signs give visitors a sense of the topography and the terror Union troops must have experienced. Ball's Bluff National Cemetery is the resting place of many who fell that October day. Guided tours are available on Saturday and Sunday, at 11 A.M. and 1 P.M., from early April through the end of November. *Ball's Bluff Road, Leesburg, VA, 21076, 703-737-7800.*

FURTHER READING

ADULTS

David T. Gilbert, *A Walker's Guide to Harpers Ferry, West Virginia,* 5th edition. Appalachian Trail Conference, 1997.

Chester G. Hearn, *Six Years of Hell: Harpers Ferry during the Civil War.* Louisiana State University Press, 1999.

Tony Horowitz, *Midnight Rising: John Brown and the Raid That Sparked the Civil War.* Henry Holt and Co., 2011.

Steven Lubet, *John Brown's Spy: The Adventurous Life and Tragic Confession of John E. Cook.* Yale University Press, 2012.

Brian McGinty, *John Brown's Trial.* Harvard University Press, 2009.

CHILDREN

Zachary Kent, *The Story of John Brown's Raid on Harper's Ferry.* Children's Press, 1988.

CIVIL WAR RICHMOND

Richmond and its environs offer a rich tableau of historical and Civil War sites. This city, founded as a fort overlooking the James River, served as the Confederate capital and was the target of two sustained Union invasions: the 1862 Peninsula Campaign and the 1864 Overland Campaign, when the Union Army began relentlessly attacking the Confederate Army on its home Virginia soil. At Richmond National Battlefield Park, visitors can see the site of the Tredegar Iron Works, overlooking the James River, which manufactured more than 1,000 artillery pieces for its army during the war. The Museum of the Confederacy and its neighboring Confederate White House can shed as much light on that short-lived government as any place in the nation.

At the outbreak of the Civil War, Richmond was the third-largest Southern city (behind New Orleans and Charleston) and shortly thereafter became the capital city of the Confederate States of America and a target of the Union Army throughout the war. During the 1862 Peninsula Campaign, Gen. George B. McClellan started at the mouth of the James River and fought his way up the peninsula east of Richmond. But erroneously believing he was outnumbered at every turn by Confederate forces, McClellan retreated south to a new base on the James, then abandoned his campaign to take the city.

Gen. Ulysses S. Grant launched his Overland Campaign in early May 1864. Over the ensuing eleven months, a number of major battles and skirmishes finally brought about the capture of an evacuated Richmond in April 1865, leading to the Confederate surrender at Appomattox and the end to four bloody years of fighting. The sheer number of battles that comprised these two campaigns against Richmond, and their names, can be confounding—the Seven Days' Battles, for example, was part of the 1862 Peninsula Campaign, which itself included a number of other engagements. But advance planning and good maps, such as those available from the National Park Service and Virginia Civil War Trails, will help ensure an informative driving tour.

The Peninsula Campaign was fraught with friction between the civilian government in Washington, D.C., and General McClellan's Army of the Potomac. President Abraham Lincoln, a self-taught military strategist, urged McClellan to attack and destroy the enemy's army, while the general insisted on seizing the Confederate capital, crafting a plan to invade Richmond from the south that involved 389 vessels; 121,500 men; 14,592 animals; and provisions for man and beast. This invasion became the largest single campaign of the Civil War and spurred a partial evacuation of the Confederate capital. "It is distressing to see how many people are leaving Richmond, apprehending that it is in danger," read Judith White McGuire's diary entry for May 3, 1862. And this abortive invasion was costly: At its end, after a little more than a month, one of every four men involved would be dead, wounded, or missing.

The ideal start to a tour of Civil War Richmond is the Richmond National Battlefield Park Civil War Visitor Center and Museum (490 Tredegar Street). Outside the visitor center stand monuments to the rich output of this industrial enterprise, the Tredegar Iron Works, which in 1860 was America's largest ironworks: a huge water wheel; "raceways," the stone-and-brick tunnels through which water flowed from the Kanawha Canal to power the foundry; and a turbine that in the 1870s replaced water wheels. All of these artifacts are accompanied by interpretive markers explaining how this massive machinery worked. Five railroads emanated from Richmond during the Civil War; two miles of track crossed the Tredegar complex alone. On this site also is the privately owned American Civil War Center, which presents the Civil War

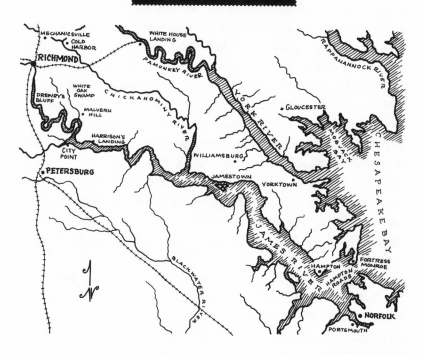

THE VIRGINIA PENINSULA

from a variety of perspectives (admission fee and parking validation). The high ground above the plaza near the entrance to the National Park visitor center yields a panoramic view of the city skyline and river, including Belle Isle, a popular island park accessible by footbridge over the James River.

Belle Isle's modern recreational allures belie its role during the war as a fetid, open-field prison camp where a thousand Union soldiers died of malnutrition and disease: "We were full of health, heart, hope and spirits," recorded the diary of J. Osborn Coburn, 38th Ohio Volunteer Infantry Regiment, after three months on Belle Isle. "Now we are down, clear down, starved out. Our flesh as well as hope and spirits are all broken or nearly so . . . we get peevish and irritable, cross, dirty and careless. Eat like beasts, our faces and hands begrimed with dirt and pine smoke." A Confederate gun emplacement is still visible on the west side. In addition to Belle Isle and Libby Prison—the other large Confederate prison in Richmond (today marked only by a plaque)—was a network of local jails, fashioned from tobacco warehouses and overseen by warden David Todd, the half-brother of Mary Todd Lincoln. Though memories of former prisoners are often distorted, one prisoner later wrote that Todd took "personal delight in human blood and suffering." Another claimed how he showered prisoners with "foul and scurrilous abuse" and entered prison yards with sword drawn, at times leaving with blood on it.

Exhibits and audiovisual programs in the visitor center convey the vivid story of Civil War Richmond, examining the war from various angles: Union, Confederate, African American, slave, and civilian, as well as its consequences for the nation's cultural and social fabric. A film on the museum's third level notes that a third of the city's 1860 population of 38,000 was black, and that the May 1862 advance of General McClellan's Union forces up the peninsula formed by the York and James Rivers deposited his men so close to Richmond that they kept time by the city's church bells.

On the museum's third level is a part of a mechanism that pumped volatile hydrogen into the aerial surveillance balloons used by both sides during the Civil War. Nearby is "Voices from the Military Front," a moving collection of recorded excerpts from letters of Union and Confederate officers and men who fought in the two Richmond campaigns. Don't miss former slave Garland H. White's powerful account of his entrance with the Union Army into an evacuated Richmond in April 1865. White was the chaplain of the 28th Infantry Regiment of the United States Colored Troops; his emotional letter describes his reunification with his mother, who had lost him as a little boy to a slave trader twenty years earlier.

Youngsters ages 4 to 13 wishing to participate in the Junior Ranger program may obtain the activity book on the entry level, where the gift shop is located. The exercises in the packet send kids on a quest to six battlefields from both Richmond campaigns and the Chimborazo Medical Museum in Richmond, with Park Service patches or badges earned upon successful completion. Periodic "cannon talks" at Tredegar allow young visitors a close look at Civil War–era artillery.

The Chimborazo Hospital, also part of the park, sits on a hill three miles east of Tredegar, on Broad Street above the James River. Knowing the Union Army would have Richmond in its sights until the end of the war, the Confederates constructed dozens of hospitals in the city, none more prominent than Chimborazo. The location of this "hospital on the hill" was ideal thanks to its elevated proximity to the river and the natural springs that supplied ample fresh water for the more than 76,000 sick and wounded Confederates treated there during the war. One item on display is a porcelain "feeding cup" for serving broth and soup to men whose injuries left them unable to feed themselves.

Richmond is easy to navigate and pleasant to explore. Built over the centuries across seven hills above the James River, many of its neighborhoods retain a nineteenth-century charm, and its southern-style eateries, antique shops, and range of shopping opportunities nicely augment a tour of its historical attractions. Before heading to the outlying battle sites, visit the Museum of the Confederacy and its sister institution, the White House of the Confederacy; stroll through Hollywood Cemetery; and take a leisurely drive down Monument Avenue. The museum's three floors offer the world's most comprehensive collection of artifacts, manuscripts, and photographs related to the Confederate era. The centerpiece of the museum complex is the White House of the Confederacy, a few yards north of the museum building. This home of Confederate president Jefferson Davis and his family during the Civil War has eleven restored rooms, representing a richly appointed and historically accurate structure from nineteenth-century America. Hollywood Cemetery (412 South Cherry Street) is the resting place of more than 18,000 Confederate soldiers; twenty-four Confederate generals (including J.E.B. "Jeb" Stuart and George Pickett); two U.S. presidents (James Monroe and John Tyler); and Jefferson Davis, the Confederacy's sole president. Scenic paths winding through its rolling hills seem most peaceful early in the morning or at sunset (check for hours prior to visiting). Young people especially will enjoy the ghost stories associated with this cemetery, such as the Richmond Vampire, said to haunt the mausoleum bearing the name of W.W. Pool. The cemetery's website offers a "find a grave" service by entering a soldier's name.

Monument Avenue, a National Historic Landmark District, is populated with huge statues of leading Virginians from the Civil War era. The first was an 1890 monument to Robert E. Lee; statues of Jeb Stuart, Thomas "Stonewall" Jackson, and Jefferson Davis soon followed. In 1993 the city added a statue of native son and tennis great Arthur Ashe. In

2007 the American Planning Association named Monument Avenue as one of the ten great streets in America—though its wide median between east and westbound traffic makes it a boulevard. Architecturally stunning homes line both sides.

Outside of Richmond is much to see as well. A complete tour of the Richmond National Battlefield Park is eighty miles, including the sites in and around the city. Those with limited time should be sure to visit these four: the visitor center at Tredegar Iron Works; the battlefields at Gaines' Mill and Malvern Hill, both part of McClellan's 1862 Peninsula Campaign; and Cold Harbor, part of Grant's 1864 Overland Campaign. While the 1862 and 1864 sites lend themselves to separate tours, these places are in close proximity to one another and are worth seeing when in the area.

McClellan's 1862 invasion route took his army northwest up the peninsula east of Richmond, east of the Chickahominy River. Confederate resistance along the way led to battles at Yorktown and Williamsburg and a host of minor skirmishes. On the march McClellan's men got a taste of Southern life: Luther C. Furst recorded seeing fleeing civilians who left everything at home, including "niggers, horses & furniture . . . The cattle, hogs & colts are running at large & our men confiscate all they want." Furst also saw escaped slaves seeking sanctuary in Union Army lines, and by putting to work these escapees, known as contraband, Union commanders unwittingly help lay the foundation for the entry of black men into the army the following year. A Lieutenant Haydon of the 2nd Michigan Infantry Regiment bought a rooster for a dollar from a "very amiable Secession lady," who, for another quarter, cooked it for him.

The battlefield tour begins east of Richmond and stretches south to the James River. The 1862 Peninsula Campaign begins on VA Rt. 360 north (Old Church Road, east of Mechanicsville), where a short drive leads to Chickahominy Bluffs. Here the Confederates began their advance toward Beaver Dam Creek, where the first of the Seven Days' Battles was fought. General Lee, after reminding a visiting Confederate president Jefferson Davis that he was in command of the engagement, ordered Davis out of the line of fire. Lee then directed Gen. Stonewall Jackson to attack Union forces on the right, commanded by Gen. Fitz John Porter, and Gen. A. P. Hill to hit Porter from the left. When Jackson

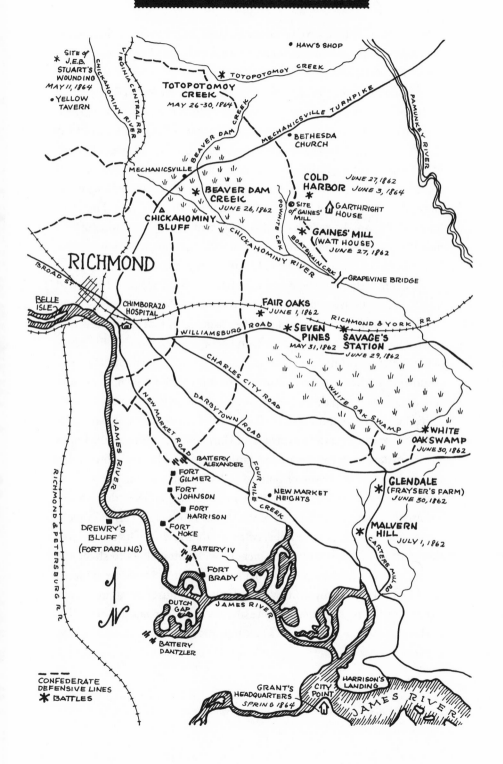

Site of J.E.B. STUART'S WOUNDING MAY 11, 1864

• Yellow Tavern

• HAW'S SHOP

✴ TOTOPOTOMOY CREEK

TOTOPOTOMOY CREEK
MAY 26-30, 1864

CHICKAHOMINY RIVER

VIRGINIA CENTRAL RR

BEAVER DAM CREEK

MECHANICSVILLE TURNPIKE

PAMUNKEY RIVER

• BETHESDA CHURCH

MECHANICSVILLE

✴ BEAVER DAM CREEK
JUNE 26, 1862

△ CHICKAHOMINY BLUFF

COLD HARBOR ✴   JUNE 27, 1862
JUNE 3, 1864

◉ Site of GAINES' MILL

⌂ GARTHRIGHT HOUSE

POWHITE CRK

CHICKAHOMINY RIVER

✴ GAINES' MILL
(WATT HOUSE)
JUNE 27, 1862

BOATSWAIN CRK

GRAPEVINE BRIDGE

RICHMOND

BROAD ST

BELLE ISLE

CHIMBORAZO HOSPITAL

FAIR OAKS
✴ JUNE 1, 1862

RICHMOND & YORK RR

WILLIAMSBURG ROAD

✴ SEVEN PINES
MAY 31, 1862

✴ SAVAGE'S STATION
JUNE 29, 1862

CHARLES CITY ROAD

WHITE OAK SWAMP

DARBYTOWN ROAD

NEW MARKET ROAD

JAMES RIVER

FOUR MILE CREEK

✴ WHITE OAK SWAMP
JUNE 30, 1862

⚔ BATTERY ALEXANDER

■ FORT GILMER

■ FORT JOHNSON

• NEW MARKET HEIGHTS

GLENDALE
✴ (FRAYSER'S FARM)
JUNE 30, 1862

RICHMOND & PETERSBURG R.R.

■ FORT HARRISON

■ FORT HOKE

DREWRY'S BLUFF
(FORT DARLING)

⚔ BATTERY IV

MALVERN
✴ HILL
JULY 1, 1862

CARTERS MILL RD

■ FORT BRADY

⬆ N

DUTCH GAP

JAMES RIVER

⚔ BATTERY DANTZLER

GRANT'S HEADQUARTERS
SPRING 1864

CITY POINT

HARRISON'S LANDING

JAMES RIVER

- - - CONFEDERATE DEFENSIVE LINES
✴ BATTLES

failed to show, Hill attacked anyway; his men surged across the Chickahominy River at the Yankees, who withdrew to Beaver Dam Creek, a mile
from Mechanicsville (this battle is known by two names—Beaver Dam
and Mechanicsville).* Today a platform overlooks the initial Confederate
position, a wooded, swampy area through which the creek runs. VA Rt.
360 north then crosses the Chickahominy swamp, where from the sanctuary of an automobile one might imagine the oppressive heat and humidity of early summer in these foreboding bottomlands—men driven mad
by stinging, biting insects; struggling through knee-high, sucking muck;
and suffering from malaria and other swamp-borne diseases. Theodore
Smith of the 32nd New York Infantry Regiment wrote to his father of "the
horrible sickness of thousands of our men poisoned in the swamps of the
Chickahominy, the loss of probably more than ten thousand."

General Porter's strong position at Beaver Dam Creek easily allowed
him to repel the frontal assault by Confederate brigades across open
fields and down the steep banks of the creek. Later that night, however,
when McClellan learned that Jackson had arrived in the vicinity, he ordered Porter to withdraw southeast to Gaines' Mill, named for the largest
landowner in the area—an ardent backer of the rebellion who reputedly
threatened to dig up the bodies of buried Union soldiers and feed them
to his hogs. McClellan's order reflected his decision to establish a new
base of operations to the southwest, at Harrison's Landing on the James
River, further from his Richmond target. With the hunted now pursuing the hunters, the battle of Gaines' Mill would be the bloodiest of the
Seven Days, with more than 15,000 combined casualties and the result
a Confederate victory. The men of the Union's 16th New York Regiment
were at particular risk from Rebel riflemen, for the wife of its colonel had
thoughtfully sent a crate of conspicuous white straw hats to shade the
boys from Virginia's intense summer sun. Pvt. Cyrus Stone remembered
that "most of the enemy firing was too high, they must have aimed at our
hats"—but the regiment suffered casualties of 40 percent as McClellan
pushed his men on to Harrison's Landing, his grandiose dream of taking
Richmond now in tatters.

---

* The Union often named battles for a topographic feature, such as a river or stream, while
the Confederates chose names of towns used as their bases.

Chronological detour alert: Between Beaver Dam Creek and Gaines' Mill, on Rt. 156, is the Cold Harbor battlefield, site of horrific fighting during Grant's 1864 Overland Campaign. Cold Harbor would mark the closest Grant would get to Richmond before its surrender in April 1865. Here on June 3, 1864, occurred murderous fighting, brutal as any single day of the war. Casualties were staggering: approximately 13,000 federal and 5,000 Confederate dead, wounded, and missing—"files of men went down like rows of blocks or bricks," a Union officer recalled. Grant finally broke the thirteen-day standoff and retreated southeast, toward Petersburg, leaving the bloodied Rebels to savor a rare victory during the last year of the war and prompting Grant to confess that his attack at Cold Harbor was the only one of the war he regretted ordering. Grant's southward movement forced Lee into a defensive position at Petersburg, to protect Richmond, a posture he retained for the remainder of the war. A small National Park Service Visitor Center at Cold Harbor features a lighted map that depicts the action at both Cold Harbor and Gaines' Mill, as both battles occurred on much of the same ground—fighting at Cold Harbor unearthed bones of those who had fallen at Gaines' Mill two years earlier. Drive or hike through the battlefield—two trails begin at the visitor center: the main interpretive trail (.9 miles) and the 2.25-mile extended loop trail both cross patchworks of well-preserved infantry entrenchments. The remains of more than 2,000 Union soldiers—many unknown—lie in the Cold Harbor National Cemetery.

Across Rt. 156 from Cold Harbor is the restored, eighteenth-century Garthright House, then owned by Confederate cavalry member Miles Garthright. His home had the misfortune to be twice in the line of fire, during the battles of Gaines' Mill and Cold Harbor when the home became a field hospital. A terrified Mrs. Garthright fled to the basement, only to watch blood drip through cracks in the floor above into her place of refuge. Though not open to the public, the small brick and frame house stands as a memorial to the ninety-seven soldiers who died from their wounds inside its walls. All were later buried in the Cold Harbor National Cemetery. A mile-long trail winds through well-preserved Union infantry lines and artillery emplacements at the adjacent county park.

The return to Rt. 156 leads to Seven Pines, site of the first battle where Union and Confederate forces faced off in the vicinity of Richmond, on May 31, 1862 (note that the auto tour does not always coincide with the chronology of the battles). The bridges over the river were largely washed away by the swollen, raging spring rains, but the Union forces made it across. No one today would envy the task of crossing the black, tar-like muck, dodging waist-high stumps that protrude from the turgid water. The Confederate attack collapsed. Gen. Joseph E. Johnston advised a young staff officer not to bother ducking at the sound of a whistling bullet: "Colonel," Johnson advised, "there is no use of dodging; when you hear them they have passed." No sooner were his words uttered than the general took a bullet in the shoulder and a shell fragment in the chest. After Johnston was carried from the field, Jefferson Davis placed General Robert E. Lee in command of the Army of Northern Virginia for the remainder of the war. Among the Union wounded was brigade commander Oliver O. Howard, who, after having his right arm amputated, was consoled by Gen. Phil Kearny, who had lost his left in the Mexican War: "General, I am sorry for you, but you must not mind it; the ladies will not think the less of you." Howard laughed heartily and observed that henceforth they could share the cost of a pair of gloves and each wear one.

At Glendale, to the southeast, another failure to coordinate his commanders cost General Lee a chance to cut the Union Army in two as it funneled through the crossroads there. Maj. Edward Porter Alexander, Lee's chief of ordnance, described the opportunity as perhaps the best the Confederates had during the entire war to end it on their terms and win their independence. And indeed the Yanks were on the run, moving as quickly as a large army could toward their new base at Harrison's Landing. At their old supply bases, Union soldiers ignited a series of spectacular bonfires, destroying whatever supplies they couldn't carry off, to prevent the Rebels from getting them. When whiskey flowing from barrels made the fires hotter, men burned themselves attempting to fill their canteens with the precious liquid.

A low stone wall now surrounds a picturesque national cemetery at Glendale, with markers for the fallen from a number of American conflicts, wind whispering through the surrounding pines often the only sound. A notebook tucked into a brick column at the entrance to the cemetery is a guide to who is buried where, including a number of unknown soldiers. The Glendale / Malvern Hill Visitor Center, adjacent to the cemetery (open seasonally), has a large map that helps visitors visualize the Glendale and Malvern Hill battles.

Lee's men would try once more to overwhelm the Union Army on Virginia soil, on July 1, 1862, at Malvern Hill to the south, but McClellan's men—employing the gently sloping ground as protection—threw heavy artillery at the Confederate attack, destroying their batteries and mowing down columns of assaulting infantry. Residents of Staunton, Virginia, a hundred miles away, claimed to have heard the cannonading. A mile-and-a-half long trail runs from the crest of Malvern Hill to the ruins of a Methodist parsonage, from which two large chimneys stand sentinel over silent fields. The bucolic view of the open, hilly terrain presents a stark contrast to the slaughter inflicted on the Confederates during this last engagement of the Seven Days' Battles. Circling vultures further call to mind the slaughter that once occurred on these fields.

Driving west on Rt. 156 / Rt. 5 leads to a line of eight earthen forts running south to north, the southernmost being Fort Brady, a Union fortification on the east bank of the James River. The other seven installations were built and manned by the Confederates to thwart Union advances up the James that could threaten Richmond from the south. These forts anchored Lee's thirty-five miles of thinly stretched defensive works, with Fort Harrison the largest of Richmond's exterior defenses. During the Petersburg Campaign, on September 29, 1864, Union soldiers crossed the James and overwhelmed the 200 Confederate defenders of Fort Harrison. A simultaneous attack at New Market Heights (not within the National Park) earned fourteen black soldiers the Congressional Medal of Honor for gallantry in leading the assault. A half-mile trail winds through Fort Harrison, with photographic interpretive markers depicting the battle action and cannon lending an aura of authenticity. The Fort Harrison visitor center is open seasonally.

The Union Army began withdrawing from the peninsula in early August 1862, its campaign an abject failure. General McClellan deflected blame: Confederate forces outnumbered him at every turn, the president refused to send adequate reinforcements, and his men and horses were exhausted. Blunders by both sides during this campaign around Richmond ensured that the Civil War would grind on for another three years.

And for the remainder of the war, Rebel soldiers mocked McClellan's "change of base" during the campaign:

Henceforth, when a fellow is kicked out of doors,
He need never resent the disgrace;
But exclaim, "My dear sir, I'm eternally yours,
For assisting in changing my base!

SIDE TRIPS

MUSEUM OF THE CONFEDERACY, RICHMOND AND APPOMATTOX, VA: This museum has three sites in two locations: The Richmond Museum and the White House of the Confederacy, adjacent to one another; and Appomattox, which opened in 2012. Collectively, this museum features the most comprehensive assemblage of artifacts relating to the Confederacy. Richmond's three floors of exhibits have hundreds of personal effects from soldiers and civilians; uniforms, equipment, and weapons; and many of Gen. Robert E. Lee's personal items he used during the Civil War. The former executive mansion of the Confederacy has been restored to its wartime appearance, looking as it did when President Jefferson Davis lived there. Highlights at Appomattox are General Lee's uniform coat and the sword that he surrendered there to Gen. Ulysses S. Grant. Audiovisual stations bring the rich human stories to life, and some exhibits explore the post-war Reconstruction period. *Richmond location: 1201 E. Clay Street, Richmond, VA, 23219, 804-649-1861. Appomattox location: 159 Horseshoe Road, Appomattox, VA, 24522, 434-352-5791 or 855-649-1861.*

JAMES MADISON'S MONTPELIER: Approximately an hour and a quarter north of Richmond—and thus of interest to those traveling to and from that city—is the ancestral home of our fourth president. Here James Madison spent the years before and after his illustrious career as the intellectual father of the Constitution, member of Congress, secretary of state, and president. Visitors can tour the mansion and inspect his impressive library and the decorative objects that reflect the personality of First Lady Dolley Madison. Montpelier's 2,650 acres include exhibits, walking trails, gardens, the first preserved and interpreted freedman's home in the United States, remains of a Confederate winter camp, and panoramic views of the Blue Ridge Mountains. An archaeology lab includes a hands-on area for kids to sift for and find artifacts. The Robert H. Smith Constitution Center at Montpelier offers a variety of seminars and free online courses about the Constitution. *11407 Constitution Highway, Montpelier Station, VA, 22957, 540-672-2728 (note: the site is not located in the town of Montpelier).*

FURTHER READING

Brian K. Burton, *Extraordinary Circumstances: The Seven Days Battles.* Indiana University Press, 2010.
Ernest B. Furgurson, *Ashes of Glory: Richmond at War.* Vintage, 1997.
Gordon Rhea, *Cold Harbor: Grant and Lee, May 26–June 3, 1864.* Louisiana State University Press, 2007.
Stephen Sears, *To the Gates of Richmond.* Ticknor & Fields, 1992.

ANTIETAM

Driving west toward Antietam National Battlefield Park on Maryland Rt. 40, the old National Pike, evokes thoughts of corn. Specifically, the corn of David R. Miller, a prosperous nineteenth-century Maryland farmer whose thirty-acre cornfield one early fall morning in 1862 became a bloody, pulsating mass of men in savage combat, being cut to ribbons by musket and artillery fire. Fighting in cornfields was not unusual during the Civil War, given the largely rural, agrarian nature of the United States at the time, but the most significant cornfield in American military history surely is David Miller's, because of that September morning just north of the town of Sharpsburg, Maryland.

The Battle of Antietam—or Sharpsburg, as the Confederates called it—remains the bloodiest day in the history of American warfare. On September 17, 1862, over 3,600 Americans died on that field. On average, one American soldier was killed or injured every other second at Antietam, while many of the 15,000 or more wounded lost limbs and sustained injuries that led to lifelong suffering and disability. Though the Union Army did not pursue the retreating Rebels into Virginia, by driving them out of Maryland they blunted both Confederate military momentum and movement toward European recognition of the Confederacy. The outcome also at last gave Abraham Lincoln the opportunity to publicly announce the

Emancipation Proclamation, to take effect on January 1, 1863, which both freed slaves in those parts of the United States that were in rebellion and laid the groundwork for black men to join the Union Army.

Antietam's pastoral setting and unspoiled beauty allow easy visualization of the battle landscape. The events that warm autumn day are less complex than say, the three-day battle of Gettysburg, and can be absorbed in a half-day's visit. The westerly route to the battlefield, over Catoctin and South Mountains, follows the route of the Union troops who marched from Washington to intercept the Army of Northern Virginia as it moved north into Maryland. The Federals caught the Confederates at Crampton's Gap, a mountain pass, on September 14, and drove them into Pleasant Valley. Union pursuit through other gaps in South Mountain came at great cost, as Gen. Jesse Reno, commanding the Ninth Corps of the Army of the Potomac, fell to a Confederate bullet. Antietam is the site associated with Gen. Robert E. Lee's famous "Lost Orders," wherein Union soldiers in Frederick discovered General Lee's battle plan, wrapped around several cigars, in which he would dispatch half of his army south to capture the Union garrison at Harpers Ferry, which threatened Lee's supply line.

The Antietam battlefield lies in the Cumberland Valley, between South Mountain, part of the Appalachian chain that forms the valley's east side, and North Mountain, several miles to the west. Unlike many Civil War battlefields today, the landscape appears much as it did in 1862. The park's visitor center, built a hundred years after the battle, stands on a rise just north of Sharpsburg, on the park's edge, and is inconspicuous from most vantage points. The narrow roads traversing the park accommodate vehicles, but visitors can easily walk or bike the grounds and in a matter of hours grasp the scale of that day's terrible events. Just west of the epicenter of the battle lies the quaint town of Sharpsburg, with the Potomac River several miles farther west.

This battle ended the first of three Confederate invasions of Maryland during the Civil War. General Lee was confident in late summer 1862. In August he thrashed Union forces under Gen. John Pope at Second Bull Run in Virginia. He began planning a move north onto Union ground with multiple objectives, including reason to think that additional Maryland men—some serving in his army already—would join his forces on the march through their slave state. When Lee crossed the Potomac into Maryland in early September, the Army of the Potomac gave hot pursuit.

Lee made his stand on prime defensive ground. Antietam Creek provided a natural barrier between the armies; South Mountain snaked southwest, parallel to the creek. The Harpers Ferry Road that ran north to Sharpsburg was one of several supply and reinforcement routes for the Confederate Army. And Lee would not be far from the safe haven of his native Virginia, on the south side of the Potomac River.

On September 8, General Lee sought to reassure Marylanders of his honorable intentions. "The people of the Confederate States have long watched with the deepest sympathy the wrongs and outrages that have been inflicted upon the citizens of a commonwealth allied to the States of the South by the strongest social, political and commercial ties," read his proclamation to Marylanders. He went on to console those who had been arrested by federal authorities and held without charge. His assertion carried a ring of truth, for Marylanders suffered more arrests early in the war for suspected disloyalty, and resultant imprisonment under Lincoln's suspension of the writ of habeas corpus, than citizens of any other state.

Not all Marylanders found Lee's proclamation soothing. Anne Schaeffer of Frederick recorded her angst at news of the Confederate approach into her town, about twenty miles east of Antietam. "No tongue or pen can describe our emotions," she wrote on September 4, 1862. "Seeing the street illuminated by a bright light, we learned the Union troops were burning the Hospital stores—making a grand bonfire in the street of all the bedding that could not be carried away, to prevent its falling into the hands of the Confederates, and the soldiers themselves were 'skedadling' as fast as their horses and their own legs could carry them." Schaeffer and her husband hid their valuables, "covered from view by ashes under an old fashioned outdoor bakeoven and not knowing what we might be called upon to endure the coming day, we lay down to rest after midnight and slept until 5 O'clock."

Antietam divides neatly into three touring phases, moving sequentially north to south to follow the battle chronologically. Start with the short film at the visitor center, which poignantly conveys the horror of

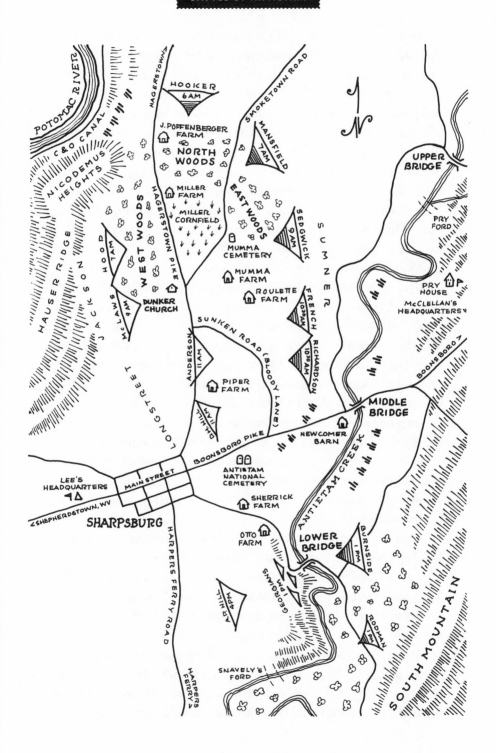

the battle through the eyes of the young men who suffered so terribly that day. One portrayed in the film is a wounded Union soldier who pulls himself up against a fence. He slowly opens his jacket and shirt, checking, perhaps, to see if he has been belly-shot—a wound men knew meant slow and painful death. He pulls an object toward his chin, a pocket watch, which may have belonged to his father, or grandfather. He gazes at it, likely knowing he will die in that spot, keepsake in hand.

An eleven-stop auto tour of nine miles is a chronological introduction to the battlefield. The first stop, on the west side of the Hagerstown Pike, is the Dunker Church, the simple meeting house of the German Baptist Brethren, pacifists who had fled persecution and settled in Germantown, Pennsylvania, in the early eighteenth century. They disdained worldly symbols such as steeples and stained glass, and their method of baptism by total immersion led to the moniker "Dunkers" (or "Tunkers," from the German "to dip"). Two miles north of Sharpsburg "was a bit of wood [since known as the West Wood], with the little Dunker Church standing out white and sharp against it," remembered Major Gen. Jacob D. Cox, an Ohio state legislator commanding the Union Ninth Corps at Antietam. "Farther to the right and left the scene was closed in by wooded ridges with open farm lands between, the whole making as pleasing and prosperous a landscape as can easily be imagined." Fighting raged around the small church throughout the morning as the two sides struggled for the strategically situated plateau on which it stood, easily visible from the Poffenberger Farm a mile to the north through the field glasses of Joseph Hooker, the Union general commanding that section of the field.

A perch on a simple wooden Dunker pew in this austere and barren building at the epicenter of so much bloodshed hardly evokes the horror it witnessed that morning. The church's windows appear today as they do in period photographs, and although destroyed in 1921 by a storm and reconstructed in 1962, its small stone front steps may have witnessed the battle.

At the north end of the field, stop 2 on the auto tour, is the North Woods and Poffenberger Farm, the starting point of the Union attack. On the morning of September 17, Union generals Hooker and Joseph Mansfield assembled men of the First and Twelfth Corps in the woods.

At dawn the Union force moved south, out of the woods into the cornfield, to assault the Confederate left flank, commanded by Gen. Thomas "Stonewall" Jackson.

The carnage in the cornfield raged for three hours. Soldiers from New York and Wisconsin were "fused into a common mass," recalled Major Rufus Dawes of the 6th Wisconsin Regiment, a unit later known as the renowned "Iron Brigade" whose performance that day earned its name. "Every body tears cartridges, loads, passes guns, or shoots. Men are falling in their places or running back into the corn." Dawes described the frantic attempts by his comrades to hide in the corn, at that time of year standing seven feet high, in the face of a fierce Confederate assault: "It is a race for life that each man runs for the cornfield. A sharp cut, as of a switch, stings the calf of my leg as I run. Back to the corn, and back through the corn, and headlong flight continues." The nine regiments commanded by Confederate general John Bell Hood suffered a staggering 40 percent casualty rate in the cornfield. Another Wisconsin soldier described the struggle in the cornfield as "a great tumbling together of all heaven and earth—the slaughter on both sides was enormous." At about 9 A.M. officers on horseback began moving through the acrid smoke to assess the carnage, riding slowly so as not to crush the injured. As the smoke cleared, they encountered more than 8,000 dead and wounded in the trampled corn.

Stop 3 is the East Woods, reached along Mansfield Avenue—the scene of the skirmishing the prior evening—and the Cornfield Trail, the northernmost trail in the park. The trail parallels the road before veering west to traverse the center of the cornfield. Butterflies, grasshoppers, and the trill of cicadas accompany autumn visitors along the mile and a half between towering corn stalks. From stop 4, on Cornfield Avenue, it is a short drive to the West Woods, where the Confederate counterattack repelled the Union assault, leaving 2,200 men dead and wounded in twenty minutes of fighting.

The Mumma Farm and Cemetery (stops 6 and 7) mark the midmorning Union advance of 10,000 men that set the stage for the clash at the Sunken Road. Union troops under Generals Israel Richardson and William H. French, moving in from the east, suffered heavy losses before finally overrunning Gen. D. H. Hill's Confederates. Lt. Thomas Livermore, of the 5th New Hampshire Regiment, recalled one of the final assaults against the entrenched rebels: "As the fight grew furious, the colonel cried out, 'Put on the war paint.' We rubbed the torn end of the cartridges over our faces, streaking them with powder like a pack of Indians, and the colonel . . . cried out, 'Give 'em the war whoop!' And all of us joined him in the Indian war whoop until it must have rung out above all the thunder of the ordance."

At midday the fighting shifted southward. A road cut into the landscape by decades of wagons hauling farm bounty to market runs through this central area of the battlefield, bisected by Richardson Avenue. The furious fighting along this Sunken Road—the Confederate defensive position known also as "Bloody Lane"—left lasting, indelible images of the Civil War: photographs of bloated, dead bodies piled in the trench (stop 8). The Union suffered more than 3,000 casualties at the Bloody Lane, and veterans would later swear that a man could walk across the corpses without once touching ground.

Visitors walking the Sunken Road might try to imagine the terror in Hill's Confederates as Union soldiers suddenly appeared on the ridge on the north side and raced down at them. Graves holding the remains of four Irish Brigade soldiers were discovered in the 1980s, just north of the Sunken Road (artifacts that identified them are in the Pry House Field Hospital Museum on Route 34). South Mountain looms in the distance above the ridge.

Gen. George B. McClellan, commanding the Union Army of the Potomac, was widely admired at the outbreak of the Civil War for his organizational and leadership skills. As the conflict ground into its second year, however, the former railroad executive came under fire from President Lincoln and the Congress for his perceived reluctance to send his men into battle (Lincoln once famously, and perhaps unfairly, asked McClellan if he might borrow the army if the General did not plan to use it.) At Antietam McClellan had concentrated the center of his force on the east side of Antietam Creek, sending units into action in numbers insufficient for a decisive victory. His conservatism was harshly criticized by those who felt that a more aggressive commander could have ended the war right there, on Maryland farmland—though few such critics were present and they knew little of the actual situation.

The lower crossing over Antietam Creek is known as Burnside Bridge (stop 9 on the auto tour). Built as Rohrbach Bridge in 1836, this limestone and granite structure resides in the annals of American military history as a memorial to the failure of Union general Ambrose Burnside to get his men across Antietam Creek. Five hundred Georgia riflemen, dug into the hill on the west side of the creek, held off Burnside's men for three hours. Commissary Sergeant William McKinley "drove a mule team into the thick of the battle, carrying hot meat and coffee to the troops," according to a biographer of the twenty-fifth American president. Looking at the ground today one can see how this was possible; career military officers still marvel at the strength of this position. An observation point overlooks the remnants of those rifle pits, so instrumental in allowing the Confederates to fight another day.

The final phase of the battle raged all afternoon. General Burnside, inventor of the breech-loading rifle, seemed cut from the same cloth as McClellan. He failed to press the attack by rushing the bridge and fording Antietam Creek, although faulty intelligence from local farmers may have prevented him from knowing that a spot higher up the creek could have allowed his men to cross and flank the Rebel riflemen. One Union officer wrote of his doubts that "Burnside has done a thing. He sent two rgts to cross the bridge, & were driven back like sheep by enemies' artillery." A third assault finally took the bridge, as Union troops approached their rear while the 51st New York and 51st Pennsylvania Regiments fixed bayonets and "rushed at a double-quick over the slope leading to the bridge and over the bridge itself, with an impetuosity which the enemy could not resist," wrote Union general Samuel Sturgis in his report. "The Stars and Stripes were planted on the opposite bank at 1 o'clock P.M., amid the most enthusiastic cheering from every part of the field where they could be seen."

Today the scene is far different. On languid summer afternoons people float leisurely on Antietam Creek aboard tubes, canoes, rafts, and kayaks. Traffic crossed that historic bridge until 1966, when a new one opened upstream, to the east side of the creek, where on the immediate left is the trailhead of the Sherrick Farm Trail. A stone wall appears in period images of the bridge, with the creek to the left; a hundred yards farther a rope swings kids from shore into the water. A glance back to the west bank conjures images of Georgia riflemen and sharpshooters on the ridge, firing with great effect into hapless Union men rushing the bridge. The Confederate advantage was greater than would appear today, as period photographs reveal a more heavily wooded position.

Burnside Bridge offers access to three other trails rarely used by visitors: the Snavelys Ford Trail to the south, the Union Advance Trail on the east side of Antietam Creek, and the Final Attack Trail on its west bank. All start on the west side at stop 9 on the auto tour. The mile-long Union Advance Trail leads to the center of the three federal assaults against the bridge and the Georgia riflemen on the other side of the creek.

In a clearing stands a monument to the 11th Connecticut Volunteer Infantry Regiment, the vanguard of the first attack on the bridge, at 10 A.M. (trail stop 3), which the Rebels answered with "the hottest fire we ever received," recalled one soldier. The enemy was "so completely concealed that they could scarcely be distinguished through the leaves from the dark background and objects around, except by the smoke of their discharged guns." From this point the creek is approximately one hundred yards south down the slope. An hour later the 2nd Maryland and 6th New Hampshire Regiments were dispatched on the double-quick along the old Rohrersville Road, on the east side of the creek, though this second Union attack quickly disintegrated in the face of withering Georgian fire (trail stop 4).

The southern portion of the battlefield, below Rt. 34, has more hills and is now heavily wooded. From Burnside Bridge the Final Attack Trail is an easy trek (under two miles) with grand panoramas of the Antietam Valley. Approximately 8,000 exhausted Union soldiers spread across these ridges and fields into a mile-wide battle line to push the Confederates from Maryland. For more than two hours the men fought violently under relentless artillery barrages.

This higher ground, untrodden by most battlefield visitors, has views of the valley and South Mountain. The nine trail stops include several monuments that cannot be seen from the roads—stop 5 honors the 16th Connecticut Regiment that bore the brunt of Gen. A. P. Hill's Confederate counterattack in a 40-acre (and lesser known) cornfield. The last, at the end of the trail, commemorates future president Sgt. William McKinley.

The devastating toll on the young of both armies is apparent at the Pry House Medical Museum, part of the National Museum of Civil War Medicine, on Rt. 34, just east of the battlefield. This was the home of the Philip Pry, a prosperous farmer, and his family. General McClellan appropriated the house as his headquarters; the barn still stands and served as a field hospital. President Lincoln reputedly took breakfast as a guest of the Prys during his visit to Antietam shortly after the battle.

The heroic efforts to treat the many wounded are vividly portrayed at the Pry House through photographs, artifacts, and written accounts. "There was not a barn or farmhouse, or store, or church, or schoolhouse, between Boonesboro, Keedysville, Sharpsburg, and Smoketown, that was not gorged with wounded—Rebel and Union," recalled Dr. Cornelius R. Agnew of the U.S. Sanitary Commission. "Even the corncribs, and in many instances the cow stables, and in one place the mangers were filled. Several thousand lie in the open air upon straw." Pvt. George A. Allen was a New Yorker detailed to a field hospital in a church in Keedysville, where boards were laid across the tops of the pews so the wounded could lie down. Allen described his grisly duties as a hospital orderly: "the bloody work of amputation commenced ... A pit was dug just under the window at the back of the church and as soon as a limb was amputated I would take it to the window and drop it outside into the pit. The arms, legs, feet and hands that were dropped into the hole would amount to several hundred pounds. On one occasion I had to fish out a hand for its former owner, as he insisted that it was all cramped up and hurt him. As soon as the hand was straightened out he complained no more of the pain in the stump."

Historians still debate McClellan's reluctance to aggressively pursue the retreating Confederates. He claimed his men were in no condition to chase an army onto enemy soil. And McClellan's intelligence sources overestimated the size of the Rebel forces, not an infrequent miscalculation during his time as a commanding general. Union general Jacob Cox later proclaimed the result of McClellan's inaction: "What might have been a real and decisive success was a drawn battle in which our chief claim to victory was the possession of the field."

But the trauma and brutality of that day might have excused reluctance for a major pursuit of Lee's army into Virginia. The history of warfare teaches that, in the heat of battle, men become unhinged by the sounds, smells, and sights of combat, the screams of the injured and dying, the opaque smoke that burns the eyes and heightens the terror. Rufus Dawes described the area between Miller's cornfield and the Bloody Lane as "indescribably horrible." A week after the battle, Dawes's fellow soldier, Lt. Frank A. Haskell, wrote his family that "all hands agree that before they had never seen such a fearful battle. I hope you may never have occasion to see such a sight as it is. I will not attempt to tell you of it." William H. Powell, a soldier in the Union 5th Corps, saw places littered with bodies so blackened they resembled African Americans; he turned his face from "marred and bloated remains."

The stillness of Antietam today contrasts sharply with the horror of that September day in 1862. Those in the small towns and fields who made their living off this gentle, rolling land suffered the effects of the battle for years. One man wrote simply of the aftermath: "You couldn't hear a dog bark nowhere, you couldn't hear no birds whistle or no crows caw. There wasn't no birds around till next spring. We didn't even see a buzzard with all the stench . . . The farmers didn't have no chickens to crow . . . It was a curious silent world."

SIDE TRIPS

FREDERICK, MD: Founded in 1745 and now Maryland's second largest city, by 1830 Frederick was a mining town known for its religious pluralism, with a dozen major churches of different denominations along Church Street, its major thoroughfare. German was the language of choice until Irish immigrants began making Frederick home in the mid-nineteenth century. Frederick's quaint streets offer plenty of historical flavor, as armies of both sides passed through the town during the Civil War. Many sites are related to that conflict, including the National Museum of Civil War Medicine on East Patrick Street and the reconstructed home of Barbara Fritchie on West Patrick Street—whose celebrated impudence in the presence of Confederate Gen. Stonewall Jackson lives on in poetic legend, even as it has been discredited. Downtown Frederick and Baker Park feature weekly summer concerts, monthly gallery walks, and children's theatrical performances. Frederick is less than an hour from Baltimore and Washington, D.C.

CRAMPTON'S GAP / GATHLAND STATE PARK, MD: Crampton's Gap, one of three passes through South Mountain, is the site of the September 14, 1862, fight that was part of the Battle of South Mountain, the precursor to Antietam. (The other two passes are Fox's Gap and Turner's Gap.) The Confederate's success at slowing the pursuing Union Army allowed them to establish strong defensive positions for the Battle of Antietam. In Gathland State Park was the home of Civil War journalist George Alfred Townsend; its major feature is the War Correspondent's Arch, a large stone monument dedicated to the memory of Civil War correspondents. Two buildings from Townsend's home remain as museums and include artifacts from the Battle of South Mountain. The Appalachian National Scenic Trail passes by the base of the monument, and a pavilion accommodates as many as a hundred picnickers.

SHEPHERDSTOWN, WV: Buildings in this oldest town in West Virginia, nestled in the lower Shenandoah Valley and just across the Potomac River from Antietam and Sharpsburg, date to the Revolutionary War. The shops and eateries along German Street are alluring, and Shepherd University is the venue for many events, including the Contemporary American Theater Festival and classical music performances. The Chesapeake & Ohio Canal, less than a mile away, and the Appalachian Trail that runs through the town offer the great outdoors in historical context. Shepherdstown is just ninety minutes from Baltimore and Washington, D.C.

FURTHER READING

Ted Alexander, *The Battle of Antietam: The Bloodiest Day* (Civil War
    Sesquicentennial Series).The History Press, 2011.
Ezra Carman, *The Maryland Campaign of September 1862,* Volume 1,
    South Mountain (edited & annotated by Thomas G. Clemens). Savas
    Beatie, 2010.

Ezra Carman, *The Maryland Campaign of September 1862,* Volume II, *Antietam* (edited & annotated by Thomas G. Clemens). Savas Beatie, 2012.

D. Scott Hartwig, *To Antietam Creek: The Maryland Campaign of September 1862.* Johns Hopkins University Press, 2012.

Perry Jamieson, *Death in September: The Antietam Campaign* (Civil War Campaigns and Commanders Series). State House Press, 1998.

Stephen W. Sears, *Landscape Turned Red: The Battle of Antietam.* Mariner Books, 2003.

12

CIVIL WAR WASHINGTON

Three miles from the White House, on a hill offering panoramic views of Washington and the Potomac River, is the Armed Forces Retirement Home, at Rock Creek Church Road, just east of New Hampshire Avenue. Abraham Lincoln spent close to a quarter of his presidency at this bucolic site, including the day before his death, in a cottage on the grounds of what was known then as the Old Soldiers' Home. He commuted daily from the White House, from early summer to late autumn along the Seventh Street Turnpike, to escape both the sultry air of swampy Washington (both climatic and political) and the deplorable condition of the White House. Lincoln received visitors, recited poetry, played checkers on the porch, and watched his son Tad cavort among encamped Union soldiers on the property, who dubbed the lad "3rd Lieutenant." Mary Todd Lincoln, more mistress of this spot than of the White House, found peace within its walls, especially in her grief over the death of her son Willie in February 1862.

Known today as President Lincoln's Cottage, this National Monument and National Historic Landmark was restored by the National Trust for Historic Preservation and opened to the public in 2008. President Lincoln first rode to the cottage on March 7, 1861, three days after his first inauguration. On this ground, amid the cool breezes of summer, Lincoln would find the strength to steer the nation through years of war, negotiate unsuccessfully with border-state congressmen to end slavery, draft the Emancipation Proclamation, and craft his 1864 reelection strategy.

Begin a visit in the Robert H. Smith Visitor Education Center. A room there gives the feel of a college seminar, as visitors sit at touch-screen consoles that describe dramatic episodes of a Civil War presidency. In "Debating Emancipation," the image of a cabinet official or document, when pressed, summons an excerpt of the Emancipation Proclamation, which, while arguably enforceable only by the Union Army's advance, changed the nature of the war by declaring all slaves in areas in rebellion "henceforth and forever free." Another selection, "Lincoln Upholds Execution of Slave Trader," recounts the fate of the only person put to death for engaging in piracy and the international slave trade. Other topics are "Running for Reelection" and "Military Turning Point." Diary excerpts from men such as treasury secretary Salmon Chase and Navy secretary Gideon Welles, members of Lincoln's cabinet, convey the drama and tension of the period.

The exhibits at the Smith Visitor Education Center give a flavor not only of life at the Old Soldiers' Home but of a Civil War Washington full of Irish and German natives. Lincoln himself was a familiar face in the city as he rode back and forth to his retreat. Poet Walt Whitman, whose home Lincoln passed on his commute, recorded his view of the commander-in-chief: "I see the President almost every day," he wrote. Lincoln appeared "rusty and dusty . . . his face with deep cut lines, seams . . . a curious looking man, very sad. We have got so that we exchange bows, and very cordial ones." One exhibit, of an 1861 map of the capital city with magnifier, gives visitors a detailed depiction of the small city of Washington, while photographs of an armed capital reflect the real danger of a Rebel incursion into the city from Virginia, just across the Potomac River. Stereoscopic viewers give three-dimensional pictures of the cottage and grounds.

But not even this sanctuary provided President and Mrs. Lincoln escape from the stark reminders of the Civil War. The two hundred wounded and disabled soldiers on the premises, the daily burials of fallen Union troops in the first national cemetery, the distant roar of cannon, and the

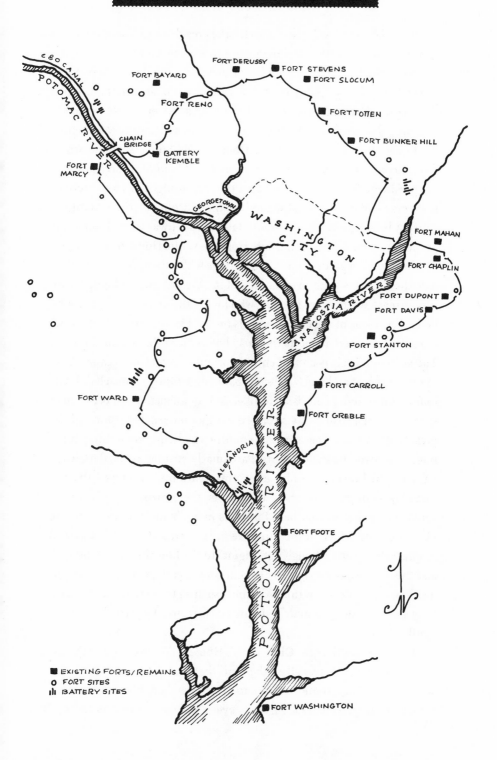

constant clatter of cavalry that escorted the president between the cottage and the White House were jarring and incessant reminders of conflict raging in the land. Battle sounds at times drew nigh, as in September 1862 when the first family heard the cannonading at Antietam. When 15,000 Confederate troops crossed the Potomac River into Maryland in July 1864, defeated a smaller Union force and turned toward Washington, the Rebels were a mere four miles from the Old Soldiers' Home, where the Lincolns were staying. Secretary of war Edwin Stanton cautioned the president "that your guard be on the alert tonight," as a mysterious horseman had been spotted shadowing the Lincoln's carriage. Stanton's worry was well placed, for a month later a bullet was fired through the president's hat as he rode one night from the White House to the cottage.

Visitors on a guided tour of the cottage will nonetheless understand why the Lincolns were so enamored of it. "We are truly delighted, with this retreat," wrote Mary Lincoln, who loved "the drives & walks around here." The focus of the cottage visit is on the Lincoln's time in it, rather than on the material objects that may have graced this seasonal retreat. The structure itself is almost entirely original, and visitors can walk in the same spaces and touch the same bannisters Lincoln himself did. The tour includes audio and visual recollections of incidents that occurred in specific rooms, such as a visitor's contemporaneous description of the president, clad in carpet slippers, entering the living room through the huge set of wood-paneled doors. Particularly striking is the dark wood paneling in Lincoln's study—after preservationists removed twenty-three layers of paint to expose the panels, the horizontal marks of the spots where shelves that held Lincoln's many books met the walls are plainly visible. Much of the furniture in the cottage is donated, period nineteenth-century (though not original to the Lincolns or the cottage), and the woodwork is original. Elements of the cottage exterior that suffered extensive deterioration over time, such as the veranda and stucco, have been restored to match pictures of it from Mary Todd Lincoln's family album.

Two miles north of the Old Soldier's Home is Fort Stevens (on Quackenbos Street, N.W.), a small earthen fort that was part of a circle of Civil War fortifications around Washington that stretched thirty-seven miles. Named for Brig. Gen. Isaac Ingalls Stevens, it stood watch over the Seventh Street Turnpike (now Georgia Avenue) that led into Washington from Silver Spring. On July 10, 1864, Washington anxiously awaited news of the whereabouts of Confederate general Jubal Early's troops. Early's more than 12,000 men had just defeated a Union force at the Monocacy River, in Frederick County, Maryland, striking terror also amidst Baltimoreans who feared he might head in their direction (he was actually en route toward the U.S capital). This audacious strike at Washington, coming late in the war, was intended to siphon federal troops to the capital from the Union siege at Petersburg, south of Richmond, at that moment gravely threatening the Confederate capital. Early furthermore hoped to liberate the nearly 30,000 Confederate prisoners from the Union prison camp at Point Lookout, at the junction of the Potomac River and Chesapeake Bay in St. Mary's County, in southern Maryland.

Federal troops in Fort Stevens spied the dust created by the marching of Early's men down the Seventh Street Turnpike on the morning of July 11. Much heavy artillery from the area's forts had been dispatched to Petersburg, so many were lightly defended. The scene of civilians and even a hospital brigade of convalescents pressed into service to supplement poorly trained reserves would have been comical had the situation not been so serious. Rebel skirmishers began firing from vacated houses and undergrowth along the road. Forts Stevens, Slocum, and DeRussy still had heavy guns, which promptly answered.

The commander-in-chief arrived to watch the action. Legend says that President Lincoln watched from atop a parapet as Rebel bullets flew near. He was urged to get down, his six-foot-four-inch frame supporting a top hat a tempting target for Confederate sharpshooters. Stories range from Capt. Oliver Wendell Holmes, not recognizing the president in the chaos, barking "get down, you fool!" to the more subdued account of Secretary of State William Seward's son, Frederick, a member of the president's party. Frederick Seward wrote that a soldier touched Lincoln's arm and begged him to get down, "for the bullets of the rebel sharpshooters may begin to come in any minute from the woods yonder." Lincoln's secretary, John Hay, recalled how "a soldier roughly ordered him to get down or he would have his head knocked off." The number of men later claiming to have been in Fort Stevens that day, helping protect the president, only seemed to grow with the years. One New York private said of the battle that Lincoln and his party "think it was a splendid sight, but we poor fellows could not see much fun in it."

Union reinforcements from Petersburg arrived in the nick of time. They pushed the Southerners back, through the former site of the Walter Reed National Military Medical Center. Men from the Government Printing Office manned the guns of nearby Fort Snyder, then "laid aside their weapons of destruction, [and] resumed their places in the office." The irony of the episode is more acute given that former vice president John C. Breckinridge, who had run against Lincoln in 1860 as a Southern Democrat, commanded the assault. Some 800 men died in the battle; 41 of the approximately 300 Union dead are buried in Battleground National Cemetery, a half mile north of Fort Stevens.

Today the fort consists of rebuilt parapets with masonry revetments that face north, the direction from which the Rebels attacked. Buildings now obstruct the open vistas the men saw those hot days in July, and neighborhood residents walk their dogs through the fort's grounds. But one can stand where Lincoln stood, back to the large American flag that flies over the ramparts, and easily imagine the 1864 landscape, the sharpshooters' smoke, and bullets thudding into dirt—and the devastating consequences for the nation had those Confederates overrun the tiny Fort Stevens and moved into the United States capital.

A contemporary map of Washington, D.C., shows a circular pattern of green patches, many of which were once other fortifications protecting the capital. Federal officials, alarmed at the Rebel thrashing of Union troops at the First Battle of Manassas in July 1861, seized privately owned fields, orchards, homes, and churches to construct these forts. In all, sixty-eight earthen forts and ninety-three batteries, or emplacements for field guns, were built on virtually every high point on what then were the outskirts of Washington. These sites, many now in urban settings, are the remnants of this defensive network, chosen by military engineers to protect turnpikes, rail lines, bridges, and shipping routes. Rifle trenches connected many, creating a formidable defensive system that made Washington the most fortified city in the western hemisphere. Telegraph wires and a relay signal system of seventy flags and torches, usually atop fort magazines and walls, allowed communication between them. A number are now parks and public spaces, with names such as Forts Reno, Totten, Slocum, and Bunker Hill to the north; and Forts Mahan, Chaplin, and Dupont to the east. South, outside the Capital Beltway, are Forts Foote, Willard Circle, and Mt. Eagle; and west, Forts Ward, Scott and, Marcy.

Much of the land for these fortifications was returned to the original property owners following the war and fell victim to the twin ravages of time and development. Others retained their original fort names and either went into the National Park system or became municipal parks, rarely leaving more than a few visible remains. Several have been partially preserved or restored. And yet, visits to even untended sites will reward those who can spot the strategic ground that was crucial for protecting the capital.

Thousands of people unknowingly traverse these long-lost fort locations daily in Washington, D.C., Maryland, and Northern Virginia. Golfers on the ninth fairway at Alexandria's Army-Navy Country Club tee off alongside the ramparts of Fort Richardson, while visitors to Fort Lincoln Cemetery, just across the Washington, D.C., line in Prince George's County, Maryland, traipse over the site of Battery Jameson. Catholic University students en route to class pass near the site of Fort Slemmer's gate.

Fort walls, or parapets, were made of dirt, the readily available, inexpensive, and effective bulwark against enemy bullets. Walls 12–18 feet thick and 18–22 feet high were stabilized by log supports called revetments. Ditches in front of the parapets and abatis—barriers of felled trees—provided further reinforcement. Subterranean magazines protected the ordnance, and bombproofs sheltered soldiers from enemy artillery. Period photographs show farmland surrounding many of the forts, requiring attacking forces to advance across open ground—often cleared in places where the Union Army cut down trees and even whole forests to create sight lines.

By the middle of 1862, some 37,000 soldiers manned the defenses of Washington. Boredom and malaria were frequently greater problems than were Rebels. Fort duty was monotonous, wrote a soldier from Fort Ethan Allen in Arlington, "unless coupled with incidents of real warfare . . . but the only thing we have to record is a remarkable dream of one of the men, in which he saw the Confederates scaling the parapet." African Americans, both free and escaped slaves (the latter known as contraband) sought refuge in some forts, often erecting tents around them.

At Fort Stanton, named for Lincoln's second secretary of war Edwin Stanton, another trooper wanted "rebs to come along and be knocked sky-high by these big guns, yawning and rusting for something to do." Another at Fort Greble used his rifle as a fishing rod, dropping a line into a large puddle in a rain-filled trench. Absent an explanation for his behavior, he was deemed insane and discharged—whereupon he shouted "that's what I was fishing for!" and jauntily departed, discharge orders in hand.

With little to worry about beyond the occasional troublemaker or Confederate raider, some defenders turned to the bottle and the temptations lurking in Washington. One Connecticut soldier complained that his "professing Christian" comrades at Fort Scott were abandoning "their religion and are now losing their character." Accounts from Fort Lincoln, which protected the upper Anacostia River valley, tell of Union officers poisoned and Southern-sympathizing Washington belles entertained.

Fort Washington, the stone behemoth thirteen miles south of the capital overlooking the Potomac River on the Maryland side, would have deterred many an enemy force. This visually striking site, in Fort Washington Park, in Prince George's County, Maryland, looms high atop a forested bluff. It offers hiking trails, a working lighthouse, and venues for fishing and picnics. When British troops marched into Washington in August 1814, during the War of 1812, and torched the Capitol, White House, and other public buildings, the Americans destroyed Fort Washington (then called Fort Warburton) to prevent the Redcoats from seizing it (see chapter 6). Ten years later the newly rebuilt installation was named for the nation's first president, and when the Civil War erupted in the spring of 1861, Fort Washington was the only fortification protecting the U.S. capital.

As worries mounted that spring that Virginia and Maryland might join the Confederacy, Army engineer George Washington Custis Lee (son of Confederate general Robert E. Lee) reported on the fort's readiness. Learning that it was manned solely by one Irish pensioner, General-in-Chief Winfield Scott snarled that the fort "might have been taken by a bottle of whiskey." The firing arcs of Washington's massive guns covered all approaches from the Potomac River, and only one shot was fired from it during the Civil War, at a gunboat that ventured too close. Fort Washington remained a fixture in the nation's coastal fortifications through World War II. Stop at the visitor center for a map and short film. Kids especially will love the tunnels and narrow passages.

Ten miles north of Fort Washington are the remains of Fort Foote, which once boasted 20-foot thick dirt walls. President Lincoln dined on peaches, cheese, and champagne here during an inspection in August 1863. Two enormous Rodman guns now sit as silent sentinels in a sur-real setting—each weighs 50,000 pounds (25 tons) and required more than 300 men to haul one up the bluffs. These giants, each operated by a twelve-man firing crew, hurled 400-pound cannon balls more than three miles.

Virginia's secession from the Union on April 17, 1861, sent Wash-ington into a frenzy. Militia troops from northern states moved quickly into Alexandria and Arlington, across the Potomac River in Virginia, and began constructing defensive fortifications. Fort Ward, one of the larg-est, protected the Leesburg and Little River Turnpike (now King and Duke Streets) approaches from Alexandria to Washington. Now operated by the City of Alexandria, located on West Braddock Road, it and Fort Stevens are the only partially restored forts in the system. Named for James H. Ward, the first naval officer killed in the Civil War, Fort Ward Museum and Historic Site gives the sense of an authentic Civil War fort, Alexandria's role as a hub for Union operations, and a taste of life inside the defenses of Washington.

Preserved elements include 90 percent of the original earthworks. The officers' quarters, ceremonial 1865 gate, and officers' hut have been re-constructed, and the Northwest Bastion restored to its 1864 appearance, based on original military engineering drawings. The viewing platform allows a close look inside its 20-foot-high walls at the recreated bomb-proof shelter that could accommodate 500 men. Large gun emplacements protrude through thick earthen walls, and infantry platforms between them allowed soldiers to lay down any necessary defensive fire. Angled rifle trenches outside the walls were to thwart enemy flanking maneuvers, and a ditch linked to a fort two miles away, so men and materiel could be deployed where most needed.

Most of the men who manned these Washington defenses lived outside their walls and spent time in them to drill and maintain their readiness for battle. One soldier at Fort Ward noted how "rebel troops could often be seen crossing the fields some three miles distant" from the cupola of the chapel at the nearby seminary. The museum features a film and items such as uniforms, letters, diaries, musical instruments, and other artifacts that describe the fort system. A striking exhibit on medical care during the Civil War consists of tools, equipment, and a discussion of both the role of women such as Clara Barton and Dorothea Dix in nursing the wounded and Alexandria as a wartime hospital center. A large period map shows the extensive circle of forts that surrounded the capital. Recounted in graphic detail is the May 1861 incident at the Marshall House Tavern in Alexandria, in which Union colonel Elmer Ellsworth, a favorite of President Lincoln's who had become famous for raising Zouave regiments, was shot dead by the secessionist proprietor while attempting to tear down his Confederate flag—an early and highly visible casualty of the war that both aroused war sentiment in the North and devastated the president.

Those with keen interest in the capital's Civil War defenses may wish to drive north to Fort Marcy on the George Washington Parkway, on the Virginia side of the Potomac River. Named for Randolph B. Marcy, Gen. George B. McClellan's chief of staff and father-in-law, this fort stood in a defensive line to protect Washington from attack via the Chain Bridge that spans the Potomac. Trails lead to clusters of cannon and earthworks and a vision of life in a spot that saw little but the routine work of drill, repairs, and parade. "Breakfast is pork, crackers and coffee, yesterday we had plenty of beans and a few small ears of corn to roast," recalled a soldier stationed at Fort Marcy. "Our rations are mostly bread and salt junk." Another wrote that they had "captured a rebel spy endeavoring to creep through to the lines. He had a rebel uniform on under his other clothes. He was sent to a fort down below our camp."

Aficionados can drive east from Fort Marcy across the Chain Bridge past the site of Fort Reno—which kept watch over the Rockville Pike—to Rock Creek Park. Across the road from the park's nature center is the trailhead leading to Fort DeRussy, which overlooked Rock Creek Valley and protected the Milk House Ford Road. Dense woods envelop what remains of the earthworks and rifle pits. The summer hum of insects brings to mind the complaint of the Rhode Island soldier who in a letter described warding off flies, bugs, and lizards stirred up during the fort's construction.

Washington, D.C., was, of course, the nerve center for planning and executing the Union war effort. The city's ban on slavery in April 1862 helped lay groundwork for Lincoln's adoption of emancipation and recruitment of black troops for the U.S. army as objectives of the Union strategy to end the war. Other than the Rebel strike in the summer of 1864 repelled by the fighters in Fort Stevens, the city was not invaded, despite its proximity to Confederate territory across the Potomac River. Sites such as President Lincoln's Cottage, Fort Stevens, and Fort Ward illustrate the rich variety of Civil War Washington, and sleuths who seek out the remnants of long-lost forts will savor an even deeper appreciation of our capital in wartime.

SIDE TRIPS

FORD'S THEATER NATIONAL HISTORIC SITE, WASHINGTON, D.C.: The campus consists of the theater (featuring a variety of performances throughout the year), museum (with rare artifacts such as the clothing Lincoln wore the night of the assassination and the derringer John Wilkes Booth used to shoot him), the Petersen House (where the room in which Lincoln died from his wounds has been recreated), and the Center for Education and Leadership (which has a winding staircase and 34-foot tower of books about Abraham Lincoln, the assassination's aftermath, and the riveting hunt for Booth). *511 Tenth Street, N.W., Washington, D.C., 20004, 202-347-4843.*

ARLINGTON NATIONAL CEMETERY, ARLINGTON, VA: The nineteenth-century mansion that overlooks the cemetery's more than 250,000 graves was to be a living memorial to George Washington from his adopted grandson, George Washington Parke Custis. Ownership passed to Mary Anna Custis Lee, wife of Robert E. Lee, who lost the 1,100-acre estate when Union troops occupied it in 1861 and established two forts on its grounds to help protect the national capital. The cemetery opened in 1864. In 1882, the U.S. Supreme Court awarded ownership to George

Washington Custis Lee, the eldest son of General and Mrs. Lee, and the following year Congress purchased it from him. The many notables resting here include President John F. Kennedy, Medgar Evers, Abner Doubleday, Joe Louis, and Walter Reed. Start at the Welcome Center, next to the cemetery entrance, for maps, guidebooks, exhibits, a bookstore, and information about locations of specific gravesites. See the ceremonial changing of the guard (on the hour) at the Memorial Amphitheater and the Tomb of the Unknown Soldier. Administered by the National Park Service; open 365 days a year. *One Memorial Drive, Arlington, VA, 22202, 877-907-8585.*

GEORGE WASHINGTON'S MOUNT VERNON, VA: George Washington lived at Mount Vernon for more than forty years. On the Potomac River in Northern Virginia, Mount Vernon is sixteen miles south of Washington, D.C., and is the most popular historic estate in America. Visitors can see the mansion, more than a dozen original structures, Washington's tomb, and nearly fifty acres of his extensive plantation. The site includes a working blacksmith shop and the Pioneer Farm, a four-acre demonstration farm with a reconstructed slave cabin and sixteen-sided treading barn. More than six acres are devoted to four separate eighteenth-century gardens. Mount Vernon has the largest number of Washington's artifacts of any in the nation, including his shoe buckles and famous dentures. The Ford Orientation Center has a short film, and the Donald W. Reynolds Museum and Education Center has twenty-five theaters and galleries that tell the story of Washington's life, with more than 500 original artifacts, eleven video presentations, and an immersion theater experience. *3200 Mt. Vernon Memorial Highway, Mt. Vernon, VA, 22309, 703-780-2000.*

FURTHER READING

Benjamin Franklin Cooling III, *The Day Lincoln Was Almost Shot: The Fort Stevens Story.* Scarecrow Press, 2013.
Benjamin Franklin Cooling III and Walton Owen II, *Mr. Lincoln's Forts: A Guide to the Civil War Defenses of Washington.* Scarecrow Press, 2009.

Adam Goodheart, *1861: The Civil War Awakening*. Alfred A. Knopf, 2011.

Virginia Jean Laas, *Wartime Washington: The Civil War Letters of Elizabeth Blair Lee*. University of Illinois Press, 1991.

Margaret Leech, *Reveille in Washington, 1860–1865*. NYRB Classics, 2011.

Matthew Pinsker, *Lincoln's Sanctuary: Abraham Lincoln and the Soldiers' Home*. Oxford University Press, 2005.

13

GETTYSBURG

"Your move," says the young soldier sitting on an ammo crate. His opponent leans forward, adjusting his artillery cap, and fingers a wooden checker. Hamsteaks sizzle on the fire behind them. A cavalry detachment rides slowly along the treeline, eyeing the enemy pickets in the distance. The soldier frowns as his opponent jumps him.

Behind the white canvas tents, a private caresses the barrel of a 12-pound howitzer (named for the weight of the shot it fires), assessing its readiness for the enemy's army encamped just over the ridge. He watches the cavalry riders, swinging swords as they maneuver horses in close quarters, and how the infantrymen reload muskets on the run. He greets visitors strolling through their camps at sunset, there to see what soldiers did during that war: clean muskets, whittle, peel potatoes, and cook over open fires. It's the annual restaging of the 1863 Battle of Gettysburg, fought on a farm close to the Gettysburg National Military Park on the weekend closest to the actual dates of the battle, July 1–3.

Civil War reenactments draw thousands of spectators and reenactors, with men and women portraying soldiers and civilians. Many seek an emotional connection with this landscape to help imagine this most crucial battlefield of the Civil War. The first three days of July 1863 were the turning point of the war, and its sacred places such as Little Round

Top, Devil's Den, and Pickett's Charge are emblazoned on our national psyche. Many visit the National Cemetery, adjacent to the battlefield, to stand where Lincoln stood as he helped consecrate this ground with his venerable Gettysburg Address of 272 words in November of that year.

Never has there been a better time to visit Gettysburg. A new museum and visitor center opened in 2008 with interactive stations, a theater featuring the film "A New Birth of Freedom," and more battle artifacts, covering the entire Civil War, on display than ever before. And most important may be a rich educational mission that reinterprets the events of those three July days, situating the battle in context by assigning equal emphasis to its origins and consequences. Museum pieces include the blood-stained litter that transported Confederate general Thomas "Stonewall" Jackson from Chancellorsville after he was felled there by friendly fire. The visitor center's nineteenth-century farm design fits the landscape beautifully, and it resides on the park's east side, on land adjacent to the battlefield (unlike the old center, a smaller space that, before razing, sat on the left flank of Pickett's Charge). The circular Gettysburg cyclorama painting, first displayed in 1884 (which, when unrolled, is longer than a football field), has been refurbished in the largest painting restoration project in North America.

The Battle of Gettysburg is arguably the most significant ever fought in America. The hills, woodlands, rocky ridges, fences, houses, and barns show the battlefield's topography much as it appeared in July 1863— though in many areas it is now more wooded, and all but a few of the thirty-eight orchards of that time have vanished. The park has a congressional mandate to preserve the line of battle, so portions of the field's almost 6,000 acres are gradually being restored to their 1863 appearance. Buildings of the period dot the landscape, as Civil War–era weaponry was, thankfully, insufficiently powerful to destroy them.

At dawn, early-rising spectators see soldiers donning their uniform jackets against a backdrop of bacon cooking over open fire and tin cup clanking against metal coffeepot. All but the hardcore reenactors eat well—most don't pursue authenticity to the point of eating the gritty corn-meal cakes and moldy hardtack that sustained many soldiers throughout the Civil War. The gunners assemble fresh charges for the guns: black powder and peat moss wrapped in aluminum foil. After breakfast they fall in for gun drill. The spectators watch the choreography of the crew. Three men clear the barrel and reload. One inserts a two-inch primer wire into the powder charge that's been rammed down the barrel. He yanks the lanyard attached to the wire. The gun explodes. The little boys racing about the camp, clad in period homespun and straw hats, stop shooting invisible enemy with their wooden guns, transfixed by this work.

In late June 1863, the Confederate Army of Northern Virginia crossed the Potomac River and marched through Maryland into Pennsylvania to strike at the enemy in his own land—less than a year after their thrust into Maryland had ended in defeat at Antietam (see chapter 11). Gen. Robert E. Lee and the Confederate government believed a triumph on Union soil would hasten negotiations and lead to Confederate independence. And there were tactical and political advantages: The invasion would relieve the pressure on Rebel armies in Virginia and the west by drawing Union reinforcements east; and a Southern victory could embolden Lincoln's political opponents who favored peace talks with the Confederacy. Lee's army would feast on the bounty of the Maryland and Pennsylvania countrysides, and his men would be positioned to threaten Harrisburg and Baltimore—whose terrified citizens, black and white, slave and free—hastily erected fortifications and barricades amid the uncertainty.

Follow the movements of these armies, drawn to fight here because nine roads converge in the town, via an eighteen-mile auto tour that traces the complex battle in chronological order over its three days. After exploring the museum in the visitor center, proceed with map in hand to stops 1–3 north and west of the town of Gettysburg to see where blood was first drawn. On July 1, 1863, Union cavalry under Gen. John Buford dismounted along McPherson Ridge to delay a Confederate advance from the northwest, along the Chambersburg Pike, until Union infantry arrived. A railroad cut, still present on the field, became a seductive defensive position for the Rebels, who after sending off an initial withering volley were overrun by Yankees firing down at them. A small memorial marks the spot where Union general John Reynolds fell to a Southern bullet—a severe blow to the Union was the loss of this Pennsylvanian on the first day's afternoon. The site, at the edge of McPherson's Woods, is often bedecked with flowers and a cluster of small American flags.

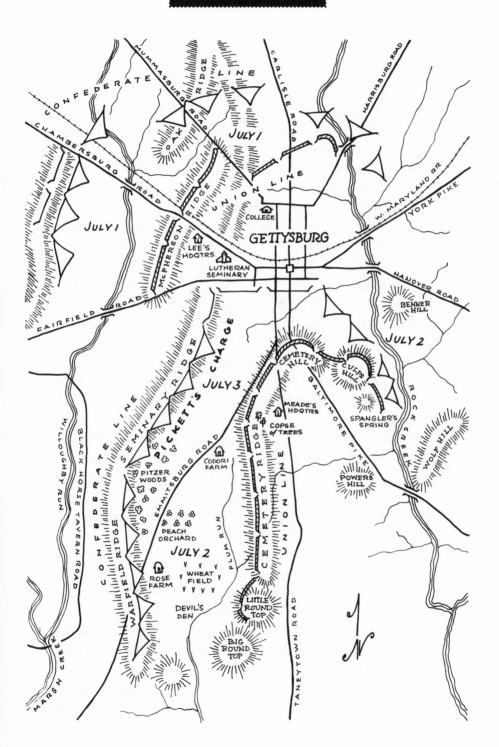

Stops 4 through 14 mark the action on the following day, July 2, and cover much ground. The first two stops are along Seminary Ridge, the high ground and heart of the Confederate position during most of the battle. Stop 5 features the Virginia Memorial and, to the east, the field where the ill-fated Confederate assault, "Pickett's Charge," against the Union center occurred on July 3. The remaining day two stops snake south on West Confederate Avenue, then north toward Little Round Top, the Wheatfield, and the Peach Orchard—the latter the site into which Union general Daniel Sickles advanced his men, thereby launching one of the war's great, unresolved debates: Did Sickles's forward move save the Union Army or invite its defeat? Sickles himself paid with his leg, which was blown off by an artillery shell. Legend—and likely only legend—says he was carried from the field with a lit cigar in his mouth. One of the Civil War's more colorful characters, Sickles dispatched the bone of his amputated leg to Washington, where he visited it annually on the anniversary of its detachment, and where today it resides on display in the Museum of Medicine and Health in Washington, D.C.

Union forces deployed, in the famous "fishhook" formation, on the high ground east of the Confederate lines, known as Cemetery Ridge (named for the cemetery south of town, where in 1863 a sign forbade firearms in this realm of the dead). Culps Hill, at the north end of this four-mile line, was the barb of the fishhook. Little Round Top, a boulder-studded hill at the south end, became its eye, tenaciously defended by Union regiments, most notably Col. Joshua Lawrence Chamberlain's Twentieth Maine Regiment, whose men garnered eternal fame for their role in its defense, and whose exploits that day were memorialized in the 1975 book, *The Killer Angels,* and in the 1993 film, *Gettysburg.*

Little Round Top's rocky summit offers a panoramic sweep of much of the second and third days' battlefield, especially from the castle-like monument to the New Yorkers who fought there. Kids love hiding amid the rock crevasses, just below the summit. Many of the more than 1,400 monuments and markers on the battlefield—the vast majority of the Union persuasion—are visible from Little Round Top. Looming in the middle is the huge Pennsylvania Memorial to the state's Gettysburg veterans who fought there. Devil's Den, the large rock formation from which Rebel sharpshooters took deadly aim at the defenders of Little Round

Top, is below on the left. Between them lies the "Valley of Death," where one soldier wrote of stampeding cattle, terrorized by the shelling.

Spectators stream into the grandstands as the Confederate infantry assembles to reenact the assault on Little Round Top. A gun crew is positioned on the ridge to support the infantry assault. The attack begins with twenty-two cannon firing *in echelon*, or sequentially, one second apart. "Gun number one, FIRE!" barks the sergeant. The gun explodes, then the next. The ground vibrates. Some spectators no doubt wish for the earplugs the gunners wear. Over the next hour the guns fire eighteen times, covering the advancing infantry. Thick smoke masks heavy Rebel casualties on the field below. A battlefield sketch artist works near the field—with photography in its infancy during the Civil War, battlefield art was the only visual information for readers eager for news of the war.

In the real fight for Little Round Top "the men rushed up the mountainside over their fallen comrades," wrote a private in the Fourth Alabama Regiment. "Minie balls were falling through the leaves like hail in a thunderstorm." A Union soldier recalled how his artillerymen's "hands and faces grew grim and black with burning powder," and that "the lines at times were so near each other that the hostile gun barrels almost touched." A Confederate officer claimed that blood "stood in puddles on the rocks." With high casualties and low ammunition, and in danger of being overrun, Colonel Chamberlain ordered his Twentieth Maine to fix bayonets—their brazen downhill charge so shocked the Confederates that the Mainers easily routed their right flank. The Rebels, confessed their commander, fled "like a herd of wild cattle." One spouted blood from a severed windpipe as he ran. The small monument to the Twentieth Maine, one of the most popular on the field, stands on the hill in woods more dense today than at the time of the battle, and a walk through them permits the imagination to see the terror of Rebel faces at the sight of charging bayonets. Monuments to lesser-known units who fought valiantly also dot the wooded hillside.

A large afternoon crowd is primed for the battle at Culps Hill, the often-overlooked site where men fought the evening of July 2 and, again, for seven hours on the morning of July 3. Rebel artillery is now deployed atop a small ridge along a tree line. The "powder monkey," the youngest member of the crew, delivers powder charges from the limber, safely behind the line. The Rebel infantry begins to move behind the guns. Flame shoots from the mouths of dozens of cannon; Union guns answer the bombardment. Lines of men drop to a knee and fire through the smoke. They rise and break into a trot, reloading as they go. Union sharpshooters appear behind a ridge, a hundred yards on the right. Mock charges explode on the field, adding flashes and columns of smoke to the clamor of cannon and musket. Men fall and writhe in pain. Others lie still. A sharpshooter's bullet sends the young flag bearer, a boy of not more than 12 named Alec, sprawling, but not before he passes the colors to an officer. "Where you hit, son?" asks a man dragging him to the rear. His reply amuses nearby spectators: "In the pancreas, Sir!" Firing ceases. Smoke lingers in the air as the artillery crews roll the big guns off the field.

At dusk on July 2 the Confederates unleashed their furious assault against the Union's right flank on Culps Hill and Cemetery Hill. Maryland Federals fought Maryland Confederates the next morning. Thirteen-year-old Maggie Mehring of New Windsor, Maryland, recorded the storm in her diary: "We heard the cannons booming very distinctly last night and it is supposed that there is a battle going on between Littlestown and Gettysburg." Confederate Harry Gilmor, a Maryland cavalry officer, told how the "brave boys fell in piles" on the forested slopes of Culps Hill. A Union general described how his cannoneers used "rammers and fence rails, hand-spikes, and stones" against Rebels who overran his artillery position on Cemetery Hill. The battle raged the night, but at first light the Yankees had held their ground.

Civilians visit at sunset. "What do you do in camp?" wonders a boy. "Is it hard to sit down in a hoop skirt?" another asks a gunner's wife. Others admire the big guns parked on the edge of camp. At dusk the soldiers remove their caps as "Taps" is played in honor of the day's fallen. A lantern walk through the camp that evening prompts thoughts about what the soldiers may have discussed around their campfires during the first two nights of July 1863: the day's action? Their fears at what morning portended? Or perhaps weightier subjects: Lincoln's prosecution of the war, Lee's string of victories, the Emancipation Proclamation of New Year's Day, 1863. Deep in the night, hard rain pounds the canvas tents.

Climb the observation tower atop Culps Hill for a grand view of the town and roads used by Confederates to converge on Gettysburg from the north. To the west is the National Cemetery, site of Lincoln's delivery of the Gettysburg Address and final resting place of many Union dead. Little Round Top is to the south. Trails from the summit lead to memorials tucked into the foliage, and to the rocky ground around Spangler's Spring at the base of the hill.

On the morning of July 3, Lee made perhaps his most crucial decision of the Civil War, and stop 15, the "High Water Mark," tells, along with stop 5, the story of this third day. Determined to attack what he was certain had become a weakened Union center, Lee massed 13,500 soldiers amid the trees along Seminary Ridge to smash it. Confederate general James Longstreet, after objecting to no avail, assigned Generals George Pickett (commanding close to half of the attacking force), J. Johnston Pettigrew, and Isaac Trimble to lead what would become known—fairly or not—as Pickett's Charge.

At 1:07 P.M.—"as suddenly as an organ strikes up in church," wrote an artillery commander—140 Confederate cannon began barraging the Union Second Corps, commanded by Gen. Winfield Scott Hancock. A hundred federal guns answered. A veteran recalled how the "tornado of projectiles" made the sky "lurid with flame, shadowing the earth as with a funeral pall."

Two hours later on that hot July afternoon, 13,000 gray-clad men stepped out of the woods and began marching toward a stand of trees a mile away, where thousands of men in blue awaited. Many knelt behind a stone wall. The Rebels, whose mile-long lines were to contract into a 600-yard width, had a mile of open ground to cover and the two rail fences to surmount on either side of the Emmitsburg Road. One prosaically recalled the "glittering forest of bayonets" and the "rustle of thousands of feet amid the stubble" of the open, mown fields.

Today the order: "Fire." Cannon comply *in echelon*. Union artillery answers. The reenacting infantry marches around the artillery onto the field. The gun crews wave their caps in tribute. "Give 'em hell, boys!" a gunner shouts. "Send them Yanks back to Boston!" Somber, unshaven men in dirty, mismatched uniforms mirror the gaunt faces of Confederate soldiers in old tintypes. Astride a horse sprinting to and fro is Gen. George Pickett, ringlets bouncing below his hat. Rebel troops begin to march. The crack of muskets fills the still, thick air. Men drop. The Union artillery pace quickens. These armies restage the most famous assault on American soil.

Some men in gray reach the trees. The reenactor portraying Confederate general Lewis Armistead, hat on the point of raised sword, leads his Virginians over the wall and smack into a swarm of blue coats. The Confederate flag waves briefly, but the incursion is short-lived. Armistead falls beside a Union cannon. Battered Rebel infantrymen stagger back across the field to their lines. The Union men chant "Fredericksburg! Fredericksburg!" recalling their slaughter six months earlier by Confederates as they marched across Marye's Heights, the open ground at that town in Virginia (see chapter 14). Many use muskets as crutches. The gunners wave their caps in salute to the returning bedraggled infantrymen.

Union commander Gen. George Meade, anticipating Lee's strategy, had reserves massed on both flanks, ready to reinforce his center if needed. More than half of the attacking Confederate force was killed, wounded, captured, or went missing in the heat of that summer afternoon. Survivors told how Lee rode among his battered men shouting "It is all my fault!" and urged them to prepare for a Union counterattack.

Visitors walking the line of this attack may be surprised at its undulating landscape—in spots the copse of trees is obscured. Start from the trees at the statue of General Lee, near both the center of that Confederate line and the spot where Lee watched the assault. Near the stone wall where the Union men waited, a sign marks the site of the rebel breach—the "High Water Mark," representing the apex of Confederate military power. The armies left a landscape of misery: More than 51,000 dead and wounded—more than ten times the number suffered on D-Day—with thousands of corpses and injured left to be cared for by Union army detachments, the United States Sanitary and Christian Commissions, and the women among the 2,500 beleaguered townspeople.

Six weeks after the Battle of Gettysburg, Marylander Augustus Shriver witnessed "a Boston Lady on the field, who with a stone smashed the teeth out of a rebel skull to take home as relics, and showing as plainly as manners could, that even to the bones of a Rebel she could not show the decency of good breeding." Gen. Daniel Sickles, after becoming a member of Congress, introduced a bill in 1895 to create the Gettysburg

National Military Park. A year later the U.S. Supreme Court issued a decision that allowed the government to seize land, in the name of battlefield preservation, on which the Gettysburg Electric Railway Company ran a trolley line, on the southern portion of the battlefield, conveying visitors to Devil's Den and the Round Tops.

The National Cemetery (stop 16) was consecrated on November 19, 1863, as a burial place for approximately 3,500 Union soldiers. Lincoln's words that day would powerfully define the new nation that emerged from the carnage of the Civil War: "That these dead shall not have died in vain, that this nation under God shall have a new birth of freedom, and that government of the people, by the people, for the people shall not perish from the earth." The cemetery is an ideal spot for parents to sum the Gettysburg experience for their children, and for each other: the significance of those three merciless days in July 1863, with its staggering 51,000 casualties; how young soldiers must have begged for sleep while trembling at the sight of enemy campfires and the horror waiting to ride with the dawn; and how the Gettysburg Address, on the heels of Lincoln's Emancipation Proclamation earlier that year, helped bring about that "new birth of freedom" for the nation.

SIDE TRIPS

THE DAVID WILLS HOUSE, GETTYSBURG: David Wills was a Gettysburg lawyer who witnessed firsthand the devastation his fellow townspeople suffered during the Battle of Gettysburg. He oversaw the creation of the National Cemetery there that was consecrated on November 19, 1863, when President Abraham Lincoln delivered the Gettysburg Address. Lincoln spent the prior night as Wills's houseguest. The Wills House, on the main town square and officially part of Gettysburg National Military Park, describes the circumstances surrounding the *Gettysburg Address* and the town's recovery from the battle. Five museum galleries and the recreated Wills law office and Lincoln Bedroom immerse visitors in the historic moments as the nation began to recover from the trauma of Civil War, almost a year and a half before Lee's surrender at Appomattox. *8 Lincoln Square, Gettysburg, PA, 17325, 877-874-2478.*

EISENHOWER NATIONAL HISTORIC SITE, PA: President Dwight D. Eisenhower purchased this farm in 1950 and spent many weekends and holidays here, often meeting with national and world leaders. The site, adjacent to the Gettysburg Battlefield, includes four farms totaling 690 acres. Eisenhower's original 230-acre farm is farmed today as it was during his time. The home is maintained as it was during the Eisenhower years and retains many original furnishings. Visitors can tour the house, enjoy an audio tour, and see the cattle barns and skeet range. Exhibits describe Eisenhower's boyhood in Abilene, Kansas, his thirty-eight-year military career, his presidency, and retirement. A half-hour program about the D-Day invasion of France in June 1944, commanded by General Eisenhower, features weapons and equipment used in the operation (summer only). Kids can join the Junior Secret Service upon completing the exercises in the Junior Secret Service Training Manual. *1195 Baltimore Pike, Suite 100, Gettysburg, PA, 17325, 717-338-9114.*

UNION MILLS HOMESTEAD, MD: The homestead of the large Shriver family for six generations is now a museum of American culture. The extensive Shriver family history and archives illuminate much about Maryland history in the eighteenth and nineteenth centuries, particularly during the Civil War, where Shrivers fought on both sides. The Homestead features historical events and reenactments throughout the year. The gristmill still produces stone-ground cornmeal and wheat and buckwheat flour and sells roasted cornmeal. Union Mills is about seventeen miles south of Gettysburg, Pennsylvania, and on the route portions of the Union Army took to the battle. *3311 Littlestown Pike, Westminster, MD, 21158, 410-848-2288.*

TANEYTOWN, MD: This historic town of almost 7,000 people, founded in 1754 and named for Raphael Taney (not U.S. Supreme Court Justice Roger B. Taney, a distant relative), is part of the striking landscape of northern Carroll County. The Taneytown History Museum provides a thorough background, and the Taneytown Historic District is on the National Register of Historic Places. Union general George G. Meade made his headquarters here at times during the Civil War. The town is thirty-five miles or less from Hagerstown, Baltimore, Westminster, Gettysburg, and Hanover, PA.

FURTHER READING

ADULTS

Edwin B. Coddington, *The Gettysburg Campaign: A Study in Command.* Touchstone, 1997.

Allen C. Guelzo, *Gettysburg: The Last Invasion.* Alfred A. Knopf, 2013.

James M. McPherson, *Hallowed Ground: A Walk at Gettysburg.* Crown, 2003.

Stephen Sears, *Gettysburg.* Mariner Books, 2004.

Michael Shaara, *The Killer Angels.* Modern Library, 2004.

Noah Trudeau, *Gettysburg: A Testing of Courage.* Harper Perennial, 2003.

CHILDREN

Jim O'Connor, *What Was the Battle of Gettysburg?* Grosset & Dunlap, 2013.

FREDERICKSBURG, CHANCELLORSVILLE, THE WILDERNESS, AND SPOTSYLVANIA

No ground in America has endured more concentrated and brutal fighting than the small area in eastern Virginia below the fork of the Rappahannock and Rapidan Rivers. From late 1862 to 1864, four major battles in the Civil War claimed more than 100,000 casualties in this heavily contested region. The 25,000 deaths in that theater represented approximately 4 percent of all Civil War deaths. These four battle sites—Fredericksburg, Chancellorsville, the Wilderness, and Spotsylvania—together comprise the 8,000-acre Fredericksburg and Spotsylvania National Military Park, which the energetic visitor can see in a long weekend. The topography of Fredericksburg is as illustrative as any Civil War site of a Napoleonic-style frontal assault on a well-defended position—in this instance, a Union attack against Confederate infantry dug in along a ridge called Marye's Heights. The Wilderness and Spotsylvania were the sites of some of the most ferocious fighting of the war, while at Chancellorsville Lee won his greatest victory but lost the indispensable Gen. Thomas "Stonewall" Jackson.

The battle of Fredericksburg in December of 1862 was the first of these four bloody clashes—Chancellorsville would come the following spring, the Wilderness and Spotsylvania a year later. Though substantial parts of these battlefields have fallen to the backhoe, vast portions remain pristine and retain well-preserved earthworks. At the Fredericksburg visitor center on Caroline Street in the historic old town are a film and selection of literature and maps on the wide variety of things to see and do in the area. The seventy-five minute trolley tour offers a thorough overview of the town's three centuries of history. Walking tours—including one designed for kids—visit some of the same sites.

A testament to Fredericksburg's embrace of its twentieth-century history is at the corner of Caroline and William Streets, location of the July 1960 lunch-counter sit-in at the F. W. Woolworth's store during the civil rights movement. African American residents of the city succeeded in peacefully desegregating that store and two others on that corner, W. T. Grant's and People's Service Drugs. Another site nearby commemorates the work of the committee to adapt Virginia's colonial laws to the new state government, in January 1777, a successful effort that included Thomas Jefferson and George Mason. The town also hosts an exciting reenactment of the battle, fought before spectators in the streets as Confederate soldiers try to halt the Union attackers who've crossed the Rappahannock River and raced up its banks to attack the entrenched Rebels. This reenactment underscores the unusual nature of this clash, fought as it was in a populated area rather than on the open ground as were so many others, and in December rather than the warm months when the armies customarily fought.

In December 1862, Union general Ambrose Burnside, pushing toward Richmond, encamped on the north bank of the Rappahannock River across from Fredericksburg, a city of 5,000 people halfway between Washington and the Confederate capital. For two weeks he awaited pontoon bridges to get his 120,000 men across the river, giving the Confederates time to dig into the hills behind the town, known as Marye's Heights, and along seven miles of riverfront. Civilians fled as Union cannon inflicted heavy damage on the city, while federal engineers began installing

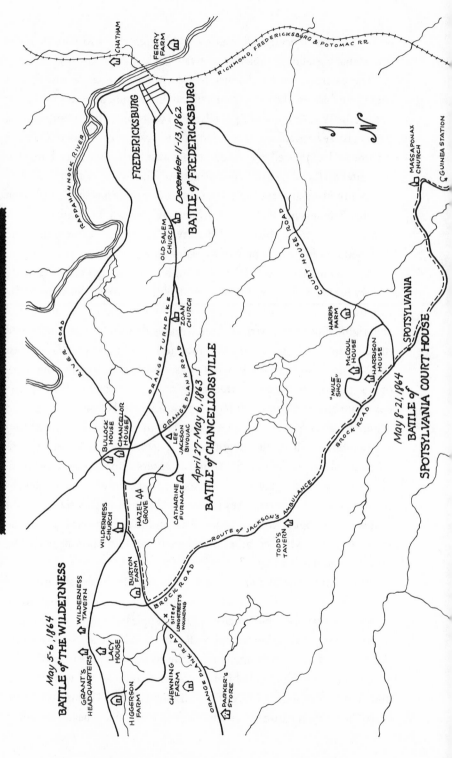

CIVIL WAR FREDERICKSBURG AND AREA BATTLEFIELDS

CHATHAM

FERRY FARM

FREDERICKSBURG

RAPPAHANNOCK RIVER

RICHMOND, FREDERICKSBURG & POTOMAC RR

RIVER ROAD

OLD SALEM CHURCH

December 11-13, 1862
BATTLE of FREDERICKSBURG

COURT HOUSE ROAD

MASSAPONAX CHURCH

GUINEA STATION

N

BULLOCK HOUSE

CHANCELLOR HOUSE

ORANGE TURNPIKE

ZOAN CHURCH

ORANGE PLANK ROAD

LEE-JACKSON BIVOUAC

April 27-May 6, 1863
BATTLE of CHANCELLORSVILLE

WILDERNESS CHURCH

HAZEL GROVE

CATHARINE FURNACE

HARRIS FARM

"MULE SHOE"

McCOUL HOUSE

HARRISON HOUSE

SPOTSYLVANIA

May 8-21, 1864
BATTLE of
SPOTSYLVANIA COURT HOUSE

May 5-6, 1864
BATTLE of THE WILDERNESS

WILDERNESS TAVERN

GRANT'S HEADQUARTERS

LACY HOUSE

BURTON FARM

BROCK ROAD

SITE of LONGSTREET'S WOUNDING

HIGGERSON FARM

CHEWNING FARM

ORANGE PLANK ROAD

PARKER'S STORE

ROUTE of JACKSON'S AMBULANCE

TODD'S TAVERN

the pontoons under cover of darkness. Rebel sharpshooters hidden in attics and cellars in houses across the river shot at the engineers, driving them back. "Such a feeling of anxiety and suspense I never experienced. I could scarcely breathe," recorded surgeon Clark Baum of the 50th New York Engineers as he watched his fellow bridge builders come under fire. A stroll on Sophia Street, along the Rappahannock, gives the view the Confederate sharpshooters had when firing at the Union engineers, and the spot where the pontoon bridges were eventually constructed—thanks to intrepid Michigan and Massachusetts soldiers who led the charge to eject the Rebel riflemen from their perches in houses along the river.

General Burnside's poor tactical judgment at Fredericksburg—a common affliction among Union generals before Gen. Ulysses S. Grant took command—led to one of the greatest Union debacles of the war. Burnside sent wave after wave of federal troops across an open field toward 2,500 Confederate infantry, who stood four deep behind a stone wall that ran along a sunken road at the base of a ridge—part of the road link between Washington, D.C., and Richmond. This Confederate position was probably the strongest natural position ever defended by Lee's army. "A chicken won't be able to cross that field when we open on it," exalted a Southern officer, whose men then inflicted heavy losses on eighteen Union brigades on the afternoon of December 13.

A half-hour's walking tour of Marye's Heights—the left-center of the Confederate line on the Fredericksburg battlefield—starts at the National Park Service visitor center, just below that sunken road and stone wall. Several houses that survived the fighting stand vigil over that field, most prominently the Innis House along the Rebel line, whose walls still bear the scars of bullets and shell fragments. The attacking federals suffered 8,000 casualties on that small field. "Our boys fired into the dense masses without the fear of missing & with a fair prospect of cutting down 2 at a time," S.H. Walker of the 48th North Carolina Infantry Regiment recalled. Union troops, ordered to hold their positions, were exposed to enemy riflemen who fired at first sight of any federal heads. Northern soldiers protected themselves behind the corpses of fallen comrades. Lt. Col. Joshua Lawrence Chamberlain of the 20th Maine Infantry Regiment, who got his men into position 80 yards from the wall, described the battleground as darkness descended. He recalled the wailing of the wounded "weird, unearthly, terrible to hear and bear," adding that "the living and the dead were alike to me." Chamberlain claimed to have heard Confederates talking behind their lines and, in a surreal passage, wrote of a loose window blind flapping rhythmically throughout the night in a nearby house whose windows had been blown out. An adjacent monument is dedicated to 19-year-old Richard Kirkland of the 2nd South Carolina Infantry Regiment, the "Angel of Mercy" who, at great risk, took water onto the field to comfort the suffering of his enemy's wounded. When Union soldiers realized his purpose, they ceased firing at him. Kirkland died in battle the following year.

Many Union dead are buried in Fredericksburg National Cemetery, while more than 3,300 Southern soldiers lie in the Fredericksburg Confederate Cemetery at the corner of William and Washington Streets. More men would die in Fredericksburg the following spring, when Union troops drove Confederate infantry from the same sunken road during the Chancellorsville Campaign. Both cemeteries are open to visitors and offer Memorial Day observances.

Fredericksburg reenacts the battle annually in December, as the two sides fight in the streets: gray-clad Rebels fire at their federal opponents from doorways and behind lamp posts. Adding to the period ambience are shopkeepers dressed in mid-nineteenth-century garb and replicas of Union and Confederate headquarters. Kenmore Plantation, the home of George Washington's sister, features soldiers' camps and a Civil War field hospital, lessons in preparing and preserving food in the mid-nineteenth century, and dancing to period music. Nearby is Ferry Farm, Washington's boyhood home across the river at Falmouth, which hosts period children's crafts and music, song, and dancing around a bonfire as part of "Christmas in the Camps." The National Park Service Visitor Center is one of many participants in the "Time Travelers" Passport Guide to Virginia's museums and historic sites, an alphabetized, color-coded guide to 120 locations, each offering a stamp to visiting youngsters, who, with six visitation stamps, can earn prizes such as T-shirts.

South of Fredericksburg, Lee Drive winds for seven miles and parallels a railroad now used by Amtrak. Maps and signs along the road describe the attacks by Union general George Meade's division, whose men poured through the marshy woods west of the tracks to breach Gen.

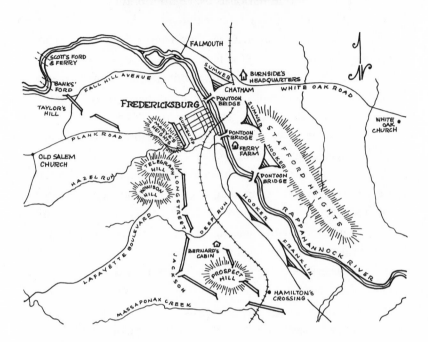

BATTLE OF FREDERICKSBURG

Stonewall Jackson's line at Prospect Hill. A granite pyramid marks the spot of the Union breakthrough. A rebel counterattack, however, forced the Yankees to retreat, prisoners in tow. The trenches on the battle line along Lee Drive lend an eerie realism to this part of the battlefield.

Chatham stands high on the east bank of the Rappahannock River, across from Fredericksburg. This majestic Georgian mansion, completed in 1771, affords a panoramic view of the city. George Washington and Thomas Jefferson were guests there, and President Abraham Lincoln visited in May 1862. Known during the Civil War as the Lacy House, Chatham was the headquarters of Union general Edwin Sumner during the assault on Fredericksburg and at other times served as a communications center—here was the first use, in a combat setting, of a magneto-electric telegraph machine, which is on display. Clara Barton helped nurse hundreds hospitalized at Chatham during and after the battle. Poet Walt Whitman visited and saw the pile of amputated limbs tossed outside through two windows on the river side of the house, at the base of two catalpha trees, whose gnarled trunks stand today. "Outdoors, at the foot of a tree, within ten yards of the front of the house, I notice a heap of amputated feet, legs, arms, hands, etc.—about a load for a one-horse cart," Whitman recalled. Clara Barton described to her cousin the atmosphere the night before the federal assault: "It is the night before a battle. The enemy, Fredericksburg, and its mighty entrenchments lie before us, the river between . . . the moon is shining through the soft haze with a brightness almost prophetic," she wrote. "For the last half hour I have stood alone in the awful stillness of its glimmering light gazing upon the strange and sad scene around me."

Chatham, under the stewardship of the National Park Service, is a fine example of an antebellum plantation house that, in its heyday, had a hundred slaves who worked the fields and as coopers, blacksmiths, coachmen, groomers, and domestics. The family of J. Horace Lacy, who acquired Chatham in 1857, had fled by the time of the battle, and Lacy would have been shocked to see what befell his home during his absence: trees cut down, slaves scattered to freedom, tents everywhere, and more than a hundred Union graves in the yard. Displays tell the story of Chatham through the ages, underscoring its role during the Civil War. Messages on the walls written by Union soldiers are preserved and deepen the sense of authenticity in this building. The short walk out the front toward the Rappahannock River reveals a replica pontoon bridge and a view of Fredericksburg that is much the same as that seen through the field glasses of Union commanders in December 1862. The steeples of city hall and two churches still dominate the skyline.

In April 1863, four months after Fredericksburg, General Burnside's successor, Gen. Joseph Hooker, marched the Union Army across the Rappahannock River at Chancellorsville, ten miles west of Fredericksburg. Though outnumbered by Hooker, Confederate general Robert E. Lee divided his army, sending Stonewall Jackson west to hit the Union right flank on May 2. As terrified deer, rabbits, and other creatures raced ahead of the Confederate advance, the Yankees retreated across the river at United States Ford, giving Lee "his finest hour" and most decisive victory of the war. The win came at a high cost. Jackson, while out conducting a reconnaissance that evening, was accidentally shot by his own men. After surgeons amputated his left arm, Lee lamented, "he has lost

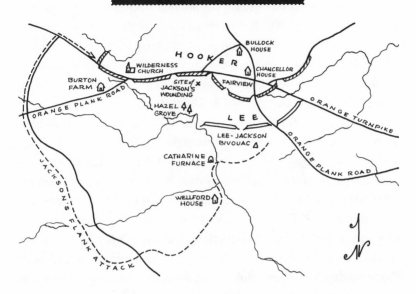

BATTLE OF CHANCELLORSVILLE

his left arm, but I have lost my right." Six miles east stands the Old Salem Church, where Confederate infantry opened fire on the Union soldiers reinforcing Hooker and forced them back across the Rappahannock. The church served as a field hospital, and marks made by more than a hundred Minie balls can be seen in its brick walls.

Much of the Chancellorsville battlefield is wooded, so the film and map available at the visitor center are essential tools for understanding the events on that terrain. The center has a number of artifacts from the fighting. The story of Pennsylvania colonel John W. Patterson and his wife, Almira Wendt Patterson, brings home the terrible consequences of the Civil War on non-combatants. Their letters to one another end with Colonel Patterson's death in 1864 at the Battle of the Wilderness. A six-mile history trail begins at the visitor center, just off VA Rt. 3, ten miles west of Fredericksburg, and ends at the site where Jackson was wounded, a hundred yards from the visitor center. The trail parallels Union and Confederate earthworks, some of which are still visible; the hardy can hike the driving tour route and see both the spot where Lee and Jackson met to draw battle plans and the Union artillery position at Fairview. Markers explain the battle as it evolved. The wounded Jackson was transported twenty-seven miles southeast by rickety ambulance to Thomas C. Chandler's Fairfield Plantation at Guinea Station, where he died on May 10, 1863. The house, now known as the Stonewall Jackson Shrine, stands on Guinea Station Road (Rt. 607), fifteen miles south of Fredericksburg. The Confederate victory at Chancellorsville paved the way for Lee's invasion of Pennsylvania the following month, where the armies met again, at Gettysburg (see chapter 13).

A year later—following Union victories at Vicksburg and Gettysburg—north and south again clashed in this region, as Gen. Ulysses S. Grant, now commanding all Union Armies, crossed the Rapidan River in another campaign to defeat Lee and capture Richmond. To do so required a march through the Wilderness, a huge expanse of dense undergrowth. The Battle of the Wilderness, on May 5–6, 1864, ignited fires that raged through the tangled thickets between the Orange Turnpike (VA Rt. 20) and the Orange Plank Road (VA Rt. 621). Terrified soldiers on both sides fought while blinded by smoke from guns and burning underbrush. Wounded men unable to move were burned alive. Exposed skeletons of the unburied Chancellorsville dead added to the horror. Over two days the Union suffered more than 17,600 casualties, the Confederates an estimated 8,000 to 12,000. This bloody engagement brought no clear winner, and Grant continued to pursue Lee's army south.

The original Confederate line lies near the site of the Wilderness Exhibit Shelter (manned in summer), where an interpreted walking trail starts and finishes. A driving tour includes eight sites, including Grant's headquarters and the spot where Confederate general James Longstreet was wounded, also by friendly fire. The two-mile Gordon Flank Attack Trail, which parallels and crosses a vast system of trenches and gun pits, follows Confederate general John Gordon's attack against the Union right flank. Just west of VA Rt. 20 is Ellwood House, a farmhouse owned by J. Horace Lacy, the owner of Chatham, and the site of both a federal headquarters and the resting place of Stonewall Jackson's left arm, which was not amputated prior to his evacuation to Guinea Station.

In the hours following the terror in the Wilderness, Grant and Lee raced to the village of Spotsylvania Court House, eight miles southeast and directly on the road to Richmond. The fight here lasted for two weeks in May 1864. In a barbaric twenty-hour period, men shot, clubbed, and bayoneted each other over hastily constructed earthworks at the Confederate position called the "Mule Shoe." Heavy fighting raged at a point where the Confederate line turned slightly to the right, known as the "Bloody Angle"—where the fighting was so intense that it felled an oak tree twenty-two inches in diameter.

The Spotsylvania Battlefield History Trail is a series of loops that can be hiked individually or in combinations; the entire trail is seven miles and starts and ends at the exhibit shelter (manned in summer). A highlight is the Bloody Angle Trail, with seven stops that can be walked in a leisurely thirty minutes through an other-worldly landscape of ridges, humps, and swales. Another loop, the McCoull-Harrison, has earthworks along Lee's last defensive line. Nearly 600 Confederate soldiers are buried in the Spotsylvania Confederate Cemetery on VA Rt. 208, just south of the battlefield. Though the battle occurred in May, winter can be a good time to tour, for crowds are thinner. Roads cut through the woods are visible throughout the year, such as the one used by Union colonel Emory Upton's men to attack the Rebel line at the Mule Shoe.

A famous series of photographs shows General Grant and his men in the yard of the Massaponax Baptist Church, conferring on church pews that had been removed so wounded men could be treated in the sanctuary. Messages scrawled on the walls by the soldiers of both sides now lie preserved beneath plexiglass. From Spotsylvania, follow VA Rt. 608 five miles east to VA Rt. 1; the church is on the northwest corner. Note that the church is not part of the park and thus may not be open to the public.

Grant would spend another bloody year on the road to Richmond, and the carnage continued. The armies endured more fighting at the North Anna River and Cold Harbor and a grueling ten-month siege at Petersburg before Union troops finally captured the Confederate capital at Richmond on April 3. Lee, his men and supplies exhausted, surrendered at Appomattox Court House six days later.

SIDE TRIPS

GEORGE WASHINGTON'S FERRY FARM, VA: Washington's family moved to this 80-acre site in Stafford County, Virginia, when he was six years old.

The name came from the ferry that transported passengers, including the Washingtons, across the Rappahannock River to Fredericksburg. The visitor center features colonial and Civil War–era artifacts found on the property and the archaeology lab, where on weekdays visitors can watch archaeologists at work. A self-guided tour includes the gardens, with the kinds of plants grown in the eighteenth century; the original site of the Washington house (identified in 2008) overlooking the Rappahannock River; and a walk down the old ferry road. Hiking trails and bird-watching can round out an afternoon's visit. *268 Kings Highway, Fredericksburg, VA, 22405, 540-370-0732.*

GEORGE WASHINGTON BIRTHPLACE, VA: This site, administered by the National Park Service, was called Popes Creek Plantation at the time of Washington's birth in 1732. He lived there until age three, when he moved with his family to Ferry Farm, on Virginia's southern shore of the Potomac River, thirty-eight miles east of Fredericksburg and approximately eighty miles downstream from Mount Vernon. The original home, likely made of brick, was destroyed by fire in 1779; the foundation was excavated in 1936. The Memorial House on the site today was built in the early 1930s to honor the memory of Washington and is representative of an early eighteenth-century middle-class Virginia planter's home. *1732 Popes Creek Road, Colonial Beach, VA, 22443-5115, 804-224-1732.*

STRATFORD HALL, VA: This home of the Lees of Virginia and the birthplace of Robert E. Lee was constructed in the 1730s by Thomas Lee. The Grand House features a collection of American and English decorative objects; several galleries offer a range of artifacts. Near the Slave Quarters are representative varieties of herbs and vegetables grown by slaves at Stratford that illuminate the plant culture they brought to America. The gardens include the Formal East Garden. Several short hiking trails give a flavor of the property, and a short walk to the Stratford Cliffs provides a panoramic view of the Potomac River. Several guest cabins are available for overnight stays. Just off VA Rt. 3, on VA Rt. 214, six miles northwest of Montross, Virginia, in Westmoreland County, and forty-two miles southeast of Fredericksburg. *483 Great House Road, Stratford, VA, 22558, 804-493-8038.*

BRANDY STATION, VA: The June 9, 1863, Battle of Brandy Station, the largest cavalry battle on the North American continent with 17,000 mounted soldiers, was the opening clash of the Gettysburg Campaign. At dawn that day, Union cavalry launched a surprise attack against their Confederate counterparts but failed to discover the latter's infantry camp near Culpeper. A five-stop auto tour with interpretive markers provides a great overview of the action on the field. Graffiti House was a field hospital during the Civil War and is now a private visitor center and museum where soldiers' inscriptions, signatures, and drawings on the walls have been identified and preserved. The battlefields of Cedar Mountain, Bristoe Station, Kelly's Ford, Mine Run, and Rappahannock Station are nearby. *19484 Brandy Road, Brandy Station, VA, 22714, 540-727-7718.*

FURTHER READING

Bruce Catton, *Glory Road: The Bloody Route from Fredericksburg to Gettysburg.* Doubleday, 1952.

Bruce Catton, *A Stillness at Appomattox.* Anchor Books, 1990 (first published 1953).

Fredericksburg and Spotsylvania County Battlefields Memorial National Military Park, Virginia. Harpers Ferry Center (a division of the National Park Service), 1999.

15

CEDAR CREEK AND
BELLE GROVE NATIONAL
HISTORICAL PARK

Virginia's lush Shenandoah Valley, stretching 150 miles from Winchester to Roanoke, is formed by the Blue Ridge Mountains to the east, the Allegheny Mountains to the west, and the Potomac and James Rivers to the north and south. The valley saw extensive fighting during the Civil War, particularly during the middle years of 1862–1864, when Confederate troops commanded by Gen. Thomas "Stonewall" Jackson and Gen. Jubal Early marched through the region with impunity, and Gen. Robert E. Lee's men used it as a route for invading the north that led to the battles of Antietam and Gettysburg (see chapters 11 and 13). The valley's rich agricultural lands also made it the "Breadbasket of the Confederacy," feeding Rebel armies throughout Virginia for much of the war.

Travelers in the valley today have rich choices of places to visit to see the stone walls, buildings, and battlefields from that time in a largely unspoiled contemporary setting. The annual battle reenactments at Cedar Creek are perhaps the best of their kind in the nation, and by being staged on the actual field lend an air of authenticity rarely seen at similar events elsewhere.

The Cedar Creek Battlefield will be, for many, the highlight of a Shenandoah Valley Civil War tour. It is the largest battle site in the valley, and the place where a significant and underrated Union victory in October 1864 helped turn the tide of the war in favor of the U.S. government. The victory was as dramatic as any in that conflict. Confederate attackers routed the sleeping federals from their tents before dawn, only to fall before a Union counterattack later in the day and lose their vital foothold in the valley for good.

Confederate units commanded by Generals Jackson and Early had until that time lived off the Shenandoah Valley's bountiful farms. The guerrilla strikes and evasive tactics employed by officers such as John Singleton Mosby, the Virginia Cavalry commander known as the Gray Ghost, kept at bay the larger enemy forces charged with expelling the Rebels from the Valley. Not until the autumn 1864 Battle of Cedar Creek did the Union finally drive the Rebels out once and for all, earning a badly needed Union victory for a Lincoln administration under intense political pressures to seek peace and recognize the Confederacy. Had the Union Army not won this victory, Abraham Lincoln may well have lost reelection in 1864 to Gen. George B. McClellan, the popular general he had twice appointed and fired earlier in the war, and whose Republican party had promised to end the war with Confederate independence if necessary.

The Cedar Creek and Belle Grove National Historical Park was created by Congress in 2002 and lies twelve miles south of Winchester, between the towns of Strasburg and Middletown. Both towns are old Virginia landmarks, and Strasburg especially retains an appealing, quaint ambience. The park is a "partnership park," meaning that the National Park Service and other organizations jointly manage its attractions and resources. While much of the park's acreage remains privately owned, some is available to the public, including the Cedar Creek Battlefield Headquarters, Hupp's Hill Civil War Park (south of the battlefield), and the Belle Grove Plantation House at its center. The park's Visitor Contact Station (7712 Main Street in Middletown, VA) is an ideal first stop on a visit to the park, offering interpretive exhibits on the history of the Shenandoah Valley, from early settlement through the Civil War. A large, three-dimensional map shows the Cedar Creek Battlefield and provides an overview of the engagement.

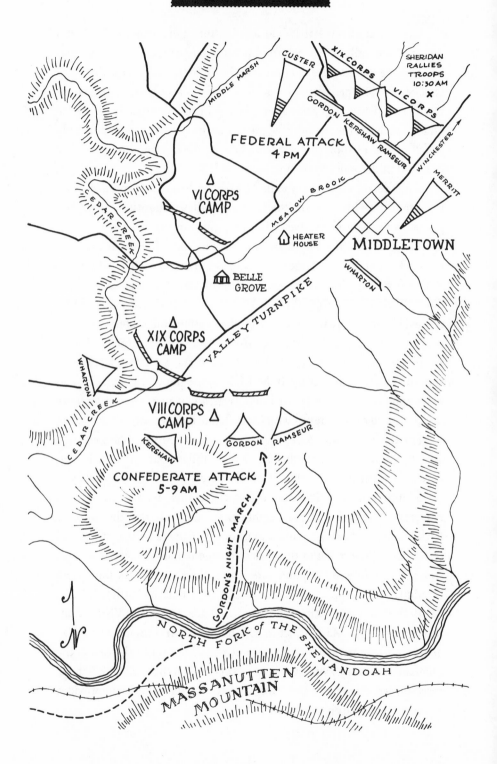

The museum at Hupp's Hill provides a colorful introduction to the Civil War in this part of Virginia, using interpretive exhibits and displays for an overview of the Battle of Cedar Creek and the 1864 Shenandoah Valley Campaign. The museum has a vivid topographical map that portrays the battle, the last in a series of clashes that began with the Third Battle of Winchester and included fights at nearby Fisher's Hill and Tom's Brook. A 50-foot mural depicts the hostilities at Cedar Creek. A camp scene features a tent, wagon, and other details of a soldier's life off the battlefield. Other intriguing items on display are musical instruments; the ID tag of Arnold Felix, a Union soldier from West Virginia; a cavalry saber excavated along the banks of Cedar Creek in the 1970s; and an 1849 Colt revolver unearthed at a Confederate picket post in 1979.

The Hupp's Hill Museum offers two short films, one of which addresses the battle. The other is an entertaining documentary about the haunted caves under portions of the battlefield, including under Hupp's Hill itself. A hospital was allegedly set up in the caves during the war, and soldiers hid among its warrens. A guide in the film claims to have seen a Confederate prisoner in the caves. Visitors may wonder if this ghost still wanders the caverns beneath the battlefield. A short walking trail that starts outside the visitor center leads to defensive trenches on the hill dug by Union troops during the Valley Campaign. A longer trail just north of Cedar Creek follows some of the most pristine Civil War earthworks that survive in the valley.

The Shenandoah Valley was ideal terrain for Confederate forces, especially for their cavalry. Their persistent presence there forced the federal government to keep troops near Washington to defend that city, troops that could otherwise have been deployed to help destroy the main Confederate Army and seize its capital at Richmond. By 1864 fighting in the valley had intensified, and the Confederates had become vulnerable. They had lost the irreplaceable Stonewall Jackson in a friendly fire incident at Chancellorsville a year earlier (see chapter 14). President Lincoln had finally found in Gen. Ulysses S. Grant a leader willing to pursue and destroy the Rebel Army; under his command Union forces had cut a swath that summer through Virginia and dug siege lines south of Richmond, at Petersburg (see chapter 16). Grant had placed Gen. Philip Sheridan in command of the Shenandoah forces; his victories in September at Winchester and Fisher's Hill had significantly curtailed Confederate operations there. Lincoln and Grant instructed Sheridan to drive the Confederates from the valley for good, and by early October he appeared to have successfully carried out his mission.

Confederate general Jubal Early believed the best defense to be a good offense. In one of the most audacious surprise attacks of the Civil War, he drove his weary army of 14,000 on an all-night march along the flanks of Massanutten Mountain to attack the sleeping Union troops at first light. At dawn on October 19, Early's men attacked; most of their adversaries were asleep in their tents along the banks of Cedar Creek. Panicked, partially dressed men ran, leaving weapons and breakfasts to the onrushing Rebel troops, who halted what was becoming a rout to eat and grab what they could, forsaking Union prisoners and jeopardizing clean victory. The scene was "a hell carnival," said one Southern soldier of the ensuing chaos.

General Sheridan, sufficiently confident that his victories earlier that autumn had given his forces control of the valley, had gone to Washington for consultations with the War Department. Quartered in Winchester as he returned from the capital, he galloped toward the battle sounds and straight into the mass of his men in full retreat. In an impressive display of Civil War generalship, Sheridan reversed the debacle and willed his men to turn certain, devastating defeat into a dramatic victory later in the day that would hasten the Southern surrender at Appomattox the following spring. "Regiment after regiment, brigade after brigade, in rapid succession was crushed, and like hard clods of clay under a pelting rain, the superb commands crumbled to pieces," wrote Confederate general John Gordon of the fighting that afternoon. "Only darkness has saved the whole of Early's army from total destruction," telegraphed Sheridan to General Grant. The fighting inspired Thomas Read's legendary poem, "Sheridan's Ride," and Sheridan's success that day took its place as perhaps the Union's most underappreciated and significant victory in the Civil War.

The Belle Grove Mansion, once the center of a 7,500-acre plantation, sits two miles north of Hupp's Hill, a half mile west of VA Rt. 11, and close to the center of the Cedar Creek battlefield. Its mansion, owned by the National Trust for Historic Preservation, was built in 1794 by Major

Isaac Hite, a slave owner who was the brother-in-law of President James Madison. Thomas Jefferson allegedly influenced its federal-period design. Paint analyses and examination of Hite family receipts have guided historic preservationists in replicating the original paint colors and carpets supplied by British manufacturers. Belle Grove was Sheridan's headquarters before and after the Battle of Cedar Creek. Throughout the fighting the terrain surrounding the mansion was home to hundreds of Union tents and campfires that filled the yard and adjacent fields, where cows now graze. One of its front columns sports an authentic bullet hole, and a divot marks the spot where a shell smashed into the front of the house. Belle Grove stands as a beautifully preserved eighteenth-century plantation house, with the gardens, ice house, smoke house, blacksmith shop, and winter kitchen that comprised such estates of the era. Limestone was quarried on the property, and a slave cemetery is 200 yards north of the manor house, adjacent to an apple orchard. Plantation records have revealed that three African Americans worked as blacksmiths at Belle Grove.

The staff at Belle Grove offers a day camp in June for children, giving them the opportunity to explore the Civil War history of the mansion and its garden and many rooms. Elements of the mansion's interior are original, including floors, Isaac Hite's desk, and his library with books on history, philosophy, and agriculture—all topics in which a cultured gentleman of that era would have been conversant. The nursery, where Union General George Custer and other officers visited wounded Confederate general Stephen Ramseur (all were classmates at West Point) as Ramseur lay dying in the bed there, after the fighting, has original furniture. The master bedroom reveals the layers of paint that have been applied over the decades, and segments of the wall are cut away to reveal the period lathing and nails. The old winter kitchen at the basement level, once the slave work area, is home to the gift shop and eighteenth- and nineteenth-century cooking demonstrations.

The Union triumph at Fisher's Hill two months earlier, in September 1864, occurred five miles south of Cedar Creek and two miles west of the town of Strasburg. Fisher's Hill lies on VA Rt. 601 in the narrowest part of the valley and, although bisected by Interstate 81, it remains in surprisingly pristine condition. A self-guided, mile-long walking tour features six stops with markers showing points of interest. Locals swear that a Confederate crow's nest is responsible for the peculiar shape of the massive oak atop Fisher's Hill.

Two annual events in the autumn merit special notice: the Battle Reenactment and the evening Soiree. The Battle Reenactment occurs in October amidst the beautiful colors of the fall Shenandoah foliage. Thousands of men in period uniforms of both Union and Confederate infantry, cavalry, and artillery reenact the various scenarios of the battle, in uncannily realistic fashion. The Soiree is a benefit Civil War ball held during the reenactment weekend under a large, lighted tent featuring period music, dancing, and dance instruction for the uninitiated. This is an ideal opportunity to plunge into a fancy, mid-nineteenth-century social affair, and visitors can either join the festivities or revel in the music and vivacious dancing from the sidelines. Children are encouraged to take part.

As with most reenactments, each five-year anniversary of this 1864 battle brings forth two or three times the usual number of participating reenactors. This spectacle occurs on ground where the battle was fought, making it one of the very few such engagements in the country held on an actual Civil War battlefield. Tents surround Belle Grove. Many civilians in nineteenth-century garb stroll the grounds. Men portray a range of characters: merchants, surgeons, and battlefield sketch artists who, in the days before photography, captured the drama of the war, illustrating it for newspaper and magazine readers around the nation. Strolling women hook arms with their officer husbands and sport their layers of nineteenth-century fashion. The rolling hills of the valley with their autumn foliage offer a colorful backdrop for the encampments of both armies, rows of heavy guns, horse stables, and tents of the sutlers— men who followed the armies, selling all manner of goods—combining to make the Cedar Creek reenactment one of the most engaging and best attended historical events in the country. (Visitors should inquire ahead of time about any special arrangements for descendants of soldiers who participated in the actual battle.)

Because Civil War armies did not fight in winter, going into winter camps during that time, most battles occurred in spring and summer, when heat, mud, insects, and disease conspired to make army life mis-

erable. Cedar Creek reenactors enjoy the cool fall weather and opportunity to wear their period greatcoats. The numerous participants pitch
rows of white canvas tents for spectators to visit before and after the
day's battles, to learn about army tactics, soldiers' lives in camp and—
of particular interest to many younger visitors—proper use of artillery,
muskets, and bayonets. The wives of the officers and soldiers are often
in camp and will readily discuss the clothing American women wore in
the nineteenth century. These encampments are wonderful opportunities
for demonstrations of musket and artillery prowess, cavalry tactics, and
displays of Civil War–era medicine—especially for imagining the horrors
inflicted by primitive surgical devices on unfortunate wounded men. In
these camps, visitors can observe the intricacies of loading muskets and
rifles, see how food was prepared, and hear how soldiers spent down
time in camp—writing and reading letters and playing games being two
popular pastimes. Visitors smell meals sizzling over open fires and peer
inside officers' tents at the cots, desks, and other personal camp items.
They watch new recruits learn to shoulder arms and march in formation.
Many families enjoy having their children photographed, sometimes in
period garb, with members of today's Union and Confederate armies.

A number of free ranger-led programs at the park explore the history and settlement of the Shenandoah Valley and the impacts of the
Civil War and the Battle of Cedar Creek on the local population. These
programs make use of living histories and features of the surrounding
landscape to tell the park's many stories. A two-hour tour over roughly
fifteen miles, in which drivers follow a ranger's vehicle, covers the Battle
of Cedar Creek in a chronological fashion. The path follows the highlights of the conflict with approximately a half dozen stops at the key
landmarks associated with the fighting. Tours begin at the Cedar Creek
Battlefield Foundation Headquarters.

The Shenandoah Valley is replete with Civil War sites. Many are part
of Gen. Stonewall Jackson's 1862 campaign, in which his forces consis-
tently evaded or repulsed larger Union armies and, in so doing, kept
enemy troops engaged that could otherwise have strengthened Union
assaults against Richmond. The principal sites in the region where
fighting resulted in Confederate success—Kernstown, Front Royal, and
Winchester—are well worth seeing when traveling in the Valley. (When

visiting in the area, bear in mind that traveling north in the Shenandoah means going "down the valley," traveling south is going "up the valley" because the Shenandoah River flows north.) But Cedar Creek remains the culminating battle of the Valley Campaign, and the place where a Union victory helped propel Abraham Lincoln to a second term in the White House just a month later.

SIDE TRIP

WINCHESTER, VA: This vital base of operations for both armies during the Civil War saw three major battles in that conflict; the final one, in September 1864, was followed a month later by the Union triumph at Cedar Creek that ousted the Rebels from the Shenandoah Valley for good. The quaint Old Town features Stonewall Jackson's Headquarters Museum, George Washington's Office Museum, the Old Courthouse Civil War Museum, and the Shenandoah Valley Discovery Museum. Guided walking tours are available. The annual springtime Shenandoah Apple Blossom Festival features the Old Town Wine & Fine Arts Festival, a carnival, dances, parades, band competitions, and a circus. *Fifteen miles north of Cedar Creek and Belle Grove National Historical Park, on I-81.*

FURTHER READING

Thomas A. Lewis, *The Guns of Cedar Creek,* 2nd edition. Heritage Associates, 1997.

Jonathan A. Noyalas, *The Battle of Cedar Creek (VA): Victory from the Jaws of Defeat.* The History Press, 2009.

Jeffrey D. Wert, *From Winchester to Cedar Creek: The Shenandoah Campaign of 1864.* Southern Illinois University Press, 2010.

16

PETERSBURG AND THE
ROAD TO APPOMATTOX

At the outbreak of the Civil War, Petersburg, Virginia's second-largest city, was a major transportation center supplying Richmond, the capital of the Confederacy, and Gen. Robert E. Lee's army, wherever it was. Five railroads went in and out of Petersburg, one of which connected with the Confederate capital. Part of Gen. Ulysses S. Grant's strategy was to sever these five rail lines and isolate Richmond, forcing it to fall and the Confederate Army to surrender. Union troops arrived in June 1864 to seize Petersburg—the culmination of Grant's bloody push south to crush the Rebel army and take Richmond—but after several assaults failed, they began a siege of the city that lasted ten months. The siege led to two of the Civil War's most dramatic moments: the explosion of the mine at the Crater and the capitulation of the Confederate Army at Appomattox Court House in early April 1865.

Confederate defenses encircled Petersburg, south of Richmond, on three sides, with the Appomattox River a natural defense to the north. Brigade Commander Joshua Lawrence Chamberlain, the Union hero of Little Round Top at Gettysburg, led his six Pennsylvania regiments on an abortive assault on June 18 against Confederate positions, so well fortified that one young Union lieutenant, seeing the awaiting Confederate forces, wrote "My heart dropped to my shoes. Cold drops stood on my forehead . . . my blood was frozen solid." During the attack, Chamberlain was shot through the pelvis, a wound that tormented him for the remainder of his life.

Begin a visit to Petersburg National Battlefield at the Eastern Front visitor center for an overview of the siege and its role in the end of the Civil War. A film introduces the action at Petersburg and its related site, City Point, where General Grant established a massive supply base at the junction of the James and Appomattox Rivers. The museum in the visitor center has a number of displays and artifacts from the fighting, including reproduced items placed in a dirt pit that show what a battlefield might look like after the battle ended. Kids can try on civilian and soldier clothing, such as caps, hats, hoop skirts, and uniform jackets. The Junior Ranger program is available at the visitor center, and Civil War trading cards are awarded at various stops in the park.

The complete thirty-three-mile battlefield tour includes the Eastern and Western fronts (four and sixteen miles, respectively), Grant's headquarters at City Point (a 15-minute drive from the visitor center), and the Five Forks Battlefield. Interpretive signs, including solar-powered audio presentations at many stops, explain the action in sequential format. Highlights along the Eastern Front include Confederate Battery 9 (stop 3) and its re-creation of earthworks, which Union colonel Charles Wainwright described on June 18, 1864: "Attacking entrenchments has been tried so often and with such fearful losses that even the stupidest private knows it cannot succeed . . . the very sight of a bank brings [the men] to a halt." This spot also features a reconstructed four-soldier winter hut—a log cabin with desk, chair, stove, table, and drinking tins— thousands of which were built during the winter siege of 1864–1865. The fortifications erected by both sides were massive, thanks to the tremendous advances in artillery since the Revolutionary War. Much of this driving tour is wooded, and picnic areas and biking/hiking trails crisscross the area.

The Union's Fort Stedman (stop 5) is typical of the thirty forts that comprised the Union siege lines south and east of Petersburg. A Confederate assault on the fort was thwarted by a Union counterattack. Stedman's earthen walls were augmented by logs and offered defenders

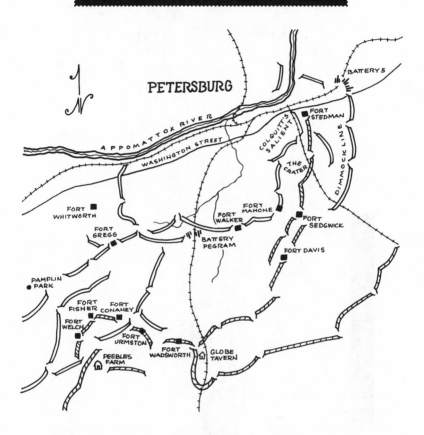

SIEGE OF PETERSBURG, JUNE 1864–APRIL 1865

refuge from shells and small arms fire from Confederate forward positions barely 300 yards away. A photograph on an interpretive sign, taken after the war, shows what life in the fort might have been like: In the center stands a black soldier holding an upright log, while to the side a white man reclines in the shade of a wagon whose side reads, "Photographic Wagon—Engineering Dept." A Union officer, Col. Theodore Lyman, explained fort construction: "The men work in the manner of bees . . . the engineer officers look as wise as possible and superintend." One soldier noted that life in these forts was no cheery affair: "Endurance without relief; sleeplessness without exhilaration; inactivity without rest; and constant apprehension requiring ceaseless watching."

Six weeks into the siege came July's Battle of the Crater (stop 8), one

LEE'S FINAL RETREAT, APRIL 1865

JAMES RIVER

RICHMOND & PETERSBURG RR

CITY POINT

SOUTH SIDE STATION

PETERSBURG

April 2

REAM'S STATION

SUTHERLAND STATION

PAMPLIN PARK

FIVE FORKS

DINWIDDIE COURT HOUSE

NAMOZINE CHURCH

April 3

SOUTHSIDE RR

Route of Lee's Retreat

BLACKSTONE

RICHMOND

EWELL CROSSES APPOMATTOX RIVER

APPOMATTOX RIVER

April 4-5
AMELIA COURT HOUSE

April 6
AMELIA SPRINGS

April 6
DEATON- VILLE

JETERSVILLE
April 5

HOLT'S CORNER

HILLSMAN HOUSE

April 6
SAILOR'S CREEK

April 6
LOCKETT HOUSE

DOUBLE BRIDGES

HIGH BRIDGE

RICE'S DEPOT

BURKEVILLE

RICHMOND & DANVILLE RR

KEYSVILLE

CHARLOTTE COURT HOUSE

April 6

CUMBERLAND CHURCH

FARMVILLE

April 7

PETERSBURG & LYNCHBURG RR

NEW STORE

April 8

CLIFTON

LEE'S REAR GUARD

April 8

APPOMATTOX

APPOMATTOX COURT HOUSE

APPOMATTOX STATION

April 9

N

★ BATTLE SITES
△ ENCAMPMENTS

of the most striking episodes of the war. This area of the battlefield had become a maze of deep trenches and tangles of branches and sharpened sticks used as defensive emplacements, known as abatis. In places the lines were extremely close, so men could not let down their guard even for an instant. Rebel sharpshooters were deadly accurate. The armies, hunkered down in their trenches, stood at a stalemate. But a group of fighting coal miners from Schuylkill County in Pennsylvania proposed a preposterous plan to their commanders: They would tunnel under Confederate lines and pack the shaft with four tons of gunpowder. "We could blow that damned fort out of existence if we could run a mine shaft under it," proclaimed a miner in the unit of Lt. Col. Henry Pleasants. "That God-damned fort is the only thing between us and Petersburg, and I have an idea we can blow it up." Plans were drawn, tools sent for. Well-rested black soldiers from the United States Bureau of Colored Troops began training to lead the infantry assault against the hapless Confederates after the explosion.

The Crater can be reached on foot via two routes. While the upper is more direct, the lower includes the mouth of the tunnel the miners constructed to burrow under the Rebel defensive lines. Colonel Pleasants wrote to his Uncle James on July 23 that he had "completed a gigantic work; and have accomplished one of the great things of this war. I have excavated a mine gallery from our line to and under the enemy's works." Pleasants's letter is a reminder that Civil War correspondence was un-censored, for Confederate interception of his short letter would surely have thwarted the plan.

"As soon as the 'high authorities' are ready . . . will blow fort, cannon and rebels to the clouds," Pleasants predicted. "The chief engineer of the Army and the rest of the regular army wiseacres said it was not feasible . . . Old Burnside stood by me. Told me to go ahead and I have succeeded," he wrote, referring to Gen. Ambrose Burnside. But this task weighed on the Pennsylvanian's conscience: "It is terrible to hurl men with my own hand at one blow into eternity, but I believe I am doing right." And he knew the danger of his words: "Be sure not to speak of this matter outside of Uncle James and Aunt Emily, until the thing is done."

Men worked around the clock, digging with bayonets until proper tools arrived. Each received a dram of whiskey after his shift. When Pleas-ants had to make precise calculations that took him perilously close to

Confederate positions, his men distracted Rebel sharpshooters by raising their caps on bayonets above the parapet walls. Rumors of tunnels wafted through both camps like soft scents on a breeze. The Rebels dug "listening galleries," vertical shafts that got agonizingly close to the tunnel but failed to detect it. Depressions in the ground reveal the locations of these listening posts. Those traversing the lower path to the Crater can inspect the tunnel's entrance and walk its route up and into the Confederate positions (the tunnel is 586 feet long, including the lateral galleries). Signs explain how the miners obtained fresh air using a vertical shaft and a wooden duct that ran the length of the tunnel with a fire at the end drawing out stale air and sucking in fresh.

The miners lit the fuse and crawled out of the tunnel. Union regiments and artillery awaited the massive explosion and orders to attack. The clock passed 3 A.M., then 3:30. Nothing. Men crept back into the tunnel to investigate. The fuse had gone out at a splice, so they relit it. "It's alright Col.—she's burning," announced one man as he emerged from the shaft.

At 4:45 A.M. on July 30, as the summer sky was lightening, the earth shot up "like an enormous whirlwind," recalled one soldier. Another likened it to "the noise of great thunders." Men and equipment flew through the air; a cannon was propelled over the Union line. But planning and leadership again failed the federals. Not only had the rested black troops who had trained to strike immediately after the explosion been pulled back the day before, the commander of the men then chosen to lead the assault was in a drunken stupor, safely away from the action. Chaos and carnage ensued as the untrained Union assault forces charged into the 30-foot deep pit. Legs of Rebel soldiers buried headfirst stuck in the air. Others, stunned at the surreal sight, could only gape.

The fighting in and around the Crater was as brutal as any in the Civil War. Men trying to climb the sides of the huge pit slipped down its steep banks and tumbled to the bottom, defenseless against withering Rebel artillery that opened up immediately. Rebel infantry regrouped around the rim eight hours after the explosion. Knowing that Confederates had sworn to execute black troops, and the white officers who led them, upon capture, white Union soldiers did the job themselves, in some instances shooting their black comrades who had joined the fray in the aftermath of the explosion. Union commanders sent orders forward that, in the chaos, made no sense by the time couriers made their way to the front.

"It is agreed that the thing was a perfect success, except that it did not succeed," Union Maj. Charles F. Adams, Jr., wryly noted after the explosion and battle in and around the Crater. "It was a stupendous failure," General Grant recalled, "the saddest affair I have witnessed in the war." Like some other historic sites that loom large in the American imagination—Dealey Plaza in Dallas comes to mind—the indentations in the ground today seem disproportionately small given the magnitude of what occurred there on that hot day in 1864. The removal of hundreds of dead men, horses, equipment, and artillery in the aftermath; damage from sightseers who tramped through following the battle; and decades of erosion have made an impressively large pit impressively smaller.

The Union siege continued through the remainder of that steamy Virginia summer following the disaster at the Crater. Temperatures reached 110 degrees. Little rain fell; the battlefield became a torturous plain of fine dust. "One's mouth will be so full of dust that you do not want your teeth to touch each other," remembered a Connecticut man. "The romance of a soldier's life disappears in a siege," mused T. M. Blythe of the 50th New York Engineers. "The change of scenery and the lively marches are gone, and the same monotonous unvaried rounds of toil take their place. Sunday and weekday are all alike." Desperate for stimulation off the battlefield, soldiers from both sides would "creep into . . . a neutral cornfield," recounted one, "for a friendly chat, for a barter, or for a game of cards!"

Enemy lines were close in some spots. "I feel quite contented this fine morning. Am out of reach of those infernal Minnie balls which the rebs send over with such spite and venom," wrote James Roantree, a white officer in the 43rd Infantry Regiment of the United States Colored Troops, from camp near Petersburg on July 2, 1864. Rations were occasionally pleasant. "Have had a bully breakfast," he wrote. "We had coffee & fried pork & fresh beef, our usual army rations. Then we had Soft bread, Condensed milk, pickled cabbage & onions, stewed beans & boiled potatoes." Roantree was killed on October 27 at the Battle of Boydton Plank Road— the last entry in his diary reads "9 A.M. just going in." His sword, cap, photograph, and officer's commission are displayed in the visitor center, along with his "Soldier's Power of Attorney" permitting his father to cast his vote in the 1864 presidential election.

Grant's Headquarters at City Point, at the confluence of the James and Appomattox Rivers, is eight miles northeast of the Eastern Front visitor center. Beginning in June 1864, Grant was on the grounds of the Eppes family home known as Appomattox Plantation, which sits on a bluff overlooking the river of the same name. He lived in a cabin that still stands, one of twenty-two built for his entourage; roughly 10 percent of Grant's cabin is original. A photograph shows Grant and two officers standing in front; personal items are visible through its windows. From this small cabin, on this site, Grant directed the largest siege ever on American soil, with battle lines extending more than thirty-seven miles around Petersburg and Richmond. Tens of thousands of troops, horses, and mules were supplied through the water and rail depots at City Point, which at its apogee was one of the busiest ports in the world, with provisions delivered daily by an average of forty steamers, seventy-five sailing ships, and a hundred barges. The depot encompassed eight wharves extending a half mile along the James River, seven hospitals (four civilian, three military), and a bakery that produced 100,000 loaves of bread each day.

The visitor center at City Point is in the Eppes House, the earliest portion of which was built in 1763. A short video presents the history of the mansion and details of its construction. A fascinating artifact displayed is a "horological device," a timing component for a bomb similar to one that Confederate saboteurs—inspired, perhaps, by the Union's exploits at the Crater—exploded in August 1864 amidst the wharves at City Point to disrupt Union supply operations. Over 40 men died and 126 were wounded in the explosion of what is believed to be the first use of a "horological torpedo," or time bomb. Also on display is the authentic front door of Grant's cabin. The ranger-guided tour of the house and grounds conveys the fascinating history of the Eppes family—which owned the land from 1635 to 1979, one of the longest continuous claims to ownership in American history, possibly longer than any other American family has owned a piece of land—and its slaves. The story of the relationship between Richard Eppes and his male slave Madison illustrates the fascinating complexity of slavery. Outbuildings include the kitchen and laundry, dairy, and smokehouse.

The shoreline has changed little since Civil War days. Archaeologists have attempted to excavate the sites of original wharves. The boardwalk invites a stroll along the water at a spot where on March 28, 1865, Lincoln—with the seemingly endless war at last nearing its end—met with General Grant, Adm. David Porter, and others. "Treat them liberally," the president instructed his subordinates, referring to the Confederates. "We want these people to return to the allegiance and submit to the laws. Therefore, I say, give them the most liberal and honorable terms." Grant would comply a few weeks later at the little town of Appomattox Court House, population 125, when he accepted Gen. Robert E. Lee's surrender.

A driving tour of the park's western front follows the path of Lee's army, along a westerly route south of the Appomattox River, after Petersburg and Richmond fell. Radio messages at each stop explain its significance (AM 1610 unless otherwise noted). On April 1, Lee had ordered Gen. George Pickett to protect the South Side Railroad and "hold Five Forks at all hazards." The South Side Railroad was Lee's remaining intact supply line for his soldiers in and around Petersburg, Union forces having cut the others. The South Side road passed Five Forks three miles to the north, and the commanders of both armies knew that Petersburg's survival depended on this rail line.

Pickett's men entrenched themselves along White Oak Road (VA Rt. 613), where remnants of a few earthworks and rifle pits can be seen just off VA Rt. 460. This portion of the Petersburg western front is the siege line comprising the battlefields west of Petersburg. When the Union forces under Gen. Philip Sheridan attacked at Five Forks, Pickett was behind the lines enjoying a shad lunch, a misjudgment compounded by his failure to appoint a commander in his absence. Five Forks was a calamity for the Confederates. Approximately 3,000 men were taken prisoner and, the following day, April 2, Gen. A. P. Hill fell to a bullet. The visitor center at Five Forks has a short film and a small number of artifacts from the battle. Kids can add to their collection of Civil War trading cards. This portion of the park features a five-stop driving tour that shows the locations of earthworks and positions of cavalry, infantry, and artillery of both sides. Stop 3 is the Five Forks Intersection, where on April 2 General Lee sent a message to Confederate president Jefferson

Davis that Richmond would have to be evacuated. Lee then gave the order to abandon Richmond and Petersburg.

The Battle of Five Forks became known as the "Waterloo of the Confederacy," earning a laudatory editorial claim from the New York *Herald* that "a more complete destruction of an army was never known." When Union forces marched into Richmond on April 3, the newspaper's editors could barely contain their glee. "Billy Smith, the Governor, Leaves His Wife to Look After His Furniture," screamed an editorial a week later, mocking Virginia's governor. "The Virginia Legislature Evacuate in a Canal Boat!" As Union troops swarmed into the Confederate capital, some of the black soldiers went to the homes of their former masters to exalt in their triumph. Confederate troops torched buildings along the James River waterfront to prevent materiel from falling to Union forces; some 900 homes and businesses were consumed by the wind-driven flames.

More than 60,000 bedraggled Rebels headed further west to the little town of Amelia Court House, where they expected to receive badly needed rations. From there Lee planned to march southwest to Burkeville and move his men even further southwest by train to Danville, to meet up with the Army of Tennessee. General Lee had reason for optimism, accustomed as he had become to the reluctance of former adversaries such as Gen. George B. McClellan to pursue him. But General Grant was different, and matters quickly went badly for the Confederates. No rations greeted the hungry men who limped into Amelia Court House on April 4, and the Army of Northern Virginia lost precious time awaiting the return of foraging parties from the countryside and Gen. Richard Ewell's troops from Richmond. Union cavalry and infantry under Gen. Philip Sheridan dug in south of Jetersville, blocking Lee's road south. Stragglers and deserters shrank the rebel ranks. "Our army is ruined, I fear" wrote Col. W. B. Taylor to his mother from Amelia Court House. "My trust is still in the justice of our cause."

General Lee turned southwest to the tobacco town of Farmville, where 80,000 rations awaited, but on April 6 his men got bogged down in the area of Sailor's Creek, where Union troops forced 7,700 of them and two generals, including Lee's son, Gen. George Washington Custis Lee, to capitulate—one of the largest battlefield surrenders at one time in North America. The gaunt and hungry Confederates again missed the opportunity to eat as the army moved north across the Appomattox River. An interactive multimedia exhibit in the museum at Sailor's Creek Battlefield Historical State Park, on VA Rt. 617 in Rice, tells the tale of this last major battle of the Civil War. A "storyteller hologram" presents one Union and one Confederate soldier telling of their experiences using animated photographs that humanize their stories. Plenty of photographs, images, and maps describe the battle action, which included hand-to-hand combat, and outcomes for both sides. Many artifacts from the clash have been recovered, for historians surmise that soldiers, sensing the end near, began gathering items to carry home. Among these is a limber chest found in a nearby barn. The park includes the Hillsman House, a 1770s-era colonial home converted into a Union field hospital to treat the wounded of both sides that became the scene of many amputations. Hillsman family slaves slipped away during the chaos. Bloodstains on the floor, reminders of the gruesome nature of the affair, and living historians bring battle and building to life. Those wishing to stretch their legs during the drive along Lee's retreat can take the 45-minute hike to Little Sailor's Creek; another option is the Confederate Overlook Trail, just under a mile (the parking area across from the Battlefield Memorial leads to the trailhead).

What remained of the Army of Northern Virginia—roughly 40,000 intrepid, calorie-starved men, now 72 hours from surrender—pushed on. Sensing the end, many slipped out of the lines and began the trek home. The following day, April 7, Lee received a message from Grant: "The results of the last week must convince you of the hopelessness of further resistance." Grant believed it his "duty to shift from myself the responsibility of any further effusion of blood, by asking of you the surrender of that portion of the C.S. Army known as the Army of Northern Virginia." Over the dissent of Gen. James Longstreet, Lee in reply inquired about surrender terms. After Union forces surrounded Lee's army, the two generals, accompanied by staff officers, met on April 9 in the parlor of the McLean House in the village of Appomattox Court House. After Grant accepted Lee's surrender, he ordered rations for Lee's men.

The visitor center at Appomattox Court House National Historical Park is in the restored county courthouse. Framed photographs of uniformed soldiers from both sides who were present at the surrender ring the wall on the first floor. Upstairs are artifacts from the surrender, including the "ordinary white towel" used as the first flag of truce, documents related to the surrender, a pencil lent to General Lee by a staff officer, and other items associated with this small town. Intriguing is the "Witness Doll," owned by 7-year-old Lula McLean. Col. Horace Porter explained its provenance: "A child's doll found in the room, which the officers tossed from one to the other, and called the 'Silent Witness.'" Two films, "Stacking of Arms" and "The Appomattox Campaign," provide an orientation to the park.

The house in which Generals Grant and Lee met was owned by Wilmer McLean, who ironically had moved his family to this peaceful town of twenty-some buildings from a home in Manassas that had been damaged in that 1861 battle, known also as Bull Run. McLean had converted the house from a tavern to a single-family home that was later disassembled for transport to Washington, D.C., to become a museum. The house never left, however, and was acquired and reconstructed on its original foundation by the National Park Service, using photographs and original architectural plans. The house and village have been restored to their 1865 appearance, and the cluster of buildings comprises the park.

Park rangers are posted in the McLean House daily from April to October, with periodic tours during the remaining months. This house tour, a highlight of the park, offers rich detail and context. The parlor of the house seems too small to have accommodated an event of such magnitude. The sofa on which a number of officers sat, including Capt. Robert Todd Lincoln, son of President Lincoln, is original, as are the table and two vases on the mantelpiece—all inanimate witnesses to the day, April 9, 1865, that symbolically ended the Civil War. Though other Confederate armies remained in the field, Lee's Army of Northern Virginia was the engine that drove the Confederacy, and men of both armies knew that its fall meant the end. General Grant offered generous terms to the vanquished enemy: Rebel soldiers could go home, rather than to prison, and keep their horses so they could work their farms. Officers could retain their side arms. None would be charged with treason. Grant recalled in his memoirs how Lee granted permission to Union officers to go inside Confederate lines to see their old army friends.

A number of the buildings from 1865 still stand in the park. The Clover Hill Tavern was home to portable printing presses that cranked out paroles for Confederate soldiers after they surrendered. Kids can turn the crank on a period printing press and, while printing their own parole, see the manual labor required to run the presses. The paroles, on paper slips 3 × 8 inches and dated April 10, 1865, state that the bearer "has permission to go home, and there remain undisturbed." These presses turned out more than 28,000 parole passes for Confederate soldiers in several days. The Appomattox History Trail runs from the site of Grant's headquarters northeast to the site of Lee's, which is a two-minute walk from Va. Rt. 24.

On April 12, some 5,000 Union troops lined the Richmond-Lynchburg Stage Road to receive the symbolic Confederate surrender. Weapons, flags, and equipment were stacked before the Union soldiers, who stood along the road from a spot east of the Peers House to the McLean House. "No man can ever describe what followed," remembered Pvt. William "Billy" Abernathy of the 17th Mississippi Infantry Regiment. "Some sat at the roots of trees and cried as if their hearts would break. Some grasped the rifle that they had carried for years and smashed them. Some cursed bitterly, some prayed." Overseeing the ceremony for the Union was Gen. Joshua L. Chamberlain, the one-time commander of the 20th Maine Regiment and later a recipient of the Medal of Honor for his actions at Gettysburg (see chapter 13). Gen. John B. Gordon, commanding Gen. Stonewall Jackson's Corps, led the solemn Confederates on horseback. With Gordon's "chin drooped to his breast, downhearted and dejected in appearance," Chamberlain ordered a bugle call, whereupon Union soldiers suddenly changed from order arms to shoulder arms. A surprised Gordon reciprocated this gesture by dipping his sword in salute and instructed his men to shoulder arms. These expressions of mutual respect were a harbinger of Lincoln's plans to embrace the return of America's Southern brethren—plans thwarted two days later by a Southern sympathizer called John Wilkes Booth.

SIDE TRIPS

THOMAS JEFFERSON'S MONTICELLO: The life of the third U.S. president reminds us that race relations remained an American problem only partially solved by the Union triumph in the Civil War and attempts by legislation and constitutional amendment to address it. Daytime and evening tours of the house, gardens, and grounds; films; and interactive exhibition galleries illuminate the enigmatic Thomas Jefferson, whose devotion to intellectual exploration, notions of liberty, and embrace of architecture were influenced by his European travels. The cellar tour includes the restored wine cellar, slave quarters, smokehouse, and kitchen. On display also is evidence of Jefferson's obsession with record-keeping that has illuminated much about socioeconomic life in the time of this slave-owner who proclaimed to the world in the Declaration of Independence that "all men are created equal." A variety of seasonal activities is available on the grounds, and kids can build models, write with a quill pen, and play eighteenth-century games at the Mountaintop Activity Center. *931 Thomas Jefferson Parkway, Charlottesville, Virginia, 22902, 434-984-9800.*

ASH LAWN–HIGHLAND: Highland was the home of James Monroe, fifth president of the United States and is today owned and operated by the College of William and Mary. Tobacco and grain were harvested here, and timber felled, by slaves. Following Monroe's death, the name of the estate was changed to Ash Lawn, but both names are used today. Living history interpretations and a variety of special events throughout the year provide a glimpse of nineteenth-century life through architecture, decorative arts, and craft demonstrations. A magnificent white oak that graced the property during Monroe's time still stands. Ornamental and kitchen gardens represent those commonly planted in the early 1800s, and the peas, beans, corn, squash, and tomatoes grown are used in Ash Lawn–Highland's open-hearth cooking program. An annual summer festival occurs at this site, which is two miles from Monticello. *2050 James Monroe Parkway, Charlottesville, VA, 22902, 434-293-8000.*

FURTHER READING

Bruce Catton, *A Stillness at Appomattox*. Anchor Books, 1990 (first published 1953).

Burke Davis, *To Appomattox: Nine April Days, 1865*. Burford Books, 2002.

A. Wilson Greene, *The Final Battles of the Petersburg Campaign: Breaking the Backbone of the Rebellion*. University of Tennessee Press, 2008.

Richard Slotkin, *No Quarter: The Battle of the Crater, 1864*. Random House, 2009.

Noah Andre Trudeau, *The Last Citadel: Petersburg, Virginia, June 1864– April 1865*. Louisiana State University Press, 1993.

Jay Winik, *April 1865: The Month That Saved America*. Harper Perennial, 2006.

INDEX

Boldface entries refer to chapter page ranges; *italic* page numbers refer to maps

Abernathy, Pvt. William "Billy," 191
Adams, Abigail, 41
Adams, Maj. Charles F., Jr., 185
Adams, John, 8; and Philadelphia, 38–39, 41, 43; and War of 1812, 59
Adams, John Quincy, 73; and Chesapeake & Ohio Canal groundbreaking, 82–84
African Americans, 139
Agnew, Dr. Cornelius R., 129
Alexander, Maj. Edward Porter, 116
Alexandria, VA, *61*, 64, *86*, 88, *135,* 141
Allegheny Mountains, 170
Allen, Pvt. George A., 129
Allentown, PA, 42
Amelia Court House, *182,* 188
American Civil War Center, 108
American Red Cross, 95
Anacostia River, *135*
Annapolis, MD, xii, *32, 61*
Antietam, Battle of, 36, 90, **120–32,** *123*
Antietam Creek, *87, 123*
Antietam Creek Aqueduct, *87,* 91
Antietam Iron Works, 104
Appalachian Mountains, 83, 85, 92
Appalachian Trail, 90, 103–4, 131
Appomattox, VA, 155, *182*
Appomattox Court House, *182,* 187, 189
Appomattox Plantation, 186
Appomattox River, 179–80, *181,* 189; and Grant's Headquarters, 186; and Lee's retreat, *182*
Ark (ship), 17, 24
Arlington, VA, *87,* 141
Armed Forces Retirement Home, 133

Armistead, Maj. George, 67
Armistead, Gen. Lewis, 154
Army-Navy Country Club, 139
Articles of Confederation, 38, 40
Ashe, Arthur, 111

Baker, Sen. Edward, 90, 106
Ball's Bluff Regional Park, VA, 90
Baltimore, ix, *32, 61,* 71, 137, 148, 156; and Baltimore & Ohio Railroad, 76, 78; and British assault against, 64–65; defense of, 59, 64–67; Irish immigrants in, 79
Baltimore & Ohio Railroad, 73–74; and Chesapeake & Ohio Canal, 82–84, *86–87,* 88, 93–94; and Harpers Ferry, 98
Baltimore & Ohio Railroad Museum, **71–81**
Baltimore Colts, 81
Baltimore Orioles, 81
Baltimore *Sun,* ix
Barney, Commodore Joshua, 63
Barton, Clara, 142, 163–64
Baum, Surgeon Clark, 161
Beaver Dam Creek, VA, *113*
Belle Grove Plantation and Mansion, VA, 171, *172,* 174–76
Belle Isle (Richmond, VA), 109, *113*
Benedict, MD, *61,* 62
Bethesda, MD, 88
Big Round Top (Gettysburg, PA), xi, *149*
Billy Goat Trail, 89
Black troops. *See* United States Bureau of Colored Troops
Bladensburg, Battle of, 60, *61,* 62, 63, 65
"Bloody Angle" (Spotsylvania, VA), 167
Bloody Lane (Antietam, MD), *123,* 126, 130

Blue Ridge Mountains, *87,* 97, *99,* 170

Blythe, T.M., 185

Bolivar, *99,* 104

Bolivar Heights, *99,* 104

Booth, John Wilkes, 18, 143, 191; and escape of, 27

Braddock, Gen. Edward, 31

Brandy Station, Battle of, 169

Brandywine, Battle of, 49

Breckenridge, John C., 138

Brent, Margaret, 23

Bristoe Station, VA, 169

Brown, Alexander, 72–73

Brown, John, 97–98, 102

Brunswick, MD, *87,* 88

Buford, Gen. John, 148

Burkeville, VA, *182,* 188

Burnside, Gen. Ambrose, 127; and Battle of the Crater, 183; and Fredericksburg, 159, 161

Burnside (Lower) Bridge, *123,* 127, 128

Butler, Col. Richard, 12

C&O Canal. *See* Chesapeake & Ohio Canal

Calvert, Lord Cecilius, 17, 22, 34

Calvert, Frederick, 33

Calvert, Gov. Leonard, 17, 23

Calvert, Philip, 22

Calvert County, MD, 28

Camden Station, 80

Capital Crescent Trail, 88

Carpenter's Hall (Philadelphia, PA), 39

Carroll, Barrister Charles, 80

Carroll, Charles (of Carrollton), 79; and first stone of Baltimore & Ohio Railroad, 71, 74, 84

Carroll, James, 73

Carrollton Viaduct, 80

Catholic University, 139

Catoctin Mountain, *87,* 121

Catoctin Ridge, 84

Caulk's Field, Battle of, *61,* 62

Cedar Creek, Battle of, xi, **170–78,** *172*

Cedar Mountain, VA, 169

Cemetery Hill, *149,* 152

Cemetery Ridge, *149*

Chain Bridge, 88, 89, *135,* 142

Chamberlain, Col. Joshua Lawrence: and Fredericksburg, 161–62; and Gettysburg, 150–51, 179; oversees Confederate surrender, 191; wounding of, 180

Chambersburg, PA, 36

Chancellorsville, VA, *160, 165,* 165–66

Charles I (king), 17

Charles County, MD, 16, 18, 28, 62

Charles Town, WV, *87,* 98

Chatham, *160,* 163–64, 166

Cherokees, xi, 33

Chesapeake & Ohio Canal, ix, x, xi, **82–96,** *86–87, 99, 123, 135*

Chesapeake and Ohio Railroad, 79

Chesapeake Bay, *19, 61, 109,* 137

Chessie, 79

Chickahominy Bluffs, 112, *113*

Chickahominy River, *109,* 112, *113,* 114

Chimborazo Hospital, 110–11, *113*

Chimborazo Medical Museum, 110

City Point (VA), *109, 113,* 180, *182*

Civilian Conservation Corps, 34–35

Clinton, Gen. Sir Henry, 13, 14

Clocker, Daniel, 25

Coburn, J. Osborn, 109

Cochrane, Vice Adm. Sir Alexander, 60, 64

Cockburn, Adm. George, 63

Cold Harbor, Battle of, *109,* 112, *113,* 167

Colonial Marines, 66

Colonial Parkway, VA, 1, 7, 9

Colonial Williamsburg, 7–9, *10, 109*

Confederate White House, 107, 111, 118

Congress Hall, 39

Conococheague Creek, 31, *88*

Constitution, U.S., 40, 42

Constitutional Convention (1787–1789), 38, 83

Continental Army, x

Cook, John, 102, 104

Copley, Anne, 25

Copley, Gov. Lionel, 25

Cornfield (Antietam, MD), 120, *123*

Cornwallis, Charles Lord, 10, 13, 14; surrender of, 1, 9

Cowpens, Battle of, 55

Cox, Maj. Gen. Jacob D., 124, 129

Cox, Samuel, 27

Crampton's Gap, 121, 131

Crater, Battle of (Petersburg), 181, 183–85

Cresap, Thomas, 93

CSX, 79

Culpeper, VA, 169

Culps Hill, *149,* 150–52

Cumberland, MD, 35, 74–75, 82, 84–85, *87,* 88, 90, 93–95

Cumberland Valley, 121

Custer, Gen. George, 175

Custis, Eliza, 44

Custis, George Washington Parke, 143

Danville, VA, 188

Davis, Jefferson, 111–12, 116, 118, 187–88

Dawes, Maj. Rufus, 125, 130

Declaration of Independence, 38, 42, 45

de Lafayette, Marquis, 41; visits Fort McHenry, 67

Dennis, Olive, 78

de Sousa, Mathias, 24

Devil's Den, 147, *149,* 150, 155

Dix, Dorothea, 142

Doubleday, Abner, 144

Douglas, Frederick, 69

Douglas, William O., 94

Dove (ship), 17, 24

Du Bois, W.E.B., 100

Dunker Church, *123,* 124

Eanes, Walter, 102

Early, Gen. Jubal, 95, 137; and Cedar Creek, 170–71, 174

Eisenhower, Dwight D., 156

Elkridge, MD, 80

Ellicott City, MD, 73

Ellicott's Mills, MD, 73

Ellsworth, Col. Elmer, 142

Emancipation Proclamation, 152, 155

English Civil Wars, 22

Eppes, Richard, 186

Eppes House, 186

Evers, Medgar, 144

Falmouth, VA, 162, *163*

Farmville, VA, *182,* 188

Federal Hill, 66

Felix, Arnold, 173

Ferry Farm, *160,* 162, *163,* 167

Few, William, 46

First Bull Run, Battle of, 190

First Continental Congress (1774), 41

Fisher's Hill, 173–74

Five Forks, Battle of, 180, *182,* 187–88

Forbes, Gen. John, 31

Forbes Road, 31

Ford's Theater, 27

Fort Ashby, 31, *32*

Fort Brady, *113,* 117

Fort Buttermilk, 31, *32*

Fort Chambers, 31, *32*

Fort Cumberland, 31, *32,* 95

Fort Duquesne, 31, *32,* 33

Fort Foote, *135,* 141

Fort Frederick, xi, **30–37,** 91

Fort Harrison, 117

Fort Lincoln Cemetery, 139

Fort Loudoun, 31, *32*

Fort Maidstone, 31, *32*

Fort Marcy, *135*

Fort McHenry, ix, xii, **59–70**

Fort Morris, 31

Fort Pitt, *32*

Fort Pleasant, 31
Fortress Monroe, *109*
Fort Stevens, *135*, 136–37, 141, 143
Fort Tonoloway, 31
Fort Ward, *135*, 141–43
Fort Washington, *61*, 64, *135*, 140
Fox's Gap, 131
Franklin, Benjamin, 39, 40, 45
Frederick, MD, *87*, 95, 130–31
Fredericksburg, VA, x, xii, **158–64**, *160*, *163*
French, Gen. William H., 125
French and Indian War, 30, 33, 34, 93
Fritchie, Barbara, 130
Front Royal, VA, 177
Furst, Luther C., 112

Gaines' Mill, Battle of, 112, *113*, 114–15
Garrett, John Work, 75, 76
Garrett farm, 27
Garthright, Miles, 115
Geocaching, 62
George III (king), 39, 45
Georgetown, 35, 82–83, 85–88, *86*, 94
Georgia Plantation, 80
Germain, Lord George, 14
Germantown, Battle of, 49
Gettysburg, Battle of, ix, xii, 36, **146–57**, *149*
Gettysburg Address, 147
Gilmor, Harry, 152
Gordon, Capt. James, 64
Gordon, Gen. John, 166, 174; surrenders at Appomattox, 191
Gosnold, Bartholomew, 5
Grant, Gen. Ulysses S., 108, 112, 115, 118, 188: and Appomattox, 189–90; moves south, 166; operations against Richmond and Petersburg, 180, 185–87; operations in Shenandoah Valley, 174; at Spotsylvania, 167; takes command of Union forces, 161, 173
Great Allegheny Passage Trail, 94

Great Falls, 83, *86*, 88, 89
Green Ridge State Forest, 92
Gruber, The Rev. John, 67
Guinea Station (VA), *160*, 166

habeas corpus, 122
Hager, Jonathan, 36
Hagerstown, MD, *88*, 156
Hamilton, Alexander, 13, 46
Hammond Hospital, MD, 28
Hampstead Hill, *61*, 65–66
Hampton, VA, *109*
Hancock, John, 44
Hancock, MD, 37, *87*, 88, 92
Hancock, Gen. Winfield Scott, 153
Hanover, PA, 156
Harper, Robert, 98, 103
Harpers Ferry, WVA, ix, x, xi, xii, 75, **97–106**, *99*
Harriet Tubman Underground Railroad Byway, x
Harrisburg, PA, *50*, 148
Harrison's Landing, *109*, *113*, 114, 116
Haskell, Lt. Frank A., 130
Hay, John, 137
Henry, Patrick, 8
Herold, David, 27–28
Hill, Gen. A.P., 112, 128; wounded at Battle of Five Forks, 187
Hill, Gen. D.H., 125–26
Historical Triangle, VA, 1
Hite, Maj. Isaac, 174–75
Hollywood Cemetery (Richmond, VA), 111
Holmes, Capt. Oliver Wendell, 137
Hood, Gen. John Bell, 125
Hooker, Gen. Joseph, 124, 164–65
Hopkins, Johns, 73
Howard, Gen. Oliver O., 116
Howe, Gen. Sir William, 49, 52, 57

Independence National Historical Park, **38–47**

Irish Brigade, 126
Iron Brigade, 125

Jackson, Andrew, 68, 84
Jackson, Gen. Thomas "Stonewall,"
    111, 147, 178: and Antietam, 125, 130;
    and Chancellorsville, 159, 165; death
    of, 166; and Fredericksburg, 162–63;
    and Harpers Ferry, 75–76, 101, 105;
    and Peninsula Campaign, 112, 114;
    and Shenandoah Valley, 170–71, 177;
    wounding of, 164–66, 173
James River, 1, 2, 4, 6, 7, 107, 109–12,
    113, 114, 117, 182, 188: and Grant's
    Headquarters, 186; Shenandoah
    Valley border, 170; supply base, 180
Jamestown, VA, 1–7, 7
Jamestown Island, 4, 7, 109
Jefferson, Thomas, 8, 159, 163; and
    Belle Grove Mansion, 175; and
    Declaration of Independence, 40,
    44; and Harpers Ferry, 97, 103; and
    Monticello, 192
Jefferson Rock, 103
Jetersville, VA, 182
Johnston, Gen. Joseph E., 116
Judge, Ona (Oney), 44
Junior Ranger Program, 10, 39, 101, 110,
    180

Kearney, Gen. Phil, 116
Kelly's Ford, VA, 169
Kenmore Plantation, 162
Kennedy, John F., 144
Kennedy Farm, 98, 99
Kernstown, VA, 177
Key, Francis Scott, 60, 62, 64, 67; as
    delegate to Canal Convention, 83
Key Bridge (Georgetown), 88
Kirkland, Richard ("Angel of Mercy"),
    162
Kirkwood, Pvt. Robert, 101
Knox, Gen. Henry, 54

Knox, Philander Chase, 54

Lacey, Capt. John, 55
Lacy, J. Horace, 164, 166
Lear, Tobias, 44
Leary, Lewis, 100
Lee, George Washington Custis, 140,
    143–44; surrender of, 188
Lee, Mary Anna Custis, 143
Lee, Mary Custis, 12
Lee, Gen. Robert E., 36, 111, 118, 170:
    and Antietam, 121–22; and Appo-
    mattox, 155, 187; becomes com-
    mander of Army of Northern
    Virginia, 116; birthplace of, 168;
    captures John Brown, 98; and
    Chancellorsville, 159, 164–66; and
    Gettysburg, 148, 154; "Lost Orders"
    of, 121; and Peninsula Campaign,
    109, 112, 117; and Petersburg, 115,
    179; retreat of, 187–89; and
    Spotsylvania, 167; surrender of,
    182, 189–91
Lewis, Meriwether, 100
Libby Prison (Richmond, VA), 109
Liberty Bell, 39, 42–43
Lincoln, Abraham, 76, 81, 163: and
    appointment of Gen. Ulysses S.
    Grant, 173; assassination of, 18, 191;
    commutes death sentence, 89;
    conflict with McClellan, 108, 126;
    Emancipation Proclamation, 121,
    134; Gettysburg Address, 155; hostile
    fire, 137; Old Soldiers' Home, 133–34,
    136; operations in Shenandoah
    Valley, 174; Pry House, 129;
    reelection prospects, 171, 178;
    suspends writ of habeas corpus, 122;
    visits defenses of Washington, 141;
    visits Philadelphia, 41, 42
Lincoln, Mary Todd, 133–34, 136
Lincoln, Capt. Robert Todd, 190
Lincoln, Tad, 133

Lincoln, Willie, 133
Little Falls, 82
Little Orleans, 84, *88*, 92
Little Round Top (Gettysburg, PA), xi,
   xii, 146–47, *149*, 150–51, 179
Livermore, Lt. Thomas, 125
Longstreet, Gen. James, 153, 166, 189
Loudoun Heights, x, *99*, 104
Louis, Joe, 144
Lyman, Col. Theodore, 181
Lyttonsville, MD, 88

Madison, Dolley, 64, 118
Madison, James, 40, 46, 118, 175
Malvern Hill, Battle of, *109*, 112, *113*, 117
Manassas, First Battle of, 138
Manassas, VA, 190
Mansfield, Gen. Joseph, 124
Marcy, Gen. Randolph B., 142
Marshall House Tavern, 142
Martinsburg, WV, 76, *88*
Marye's Heights (Fredericksburg, VA),
   xii, 154, 158–59, 161, *163*
Maryland Heights, 90, *99*, 100, 104
Mason, George, 8, 159
Massanutten Mountain, *172*, 174
Massaponax Baptist Church, *160*, 167
Mather Gorge, *87*, 89
McClellan, Gen. George B., 10, 188;
   and Antietam, 126, 129; and 1864
   presidential candidate, 171; and
   Peninsula Campaign, 107–8, 110,
   112, 114, 117–18
McComas, Henry, 66
McGuire, Judith White, 108
McKinley, Sgt. William, 127, 128
McLean, Wilmer, 190
McLean House, 191
Meade, Gen. George, 154, 156, 162
Mechanicsville, Battle of (Beaver
   Dam), *113*, 114
Mehring, Maggie, 152
Middletown, VA, 171, *172*

Miller, David, R., 120
Mine Run, VA, 169
Monmouth, Battle *of*, 57
Monocacy, Battle of, 90
Monocacy Aqueduct, 83, *87*, 90
Monocacy River, *32*, 77, *87*, 90, 137
Monroe, James, 111, 192
Monticello, 191–92
Monument Avenue, Richmond, VA,
   111–12
Morgan, Col. Daniel, 55
Morris, Robert, 43
Morse, Samuel, 76
Morse Code, 77
Mosby, John Singleton ("Gray Ghost"),
   171
Mount Joy (Valley Forge), *50*
Mount Misery (Valley Forge), *50*
Mount Vernon, VA, 49, 144, 168
Mt. Clare, 71, 73–76, 80
Mudd, Dr. Samuel, 18, 27
Muhlenberg, Gen. Peter, 52
"Mule Shoe" (Spotsylvania), *160*, 167
Murphy-Chambers Farm, *99*
Museum of the Confederacy, 107, 111

National Association for the Advance-
   ment of Colored People, 100
National Cemetery (Gettysburg), 153,
   155
National Constitution Center
   (Philadelphia), 45
National Harbor, 88
National Oceanic and Atmospheric
   Administration, 62–63
National Pike, 120
National Road, 72, 95
Negro Leagues (baseball), 81
Nelson, Gov. Thomas, Jr., 11, 13
Niagara Movement, 100
Norfolk, VA, *109*
North Anna River, 167
North Mountain, *88*, 121

North Point, Battle of, *61*, 66
North Point State Park, 60, 64–65
Nova Scotia, 66

Ohio River: and Baltimore & Ohio
    Railroad, 72, 74; and Chesapeake &
    Ohio Canal, 82–83
Ohio Valley, 33, 35, 98: and Baltimore &
    Ohio Railroad, 73, 76; and Chesa-
    peake & Ohio Canal, 82–85, 94
Old Soldiers' Home, 133–34, 136
Oldtown, MD, 93
Overland Campaign (1864), 107–8, 112,
    115

Paine, Thomas, 52
Pamunkey River, *109, 113*
Paoli, Battle of, 49
Passage Trail, 94
Patapsco River, *20*, 60, 64, 67; and
    Thomas Viaduct, 80
Patterson, Almira Wendt, 165
Patterson, Col. John W., 165
Patterson Park, 66
Patuxent River, *20*, 28, 62, 63, 64
Paw Paw Tunnel, 83, *88*, 92–93, 94
Peach Orchard, *149, 150*
Peale, Charles Willson, 80
Peninsula Campaign (1862), 107, 108, 112
Penn, William, 42, 46
Pennsylvania State House, 40
Percy, George, 2, 5
Petersburg, VA, *109*; and siege of,
    179–86, *181*
Pettigrew, Gen. J. Johnston, 153
Philadelphia, 48–49, *50*, 51, 54
Pickersgill, Mary, 68
Pickett, Gen. George: and Battle of
    Five Forks, 187; burial site of, 111;
    and Gettysburg, 153
Pickett's Charge, xii, 147, *149, 150*, 153
Pig Point, *61*, 63
Pine, Robert Edge, 80

Piscataway Indians, 26
Pitcher, Molly, 57
Pittsburgh, 82, 84, 94
Pleasants, Col. Henry, 183
Pocahontas, 7
Poffenberger Farm (Gettysburg, PA),
    123, 124
Point Lookout, MD, 95, 137
Point of Rocks, MD, 74, 84, *87*
Pool, W.W., 111
Pope, Gen. John, 121
Pope, Nathaniel, 23
Pope's Creek Plantation, 168
Porter, Adm. David, 187
Porter, Gen. Fitz John, 112, 114
Porter, Col. Horace, 190
Port Royal, VA, 28
Potomac National Heritage Scenic
    Trail, 94
Potomac River, xii, *19*, 28, *32, 61*, 64,
    87–88, 96, *99, 123, 135*, 143, 144, 168;
    and Antietam, 121–22, *123*; and
    Baltimore & Ohio Railroad, 73–74;
    and Chesapeake & Ohio Canal,
    82–84, 88, 89–93, 96; and Fort
    Frederick, 31, 33, 34, 35, 37; and
    Gettysburg, 148; and Harpers Ferry,
    97–98, 100, 104–5; Shenandoah
    Valley border, 170; and Washington,
    D.C., 133–34, 136–37, 140
Pott, Dr. John, 2
Potts, Isaac, 54
Powell, William H., 130
Powhatan Indians, 2, 6, 15
Pratt Street Riot, Baltimore, 69, 75
President Lincoln's Cottage, 133, 143
President's House (Philadelphia), 39,
    43–44
Prince George's County, MD, 140
Project Lead Coffin, 22
Pry, Philip, 129
Pry House Field Hospital Museum,
    123, 126, 129

Quakers, 41

Ramseur, Gen. Stephen, 175
Rapidan River, 158, 166
Rappahannock River, *109*, 158–59, *160*, *163*, 164–65, 168
Rappahannock Station, 169
Read, Thomas ("Sheridan's Ride"), 174
Red Caps (Baltimore & Ohio Railroad), 78
Reed, Walter, 144
Relay, MD, 80
Reno, Gen. Jesse, 121
Revolutionary War, 48
Reynolds, Gen. John, 148
Rhode Island, 38
Richardson, Gen. Israel, 125
Richmond, VA, 107–12, *109*, *113*, 179, 188
Richmond Vampire, 111
Ridgely family, 69
Rittenhouse, David, 47
Roanoke, VA, 170
Roantree, James, 185
Rock Creek, *86*, 88
Rockefeller, John D., Jr., 8
Rockville, MD, *87*
Roman Catholic Church (Maryland origins), 21
Roosevelt, Franklin D., 78
Ross, Gen. Robert, 64; death of, 66
Royal Navy, 59
Ruth, George Herman "Babe," 80

Sailor's Creek, VA, Battle of, *182*, 188–89
Salty Dog Tavern, 104
Schaeffer, Anne, 122
Schuylkill County, PA, 183
Schuylkill River, 48, *50*, 54–57
Scott, General-in-Chief Winfield, 140
Seaboard Coast Lines, 79
Second Bull Run, Battle of, 121
Second Continental Congress

(1775–1781), 38, 40, 41, 44
Seminary Ridge, *149*, 153
Seven Days' Battles, 108, 114, 117
Seven Pines, Battle of, *113*, 115
Seward, Frederick, 137
Sharpe, Gov. Horatio, 33, 34
Sharpsburg, MD, *87–88*, 120–22, *123*, 124, 131
Shenandoah River, xii, *32*, 90, *172*, 178; and Harpers Ferry, 97, *99*, 100, 103, 105
Shenandoah Valley, 170–71, 173, 177–78
Shepherd, Heyward, 98
Shepherdstown, WV, xi, *87*, 91, *123*
Sheridan, Gen. Philip, 105; and Battle of Five Forks, 187; and Cedar Creek, 173–75; and Jetersville, 188
"Sheridan's Ride" (poem), 174
Shriver, Augustus, 154
Shriver Home (Union Mills, MD), 156
Sickles, Gen. Daniel, 150, 154
Signal Corps (Civil War), 77
Silver Spring, MD, *86*, 88
Smith, Gov. Billy, 188
Smith, Capt. John, 2
Smith, Maj. Gen. Samuel, 65, 68
Smith, Theodore, 114
Smithsonian Institution, 72; partnership with B&O Railroad Museum, 74
Smithsonian Museum of Natural History, 67
Solomons Island, MD, 62, 63
South Mountain, *87*, 121–22, *123*, 126, 128, 131
Spong, Sam, 85
Spotsylvania, VA, *160*, 166–67
St. Clement's Island, MD, 17, *19*, 26–27
St. Mary's City, MD, xii, **16–29**, *19*, *20*
St. Mary's College of Maryland, 17
St. Mary's County, MD, 137
St. Mary's River, 16–17
St. Paul's School, xviii

St. Thomas of Jenifer, Daniel, 46
Standard Time Act, 75
Stanton, Edwin, 76, 140
Star-Spangled Banner, 60
Star-Spangled Banner National
  Historic Trail, **59–70**
Starving Tyme, 5
Staunton, VA, 117
Stevens, Brig. Gen. Isaac Ingalls, 136
Stone, Pvt. Cyrus, 114
Storer College, 100, 103, 104–5
Strasburg, VA, 171, 175
Stuart, Lieut. "Jeb": burial site of, 111;
  captures John Brown, 98; wounding
  of, *113*
Stuckenberg, John H.W., 103
Sturgis, Gen. Samuel, 127
Sunken Road (Antietam, MD), *123,*
  125–26
Sunken Road (Fredericksburg, VA), xii,
  163
Surratt House Museum, 27
Susquehannock Indians, 21, 24

Taney, Raphael, 156
Taney, Justice Roger B., 156
Tangier Island, VA, *61,* 62
Taylor, Col. W.B. (Walter), 188
telegraph, 76–77
Thacher, Dr. James, 14
Todd, David, 110
Townsend, George Albert, 131
Tredegar Iron Works, 107–8, 110, 112
Trimble, Gen. Isaac, 153
Trowbridge, John, 105
Tubman, Harriet, 100
Turner's Gap, 131
Tyler, John, 111

Underground Railroad, xiii
United States Armory, Harpers Ferry,
  98
United States Bureau of Colored

Troops, 63, 110, 143; and Battle of
  the Crater, 183, 185
Upton, Col. Emory, 167

Valley Forge, PA, ix, x, **48–58,** *50*
Varnum, Gen. James, 56
Virginia Company, 3, 6
Virginius Island, 103
von Steuben, Baron Friedrich, 56

Wainwright, Col. Charles, 180
Waldo, Albigence (surgeon), 55
Walker, S.H., 161
Wallace, Gen. Lew, 95
Ward, James H., 141
War of 1812, xi, **59–70,** 140
Washington, Bushrod, 83
Washington, D.C., 39, 42, *61, 87,* 133,
  135, 150, 161: assault against, during
  Civil War, 90, 95, 137–38; Baltimore
  & Ohio Railroad service to, 73;
  burning of, during War of 1812,
  62–64; defense of, during Civil War,
  135, 141–42; and immigrants, 134;
  slavery banned in, 143
Washington, George, x, 31, 33, 93, 103,
  143, 163, 178: birthday and Liberty
  Bell, 43; as co-founder of Potow-
  mack Company, 73; at Constitu-
  tional Convention, 38–40, 45, 46;
  field tent of, 12; slaves of, 43; surveys
  Potomac River Valley, 83; and
  Yorktown, 1, 14
Washington, Martha, 44, 54
Washington County, MD, 33, 36
Washington Navy Yard, 64
Washington Post, 94
Wayne, Gen. "Mad Anthony," 53
Wells, Daniel, 66
Western Maryland Rail Trail, 36–37, 92
Western Maryland Railway Station, 95
Western Union, 77
Westminster, MD, 156

Wheatfield, *149,* 150
Wheeling, WV, 74
White, Andrew, 21
White, Chaplain Garland H., 110
White House, *61,* 133; burning of, 64, 140
Whites Ferry, *87,* 90
Whitman, Walt, 134, 163–64
Wicomico County, MD, 21
Wilderness, Battle of, *160,* 166
Williams, Nathan, 34
Williams, Samuel ("Big Sam"), 34
Williamsburg, VA. *See* Colonial Williamsburg

Williamsport, MD, 83, *87,* 88, 91, 96
Wills, David, 155
Wills Creek, 31, *88*
Winchester, VA, 170–71, *172,* 174, 177
Winder, Brig. Gen. William, 63
Wolseley, Anne, 22

Yoacomaco Indians, 20–21
York, PA, 57
York River, 1, *4, 9,* 10, 13–14, *109,* 110
Yorktown, VA, *9,* 9–14, *109,* 112
Youghiogheny River, *32,* 83

Zouave Regiments, 142